NIGHT+DAY
AMSTERDAM

Neil Carlson

PULSE GUIDES

Pulse Guides' **Night+Day Amsterdam** is an independent guide. We do not accept payment of any kind from events or establishments for inclusion in this book. We welcome your views on our selections. Please email us: **feedback@pulseguides.com**.

The information contained in this book was checked as rigorously as possible before going to press. The publisher accepts no responsibility for any changes that may have occurred since, or for any other variance of fact from that recorded here in good faith.

Distributed in the United States and Canada by National Book Network (NBN). First Edition. Printed in the United States. 30% postconsumer content. Copyright © 2006 ASDavis Media Group, Inc. All rights reserved. ISBN-10: 0-9766013-3-8; ISBN-13: 978-0-9766013-3-3

Credits

Executive Editor	Alan S. Davis
Editors	Anita Chabria, Christina Henry de Tessan
Author	Neil Carlson
Copy Editors	Kelly Borgeson, Elizabeth Stroud
Maps	Chris Gillis
Production	Jo Farrell, Henry Chen, Samia Afra

Photo Credits: (Front cover, left to right) Les Byerley (martini), courtesy of SupperClub, and Mary Lou D'Auray (bicycles); (Back cover, left to right) courtesy of Stedelijk Museum CS, Bimhuis, Bazar, and Jimmy Woo (p.44); (Inside cover, top to bottom) courtesy of the College Hotel, Odeon, and the Van Gogh Museum; (p.4) Mary Lou D'Auray; (p.8) Neil Carlson.

Special Sales

For information about bulk purchases of Pulse Guides (ten copies or more), email us at bookorders@pulseguides.com. Special bulk rates are available for charities, corporations, institutions, and online and mail-order catalogs, and our books can be customized to suit your company's needs.

NIGHT+DAY
The Cool Cities series from **PULSE**GUIDES

P.O. Box 590780, San Francisco, CA 94159
pulseguides.com

Pulse Guides is an imprint of ASDavis Media Group, Inc.

The Night+Day Difference

The Pulse of the City

Our job is to point you to all of the city's peak experiences: amazing museums, unique spas, and spectacular views. But the complete *urbanista* experience is more than just impressions—it is grown-up fun, the kind that thrives by night as well as by day. Urban fun is a hip nightclub or a trendy restaurant. It is people-watching and people-meeting. Lonely planet? We don't think so. **Night+Day** celebrates our lively planet.

The Right Place. The Right Time. It Matters.

A **Night+Day** city must have exemplary restaurants, a vibrant nightlife scene, and enough attractions to keep a visitor busy for six days without having to do the same thing twice. In selecting restaurants, food is important, but so is the scene. Our hotels, most of which are four- and five-star properties, are rated for the quality of the concierge staff (can they get you into a hot restaurant?) as well as the rooms. You won't find kids with fake IDs at our nightlife choices. And the attractions must be truly worthy of your time. But experienced travelers know that timing is almost everything. Going to a restaurant at 7pm can be a very different experience (and probably less fun) than at 9pm; a Champagne boat cruise might be ordinary in the morning but spectacular at sunset. We believe providing the reader with this level of detail makes the difference between a good experience and a great one.

The Bottom Line

Your time is precious. Our guide must be easy to use and dead-on accurate. That is why our executive editor, editors, and writers (locals who are in touch with what is great—and what is not) spend hundreds of hours researching, writing, and debating selections for each guide. The results are presented in four unique ways: The *99 Best* with our top three choices in 33 categories that highlight what is great about the city; the *Experience* chapters, in which our selections are organized by distinct themes or personalities (Cool, Hip, and Classic); a *Perfect Plan* (3 Nights and Days) for each theme, showing how to get the most out of the city in a short period of time; and the *Black Book*, listing all the hotels, restaurants, nightlife, and attractions, with key details, contact information, and page references.

Our bottom line is this: If you find our guide easy to use and enjoyable to read, and with our help you have an extraordinary time, we have succeeded. We review and value all feedback from our readers, so please contact us at **feedback@pulseguides.com**.

From the Publisher

When I retired (or thought I had) ten years ago, I set out on a journey to find the 100 most fun places to be in the world at the right time—from Fantasy Fest in Key West, Florida to Songkran Water Festival in Changmai, Thailand. The result was a series of two guidebooks—one for North America, one for Europe, Latin America and Asia—named *The Fun Also Rises* after Ernest Hemingway's *The Sun Also Rises*, which helped popularize what has become perhaps the most thrilling party on earth, Pamplona's Fiesta de San Fermín, also known as the Running of the Bulls.

For each event I had three-day itineraries, event information, and listings of the city's hotspots. For some of the cities, including Amsterdam (Queen's Day), there wasn't space to describe all the places I thought a sophisticated traveler MUST go to. Thus begat the **Night+Day** series.

Night+Day guides, the first travel series from Pulse Guides, present the best that a city has to offer—hotels, restaurants, nightlife, and attractions that are exciting without being stuffy. **Night+Day** is designed for Gen-Xers to Zoomers (Boomers with a zest for life), who know that if one wants to truly experience a city, the night is as important as the day.

Unlike guidebooks that are neither informative nor exciting enough to capture peak experiences—whether for world-class events or a night on the town—Pulse Guides aims to publish extraordinary guides for extraordinary travelers. Woody Allen's quip, "90% of success is just showing up," got me thinking in mathematical terms about peak experiences: 50% (not 90) for just showing up in a new city; 75% with research; throw in the serendipity factor—meeting that special someone or witnessing a unique event—gets you to 90%; with **Night+Day** we hope to put you at 100%.

Pulse Guides abides by one guiding principle: *Never settle for the ordinary*. We hope that a willingness to explore new approaches to guidebooks, combined with meticulous research, provides you with unique and significant experiences.

Wishing you extraordinary times,

Alan S. Davis, Publisher and Executive Editor
Pulse Guides

P.S. To contact me, or for updated information on all of our **Night+Day** guides, please visit our website at **pulseguides.com**.

TOC

About the Author

 Originally from Toronto, **Neil Carlson** lived in Vancouver before moving to Amsterdam, where he's the Travel, Art, and Design Editor of *Highrise Magazine* and a freelance journalist whose work has appeared in numerous publications including *Getaway* and *Slate*. When he's not in Amsterdam or Vancouver, you can find him indulging in his passions for architecture, design, jazz, hiking, camping, kayaking, and exploring the nether reaches of the world. Neil has traveled to over 40 countries, but for the time being he has chosen to settle in Amsterdam.

Acknowledgments

Thanks to Constant Broeren of the Amsterdam Tourism & Conventions Board. Thank you to Isabelle le Neillon, the concierges of the Dylan, Robert from the Krasnapolsky, and Renate from the Lloyd Hotel, for their help in opening this city's doors. My thanks to Alexander, Maureen, Martijn, Sioe Yien, Rookje, and Maud, all of whom helped me explore the Netherlands. Thank you to Kyle, Cynthia, and Ben for sending me to my adopted home city. Thank you to Alan, Christina, and Anita for their patience and guidance, and a very special thanks to Charel van Dam of the Netherlands Board of Tourism and Conventions whose gracious assistance and valuable insights made this book possible. My most heartfelt gratitude is reserved for Joyce—for motivating me to visit and move to the Netherlands—to my uncle and aunt, Bruce and Gail, for taking me to Yemen as an eight year old, and to my mom for not stopping them: I've had the travel bug ever since.
Neil Carlson

Introduction

Amsterdam: What It Was

Amsterdam. Venice of the North. City of water. City of diamonds.

If you're looking for the glory of past centuries, the Netherlands has plenty of it. Celtic and Germanic tribes, the Romans, the Franks and Frisians, the Vikings, Charlemagne, and the Spanish have all plundered or ruled the place at one time or another. Nevertheless, while much of Holland has a lengthier history of human settlement, Amsterdam itself is relatively young. The city was founded in the 12th century as a fishing village near the mouth of the river Amstel, and it wasn't long before the settlers left their mark on the city that was to come. First, they built a dam that led to the community's name, *Amstelledamme*, meaning the "Dam on the Amstel." Then they engaged in trade with passing vessels, all the while imposing tolls on ships that sought to use the river for trade. In doing so, the fledgling settlement quickly earned a reputation as being home to shrewd businessmen who were happy to welcome foreign trade and, by proxy, foreign people along with it.

After 1300 the city grew rapidly. Amsterdam continued to emerge as a hub for business between the Baltics and Southern Europe and its merchant class grew increasingly rich and powerful. Ultimately, a power struggle resulted between these merchants and the Spanish lords who ruled Holland on behalf of the Roman Empire. Religious differences, disputes over taxes, and the fact that the King's army was quick to employ brutal tactics to crush dissent only added fuel to the fire (as did the introduction of the Inquisition). Change was inevitable. King Philip II was deposed, and the much loved William I of Orange-Nassau became the magistrate of the seven United Provinces with the Union of Utrecht in 1579. In addition to bringing a measure of peace to the region, his leadership also formalized Holland's commitment to tolerance. Raised as a Lutheran and educated as a

Key Dates	
12th C	Amsterdam founded
1576	William I of Orange-Nassau takes power from Spanish
1579	Union of Utrecht formalizes secession from Spanish rule
1585	Golden Age begins
1672	Golden Age ends
1795	French occupation begins
1815	Kingdom of Netherlands formally established
WWII	Jewish population decimated
1945	Hunger Winter
1968	Student protests spark beginnings of liberal social era

Catholic, William was wildly popular, and he respected freedom of religion so much that he came to be known as William the Silent for his policy of avoiding not only religious favoritism, but any topic that seemed to be too controversial or divisive.

That policy proved incredibly attractive to Europe's disenchanted masses: Between 1570 and 1640, Amsterdam's population increased from 30,000 to over 135,000. Booming international trade brought wave after wave of immigration, and the persecuted sought refuge in the city. Protestant settlers like the French Huguenots flocked to Amsterdam, as did Portuguese Jews, who, having fled the Spanish Inquisition, settled here and laid the foundations of the diamond-cutting industry that thrives to this day.

At the highpoint of the Golden Age (1585-1672), bolstered by the Dutch dominance on the high seas, the wealth of its colonies (Suriname and Batavia—later Indonesia—being the two most significant), and the Dutch East India Company's overseas spice trade, Amsterdam emerged as one of the world's wealthiest cities. Dutch banking notes were recognized worldwide as legal tender, and between 1613 and 1663, much of the city's characteristic appearance took shape. Historical buildings like the Dam Paleis (then the town hall), the Zuiderkerk, and the Westerkerk were built; stately houses and offices sprang up; and the business community financed many of the city's famous picturesque canals. While the Golden Age was the heyday of Amsterdam's commercial success, it also marked the highpoint in its cultural life. Patronage of the arts flourished. Philosophers like Baruch, Spinoza, and Descartes made the scene in Amsterdam; small but rich traditions in literary arts and printing emerged; Jan Steen, Frans Hals, and Vermeer ushered in the age of Dutch master painting; and Rembrandt produced *The Night Watch*.

The Golden Age came to an end in 1672, when both the French and the English attacked the country simultaneously. While Amsterdam's economy didn't crash, the 18th century ushered in a period of financial decline and in 1795 the country was brought to its knees: France occupied the Netherlands, and Amsterdam suffered from recession.

The 19th century brought a new hope for recovery. In 1815, the Kingdom of the Netherlands was formally established, prompting an economic recovery along with a surge of developments in architecture, infrastructure, and industry. Dutch revival styles sprang up in Gothic-, Renaissance-, and Baroque-inspired buildings, such as Cuypers' Centraal Station and Rijksmuseum and van Gendt's Concertgebouw. At the same time, Amsterdam was linked to the Rhine by way of the Amsterdam-Rijn Canal, and the Industrial Revolution ensured that the economy once again boomed. Another wave of immigration arrived on Amsterdam's shores, and the city expanded beyond the Singelgracht, as large, poorly built working-class neighborhoods, like the Jordaan, seemed to rise overnight.

Due to its neutrality, Amsterdam escaped World War I relatively unscathed, but between 1920 and 1940 the city was irreversibly scarred: Haphazard development meant that many historic buildings were destroyed and canals were filled in to accommodate the rising popularity of automobiles. Nonetheless, things would only get worse as World War II and two of the darkest episodes in Amsterdam's history loomed ahead.

At the highpoint of the Golden Age (1585-1672), bolstered by the Dutch dominance on the high seas, the wealth of its colonies, and the Dutch East India Company's overseas spice trade, Amsterdam emerged as one of the world's wealthiest cities.

First, despite some resistance by locals—notably dockworkers who staged a strike in February 1941—the entire Jewish population, so pivotal in trade, business, and culture, was virtually wiped out: 100,000 of Amsterdam's Jews, the most famous being Anne Frank, were deported and killed, and the Jewish Quarter (today's Waterlooplein area) was decimated. Secondly, in the bitter cold "Hunger Winter" of 1945, a German blockade of the city saw residents resort to eating tulip bulbs in order to survive. Train tracks were stripped of their wood to provide fuel for fires, to no avail as the elderly froze in unheated apartments and children were subject to diseases unknown in modern times.

In five short, violent years, Holland went from one of the healthiest countries on earth to one of immense suffering. But following World War II, Amsterdam was determined to rise again. Participation in NATO and the laying of the groundwork for the European Union helped Amsterdam's port to re-emerge as a hub for shipping commodities, and with the bitter memories of World War II fresh in the minds of the Dutch, the country looked inwards, planting its feet on a socially progressive path. In 1968, the Provos (short for Provocatives) emulated student activists in Berkeley, California, and in Paris, rioting for accessible education, housing, and social justice. Simultaneously, significant local powers—chiefly the planning and execution of social policies—were transferred to neighborhood councils whose aims are largely the preservation of a high standard of living. As a result, the last 30 years are rightly seen as both a period of radical change and the time that has most defined modern life in Amsterdam.

Night+Day's Amsterdam Urbie

Night+Day cities are chosen because they have a vibrant nightlife scene, standard-setting and innovative restaurants, cutting-edge hotels, and enough attractions to keep one busy for six days without doing the same thing twice. In short, they are fun. They represent the quintessential *urbanista* experience. This wouldn't exist but for the creativity and talents of many people and organizations. In honor of all who have played a role in making Amsterdam one of the world's greatest cities, Night+Day is pleased to give special recognition, and our Urbie Award, to an organization whose contribution is exemplary.

THE URBIE AWARD: Concrete Architectural Associates
As much as the Golden Age can be credited with giving this city its worldwide reputation as a hotbed for classic arts and culture, Rob Wagemans and his colleagues at Concrete Architectural Associates can be regarded as having cemented Amsterdam's place in the global-cool modern consciousness. Their design for the now-famous SupperClub restaurant and lounge earned them instant accolades, and from that point onwards this city hasn't looked the same.

Concrete's design sensibilities mean that the décor shares top billing with gorgeous, worldly patrons, and the room—be it a restaurant, bar, lounge, dance club, or all-in-one space—is not only a staging ground for a chic evening of dining and dancing, but a scene-stealing backdrop for the emerging modern international culture. Nightclubs like the high-wattage More are instant classics, restaurants like Blender and Envy have appeal with the culinary savvy, hyper-stylish crowd, and conceptual dining-lounge spaces like the SupperClub Cruise ship transcend cultures as much as they do conventions.

Perhaps the greatest measure of Concrete's contemporizing influence on Amsterdam's public spaces is the proliferation of up-to-the-minute design beyond the traditional domain of restaurants and bars: Measure the city-wide embrace of Concrete's work where even mundane retail spaces are rendered magnificent—the most obvious example being the stunning design for the Lairesse Pharmacy, which garnered Concrete a prestigious Lensvelt Architecture Prize. Their reputation has a global reach, and more recently their style does too: witness SupperClubs in Rome and San Francisco, and the Bremen, Germany's Hotel ÜberFluss. But it's Amsterdam that Wagemans loves, and as he's said, "Everything that makes life worth living you can find here."

Amsterdam: What It Is

Today's Amsterdam is a crowded melting pot: Almost 1.5 million people live in the greater region (750,000 in the city proper), and with over 173 nationalities present, you're bound to meet people from all corners of the globe. Almost 45 percent of the population belongs to a cultural minority group, and there are communities from Holland's former colonies (Indonesia gained independence in 1949, and Suriname did so in 1975) as well as significant Moroccan and Turkish populations who were recruited in the 1970s to satisfy a need for labor. Likewise, recent European Union legislation has resulted in an influx of European migrants, and even though 10 percent of the working population of 400,000 is already involved in the information technology sector, the growing demand for educated workers continues to encourage new arrivals.

Amsterdam's residents enjoy first-class universal health care, social equality including legalized civil marriages for same-sex couples, a generous welfare system, and the right to education, with the result that stereotypical urban blight—violent crime and crushing poverty—is virtually nonexistent on the city's streets. In fact, as the rebellious but social-minded spirit of the Provos lives on in Amsterdam, you're more likely to witness a semi-festive protest march than you are an act of violence. The locals do have a reputation for outspokenness, and they continue to argue for a balance between social pragmatism and individuals' rights, which illustrates the thinking behind the decriminalization of prostitution and soft drugs. But what may seem ridiculously liberal to foreign observers is trumpeted as a success here in Amsterdam: Death by an overdose of hard drugs is much less likely in Holland than it is elsewhere in Europe, the overall number of drug addicts appears to have dropped, and even the number of "coffeeshops" legally selling soft drugs is on the decline. Sure, it's far from perfect, but Amsterdam's "harm reduction" approach has gained a worldwide reputation as a model for confronting the drug issue.

Similarly, careful urban planning has allowed the development of streets where shops and cafes seem to mingle seamlessly with creative businesses and cultural venues, and where cars still take a backseat to bicycles. These remain Amsterdam's preferred mode of transport, and with over 400 km (250 miles) of bike paths, it's easy to understand why.

As good as things seem, Amsterdam is not immune to the occasional identity crisis, and the latest soul searching, prompted by the 2004 murder of a controversial filmmaker at the hands of a Dutch Muslim immigrant of Moroccan descent, has caused some residents to wonder aloud "Where is this city going?" Current hot topics include the assimilation of immigrants (especially Muslims), Holland's role in the European Union, the responsible use of the freedom of speech, and the preservation of "Dutch values" in an increasingly multicultural society. But surprisingly, the one topic that never seems to be on the table is the pervasiveness of English. Sure, the Dutch still speak Dutch, but you won't need to: Almost everyone is bilingual.

In contrast to the flexible approach to language, the Dutch have one principle that they won't compromise on, and that is *gezelligheid*. It's best translated as the coziness that's achieved through a mellow, charming atmosphere, and Amsterdammers love it. You're bound to encounter it during your stay. More often than not, first-time visitors misinterpret the Dutch efforts in pursuit of *gezelligheid* as poor service, but if you pay attention, you'll avoid looking like a newcomer: You'll have to ask for a menu in a restaurant because waiters don't want to appear to be rushing your dinner along. You'll definitely have to ask for the check at the end of a meal because leaving it on the table would have the appearance of pushing you out the door. Consistent with the socially progressive ethos, flashy personalities, classism, and showing off in general are looked down upon, and the nightlife scene, in particular, is much more democratic than it is elsewhere in Europe.

Amsterdam's residents enjoy first-class universal health care, social equality including legalized civil marriages for same-sex couples, a generous welfare system, and the right to education, with the result that stereotypical urban blight—violent crime and crushing poverty—is virtually non-existent on the city's streets.

But enough with the history. You're here for fun, and and no matter what your interests or tastes, Amsterdam is ready to show you it has something for everyone. Whether you've come to check out the of-the-moment design and architecture that 21st–century Amsterdam has come to symbolize, or you're here to feed your inner Rembrandt and revel in historic glory, Amsterdam bids you a hearty welcome.

Welcome to fabulous Amsterdam ...

THE 99 BEST of AMSTERDAM

Who needs another "Best" list? You do—if it comes with details and insider tips that make the difference between a good experience and a great one. We've pinpointed the 33 categories that make Amsterdam exciting, magnetic, and unforgettable, and picked the absolute three best places to go for each. Check out the next few pages of our favorite ways to play in this invigorating city—the glamorous lounges, happening cultural scenes, stellar architecture, don't-miss museums, and liveliest places to see-and-be-seen.

Best After-Work Drinks

#1–3: Stop in for a quick one or set up camp for the night. Starting at about 5:30pm, these fun and friendly bars attract an after-work crowd that's in no rush to get home.

Café Luxembourg*
Spui 24, Nieuwe Zijde, 620-6264 • Classic

The Draw: One of the city's best brown cafes (local watering holes typically with tiny Persian-carpet beer mats, dark wood, and lots of neighborhood revelers) is also a hot spot for gathering after the office closes.

The Scene: The world's international press has spread the word on Luxembourg's fine menu of Dutch classics, competent bartenders, and authentic brown bar décor. Nevertheless, attracted by the reading table and bustling singles scene, lots of regulars still call it theirs. *Sun-Thu 9am-1am, Fri-Sat 9am-2am.* ≡

Hot Tip: When it's busy, stock up on your drinks; you won't see your server again anytime soon.

Café 't Schuim*
Spuistraat 189, Nieuwe Zijde, 638-9357 • Hip

The Draw: Creative 20- and 30-somethings jockey for space and drinks in a fun, lively atmosphere.

The Scene: Comfortable chairs and sofas provide the perfect vantage point for scanning the crowd in this large restaurant-bar. In addition to the huge selection of premium vodkas, a boisterous crowd and laid-back singles scene make it an Amsterdam favorite. *Sun-Wed 11am-1am, Thu-Sat 11am-3am.* ≡

Hot Tip: 't Schuim has a well-earned reputation for its excellent coffee.

Café Wildschut*
Roelof Hartplein 1-3, Museumplein, 676-8220 • Classic

The Draw: Drink a cold one on a large terrace that's always buzzing by 6pm.

The Scene: Patrons in this Art-Deco cafe tend to be "starters"—young professionals at the beginning of their careers—or business types who live in the up-and-coming residential areas nearby. The singles scene rages on Friday nights, from after work until late, so don't leave too soon. *Mon-Thu 9am-1am, Fri 9am-3am, Sat 10am-2am, Sun 10am-1am.* ≡

Hot Tip: Close to the Concertgebouw, Wildschut is ideally situated for pre- (or post-) concert drinks.

Always-Trendy Tables

#4–6: Who says hot spots always cool down? Sure, up-to-the-minute décor and menus often don't have staying power, but by serving excellent cuisine in stylish settings, these enduring eateries continue to attract chic crowds.

Cinema Paradiso
Westerstraat 184-186, Jordaan, 623-7344 • Cool

The Draw: Strut your calculatedly informal-glamorous stuff—and check out the competition—in the company of Amsterdam's who's-who.

The Scene: International soccer stars, Dutch A-listers, and Amsterdam fashionistas by the gorgeous tableful vie for attention, drawing the focus away from the simple interior and uncomplicated, seafood-heavy Italian cuisine. *Tue-Sun 6-11pm*. € ≡

Hot Tip: Come early for a drink; they don't accept reservations and you're guaranteed to wait for your table.

The Dylan (formerly Blakes Amsterdam)
Keizersgracht 384, Jordaan, 530-2010 • Cool

The Draw: Schilo van Coevorden's legendary East-West cuisine—think fillet of veal with shanso pepper, udon noodles, and black bean sauce—promises a food-induced nirvana.

The Scene: Celebrities, locals, and jet set visitors jockey for tables. Attentive servers and a cool but warm design scheme featuring rich fabrics and dark colors complete the Zen-like sensory feast. *Daily noon-2pm and 6:30-10:30pm. Tea 3-5pm.* €€€ ⊟

Hot Tip: Request one of the two tables with courtyard views.

SupperClub*
Jonge Roelensteeg 21, Nieuwe Zijde, 344-6400 • Cool

The Draw: It's arguably the birthplace of the modern design lounge phenomenon that has spread across Europe and the US.

The Scene: Five-course tasting menus, DJs, day beds, and massages in the all-white space are integral parts of the SupperClub experience, as are staff members as beautiful as the international clientele. *Sun-Thu 8pm-1am, Fri-Sat 8pm-3am, private lounge open nightly from 7pm.* €€ (set menu) ≡

Hot Tip: Experience it on a Friday or Saturday when live music and performance artists make the scene.

Art Museums

#7–9: One of Amsterdam's big draws is its wealth of world-class art museums. From Rembrandt and Van Gogh to Mondriaan and the next wave of installation artists, you'll find Dutch masters of all centuries at these heavyweight art institutions.

Rijksmuseum

Jan Luijkenstraat 1, Museumplein, 674-7000 • Classic

The Draw: A massive collection of Golden Age paintings, it includes such masterpieces as Vermeer's *The Kitchen Maid*, and *The Jewish Bride* and *The Night Watch*, both by Rembrandt.

The Scene: The imposing building designed by Pierre Cuypers and completed in 1885 houses one of the world's most significant collections of paintings and creates the perfect atmosphere for old-world culture. *Daily 9am-6pm, Friday till 10pm.* €

Hot Tip: Come on a weekday to avoid the crowd, opt for the informative audio tour, and jump the line by purchasing an entrance ticket in advance at the AUB ticket office. (see p.161)

Stedelijk Museum CS

Oosterdokskade 5, Eastern Harbor, 573-2911 • Hip

The Draw: Groundbreaking art, in various media, from today's hottest artists.

The Scene: Temporary exhibits featuring the world's up-and-coming artists make this always-changing venue on an industrial site minutes from Centraal Station the perfect postmodern stand-in while the Stedelijk Museum CS undergoes renovations. *Daily 10am-6pm.* €

Hot Tip: Call or check the website (stedelijk.nl) for a list of the evening lectures: Often in English, the subjects range from aesthetics to robotics to food.

Van Gogh Museum

Paulus Potterstraat 7, Museumplein, 570-5200 • Classic

The Draw: The world's largest Van Gogh collection contains a wealth of iconic works by the artist: *Sunflowers, The Potato Eaters*, and *Self-Portrait as an Artist* are standouts.

The Scene: With a main building designed by Gerrit Rietveld and an exhibition hall designed by Kisho Kurokawa, the museum is the perfect light and airy showcase for boldly colored masterpieces. Even the most jaded art snob has to be impressed. *Sat-Thu 10am-6pm, Fri 10am-10pm.* €€

Hot Tip: Come early in the day (right at 10am) to avoid the largest crowds. Look for the perfect gift at the museum shop. It has a comprehensive selection of books, stationery, posters, and reproductions.

Beer-Lovers Spots

#10–12: Heineken and Grolsch are the most famous beers from this country. But Holland has a rich and proud brewing history and its people have a love for the brown drink. Don't hesitate to ask the patrons and bartenders to recommend their favorites.

't Arendsnest

Herengracht 90, Jordaan, 421-2057 • Classic

The Draw: Every brewery in the Netherlands is represented here—it's the only pub in the country selling exclusively Dutch beer.

The Scene: Peter the bar owner is a certified "beer specialist," but the patrons know their stuff too. The 30-something crowd is warm, friendly, and happy to share their opinions on the best of Dutch brews. *Sun-Thu 4pm-midnight, Fri-Sat 4pm-2am.* ≡

Hot Tip: Order anything but Grolsch or Heineken, which will make you stand out like a rank amateur.

Café Gollem

Raamsteeg 4, Nieuwe Zijde, 626-6645 • Classic

The Draw: Amsterdam's first specialty beer bar has 200 beers on hand representing a cross section of Europe's finest Krieks, Lambics, and Trappist brews.

The Scene: The low lighting, beer banners, and acres of dark wood won't win any design awards, but face it, that's not why you're here. The crowd is hip but diverse since all beer lovers eventually find their way to Gollem. *Sun-Thu 4pm-1am, Fri-Sat 2pm-2am.* ≡

Hot Tip: Order your brew of choice in a guik, a traditional stone chalice.

Heineken Experience

Stadhouderskade 78, De Pijp, 523-9666 • Hip

The Draw: Learn about Heineken's history, gain a richer appreciation for the craft of brewing, and have a beer or two while you're at it.

The Scene: Visiting this historical brewery-turned-museum is a rite of passage for vacationing students and British tourists on stag weekends, but don't let that scare you away. The self-guided tour offers an informative and fun look at Holland's most famous brand. *Tue-Sun 10am-6pm.* Note: Last tickets are sold at 5pm. €

Hot Tip: Buy a souvenir "Biertje?" T-shirt. Only a local would know that the phrase, originally part of a Dutch Heineken ad campaign, has entered the Dutch vernacular as a synonym for "Wanna beer?"

Brunches

#13–15: Having an elaborate breakfast seems downright foreign to most Dutch, so satisfying the urge to splurge on Sunday morning takes a bit of inside knowledge. These new places are starting a trend with diverse brunch menus and bustling scenes.

Brasserie van Baerle

Van Baerlestraat 158, Zuid, 679-1532 • Cool

> The Draw: Beautiful brunches with a cosmopolitan, Parisian vibe make it a constant favorite.
>
> The Scene: Old money, new money, local celebrities, and informed visitors all make an appearance at this staple on the "let's-do-lunch" circuit. The scarcity of great Sunday brunch spots coupled with oenologist Floor van Ede's wine list means you have to book ahead. *Mon-Sat noon-11pm, Sun 10am-11pm, brunch Sun 10am-1pm. €€* ≡
>
> Hot Tip: Beg for a table in the charming, shaded garden.

La Sirene

Apollolaan 2, Zuid, 570-5724 • Classic

> The Draw: Enjoy a standout champagne brunch at the junction of five canals.
>
> The Scene: Focusing on seafood, Rob Blaauboer's brunch menu promises sophistication and old-world charm, drawing a classy crowd of smart locals and visitors alike. *Mon-Sat noon-2:30pm and 6-10pm, Sun noon-2:30pm. €€€* ≡
>
> Hot Tip: It's all about the water: Arrive by water taxi at the hotel's private marina and head straight to the garden terrace.

Wolvenstraat*

Wolvenstraat 23, Jordaan, 320-0843 • Hip

> The Draw: Amsterdam's in-the-know breakfast spot attracts clubbers and the terminally hip.
>
> The Scene: With delicious, uncomplicated food and long hours, this low-attitude design-lounge attracts an overwhelmingly local crowd. Work on a Powerbook, flip through the latest copy of *Wallpaper*, or sit back and enjoy the mellow tunes. You'll fit right in. *Mon-Fri 8:30am-1am, Sat 10am-2am, Sun noon-1am. €* ≡
>
> Hot Tip: Ask the well-connected staff for the inside scoop on the night's most promising parties and gallery openings.

Coffeeshops

#16–18: Coffeeshops aren't here for your java fix, but they will hook you up with other vices—in this city, coffeeshops are places where marijuana is sold off menus kept discreetly behind the bar. Just ask, but be warned: More than one tourist has overestimated their capacity to handle what is often the strongest pot you've come across since Woodstock.

Coffeeshop de Dampkring
Handboogstraat 29, Nieuwe Zijde, 638-0705 • Classic

The Draw: This classic spot is a perennial favorite among Cannabis Cup voters.

The Scene: An old-school den with a solid reputation for quality and variety, De Dampkring aims to please and succeeds. They have a rare license to serve alcohol, the staff are friendly, the music is mainstream, and the patrons are too. *Sun-Thu 10am-1am, Fri-Sat 10am-2am.*

Hot Tip: Try the "Ocean's Twelve," named in honor of the movie that was partially shot inside and whose cast is known to make cameo appearances.

Dutch Flowers
Singel 387, Jordaan, 624-7624 • Classic

The Draw: Rare and high-grade, uh, products, including cigars.

The Scene: A city-center location and a menu of hard-to-find specialties make it well-loved by locals and tourists alike who are looking for the real deal. The alcohol license (one of only a few) increases the chill-out factor. *Sun-Thu 10am-1am, Fri-Sat 10am-2am.*

Hot Tip: Come during fine weather—the canal-side terrace is the perfect Amsterdam spot for relaxing and watching the day float by.

Kadinsky
Three Locations: Rosmarijnsteeg 9, Langebrugsteeg 7A, and Zoutsteeg 14, Nieuwe Zijde • Hip

The Draw: Hip without being self-conscious, Kadinsky has an interior that's uniquely contemporary and modern, making it the only coffeeshop with designer appeal.

The Scene: Less commercial than the big-name places, located near some great nightlife options, and more refined than its competition, Kadinsky attracts a cooler, more creative, and stylish crowd. *Daily 10am-1am.*

Hot Tip: Come here to try "space cakes," Amsterdam's infamous brownies.

Contemporary Art Spaces

#19-21: This city's creative reputation might be founded on Rembrandt and Van Gogh, but if you want to check its artistic pulse, head to its contemporary exhibition spaces. Showcasing exciting work from Holland's hottest artists alongside international stars—some rising, others firmly established—they offer an enticing glimpse into the future.

De Appel Centre for Contemporary Art

Nieuwe Spiegelstraat 10, Canal Belt, 625-5651 • Hip

The Draw: De Appel features unconventional exhibitions featuring the hottest up-and-coming artists from the Netherlands and beyond.

The Scene: Hip meets highbrow as scenesters of all ages show up to take measure of the boundary-busting art world and to meet tomorrow's brightest stars. Edgy exhibitions focused around alternative themes add a slightly subversive touch to the ambience. *Tue-Sun 11am-6pm, Tue nights by reservations only.* €

Hot Tip: Visit on a Tuesday night when impromptu exhibitions and stimulating lectures by visiting luminaries enhance the schedule.

De Balie

Kleine Gartmanplantsoen 10, Canal Belt, 553-5100 • Hip

The Draw: View new media, photography, design, films, and decorative arts in the company of what is possibly Amsterdam's most creative-hip crowd.

The Scene: In-the-know trendsetters show up to be challenged by the art, by the symposiums that fill up the agenda, and by each other—although the latter happens in the cafe over beer—providing the perfect opportunity for conversations with gorgeous and creative locals. *Opening times vary according to events and exhibitions. Cafe Sun-Thu 10am-1am, Fri-Sat 10am-2am.* €

Hot Tip: You don't have to attend an art exhibition to make use of the cafe; just steps from the Leidseplein, and boasting a sidewalk terrace, it's an insider alternative to the area's more touristy options.

Loods 6

KNSMlaan 143, Eastern Harbor, 418-2020 • Cool

The Draw: A contemporary art mecca offering exhibition spaces occupied by art collectives, it also has 10 design boutiques, and over 50 studios and galleries, all under one roof.

The Scene: Art Basel the Dutch way: Serious aficionados browse high-end—and highbrow—exhibitions and ateliers, and shop for must-have pieces, rounding out their collections. *Mon-Fri 9am-5pm. Evening hours vary, call for schedule.*

Hot Tip: Time your visit to coincide with an exhibition opening or one-off event to catch the crowd at its most buzzing.

Dance Clubs

#22–24: Amsterdam loves to kick up its heels. Big-name international DJs are always dropping in to spin house, trance, hip-hop, disco, and even salsa. Like everything in Amsterdam, there's a spot for any taste.

Club Magazijn

Warmoesstraat 170, Oude Zijde, 669-4469 • Hip

The Draw: Mingle with the city's most approachable and chilled-out dance crowd.

The Scene: People are here for two reasons only—to dance and to have fun. It shows. High on the hip-factor, yet low in attitude, the attractive crowd is warm, welcoming, and interested in music much more than showing off. *Wed 9pm-3am, Thu 10pm-3am, Fri-Sat 10pm-4am, Sun 9pm-3am.* C≡

Hot Tip: Relaxed doesn't mean come-as-you-are; dress casual-trendy and you'll make a great impression.

Escape deLux

Rembrandtplein 11, Rembrandtplein, 622-1111 • Cool

The Draw: Good-looking 30-somethings rule this sophisticated space.

The Scene: Not to be confused with Escape, which shares the same entrance, this club within a club seems to exclude anyone under the age of 25, so there's never the risk of students taking over. That suits the regulars just fine, thank you. Dress up and shake it to inspired house, dance classics, and disco. *Thu 11pm-4am, Fri-Sat 11pm-7am, Sun 11pm-4am.* C≡

Hot Tip: Amsterdammers often appear to be dancing to the beat of their own drummer, but here you can see it first hand. Peer through the windows to the separate club below where you can watch, but not hear, the evening's entertainment.

Panama

Oostelijke Handelskade 4, Eastern Harbor, 311-8686 • Cool

The Draw: Visiting celeb DJs like Sander Kleinenberg, Frankie Knuckles, and Tiësto complement an exceedingly capable stable of "DJs-in-residence."

The Scene: Thirty-ish dance aficionados get their groove on in two rooms, one with hip-hop and soul music, and the other—the main attraction—with house music and two bars. *Thu-Sun; times and prices vary according to events.* C≡

Hot Tip: Although the food isn't great, you can avoid the door line for the club by eating at the restaurant until the dance spaces open.

Best

Dutch Design

#25–27: Dutch designers are famous for their enlightened fusion of form and function. At the lairs of these masters, you're guaranteed to see some outstanding and creative takes on traditional items.

Droog Design
Staalstraat 7b, Oude Zijde, 523-5059 • Hip

The Draw: Modern icons from Holland's hottest collection fill this stylish space.

The Scene: Droog's new home shows works by Marcel Wanders, Tejo Remy, and a host of other big-name designers. Equal parts exhibition space and showroom, everything is for sale. *Tue-Sun noon-6pm.*

Hot Tip: Amsterdam's creative set makes the scene at Droog's openings. Call ahead for the agenda of events.

The Frozen Fountain
Prinsengracht 645, Canal Belt, 622-9375 • Cool

The Draw: Specialized collections of contemporary furniture and home accessories with a focus on Dutch crafts lure a sophisticated crowd.

The Scene: Stylish, moneyed locals and international design enthusiasts browse brands alongside installations and commissioned art pieces in a canal-side showroom. *Mon 1-6pm, Tue-Fri 10am-6pm, Sat 10am-5pm.*

Hot Tip: For those who love fine contemporary ceramics and linens, this is a great spot to buy from the Netherlands' top fabric and craft mavens.

Platform 21 Amsterdam Design Center
Prinses Irenestraat 19, Zuid, 344-9449 • Cool

The Draw: A hot artistic crowd gathers to check out the latest in new culture.

The Scene: Academia meets the street. The fashion and design exhibitions attract a broad—although universally creative—section of society. Lectures and symposiums range between the practical and the esoteric, turning Amsterdam's artistic class into philosophers. *Agenda varies according to exhibition calendar.*

Hot Tip: Some events here require tickets, especially the excellent debates, panels, and lectures that draw the city's hippest design crowd. Check for updates on the website (platform21.com), and note that this site is also considered part of the gallery, and has "exhibits" of its own.

Dutch Dining

#28–30: Even if you don't know your stamppot from your hutspot, don't pass up the chance to try Holland's native cuisine. It's flavorful stuff, and a well-established interest in locally sourced products has made Amsterdam a leader in organic, innovative options.

De Kas
Kamerlingh Onneslaan 3, East, 462-4562 • Classic

The Draw: De Kas means "the greenhouse" in Dutch, and that's where you'll be eating. To ensure freshness, the ingredients of every 5-course meal are grown on site or on the restaurant's private farm.

The Scene: This picturesque spot located in the middle of a park will leave you thinking you've left the city for the countryside. The presence of Amsterdam's who's who will remind you that you're not far from the center of the action. *Mon-Fri noon-2pm and 6:30-10pm, Sat 6:30-10pm.* €€ (set menu) ≡

Hot Tip: Book the chef's table and ask for a tour of the greenhouse. It accommodates 2-4 people at €125 each, which includes four courses and wine pairings.

Saskia's Huiskamer
Albert Cuypstraat 203, De Pijp, 862-9839 • Hip

The Draw: You'll feel like part of a hip family on Friday and Saturday nights when Saskia invites guests into her informal dinner space.

The Scene: Amsterdam's trendsetters are happy to eat whatever Saskia dishes out, which is perfect since everyone is served the same delicious, 4-course menu that draws upon Holland's finest culinary traditions. In another nod to egalitarianism, you dine sitting shoulder to shoulder with strangers at a long table for 20, guaranteeing your chances of meeting some locals. *Fri-Sat at 7:30pm by reservation only.* €€ (set menu) ▯≡

Hot Tip: Put the book down and call for a reservation. Now.

d' Vijff Vlieghen
Spuistraat 294-302, Nieuwe Zijde, 530-4060 • Classic

The Draw: Its "New-Dutch cuisine" promises organic ingredients and modern takes on classic dishes like lamb and saddle of rabbit, but the real draw is the atmospheric location.

The Scene: Set in five authentic 17th-century buildings, the candlelit dining experience and top-notch service continues to attract A-list clients who appreciate tradition. *Daily from 5:30pm.* €€ ▬

Hot Tip: Call ahead to request a table in the Rembrandt Room, where you'll find four original etchings handmade by the master himself.

Dutch Drinking

#31–33: Combining time-honored distilling traditions with friendly, up-to-date locals and well-informed barkeeps, these Amsterdam institutions are the perfect gateway into the laid-back world of jenevers (Dutch gins) and liquors.

De Admiraal

Herengracht 319, Jordaan, 625-4334 • Classic

The Draw: A large roster of liquors, jenevers, beers, and wines means there's something for everyone—and everyone shows up.

The Scene: Friendly. From the guy behind the bar to the woman standing next to you, this is a congenial crowd that enjoys their drink. Factor in the period décor and it's easy to see why this is a perennial favorite among a cross-section of 30-something locals and visitors alike. *Mon-Sat 4:30-10:30pm.* ☰

Hot Tip: Get it while you can! This is the only bar offering the wares of Amsterdam's last independent distiller, van Wees.

Café Hoppe

Spui 18-20, Nieuwe Zijde, 420-4420 • Hip

The Draw: A lively crowd, which often spills out into the street, makes this a casually fun spot to drink.

The Scene: The interior—dark wood and sand on the floor—suggests the past without being passé. Young businessmen coexist with hip 20- and 30-somethings, and a lively pick-up scene develops nightly. *Sun-Thu 8am-1am, Fri-Sat 8am-2am.* ☰

Hot Tip: Don't be fooled by the early opening hours. The crowd begins to build right after work, so come in the early evening.

Het Proeflokaal Wynand Fockink

Pijlsteeg 31, Nieuwe Zijde, 639-2695 • Classic

The Draw: Sip house-brand liquors and jenevers in a 400-year-old "tasting bar" that remains the city's most traditional.

The Scene: It's standing room only in this hidden gem, but that doesn't deter the scores of professionals who drop in for a tipple. The dark brown wooden bar oozes history, the crowd is warm, and the barkeep has an encyclopedic knowledge of spirits. *Mon-Sun 4-9pm.* ☰

Hot Tip: You won't recognize much on the menu so let the bartender-guru surprise you.

Fine Dining

#34–36: Fine dining here competes with anything the culinary capitals of Europe can offer. Whether it's a white-tablecloth classic you're looking for, or something more extraordinary—like an ultra-exclusive chef's table—Amsterdam has a place for you.

La Rive

Professor Tulpplein 1, Canal Belt, 520-3264 • Classic

The Draw: Sophisticated clientele, an elegant setting, and Edwin Kats' 2–Michelin-star classic French cuisine make it one of the city's best.

The Scene: A must for discerning diners, La Rive is ground zero for Amsterdam's most demanding traditionalists. Crisp white linens, a 3,000-bottle wine room, and a range of Cuban cigars are merely side attractions to the food and who's-who crowd—business movers and shakers and royalty among them—in the city's grand dame of restaurants. *Mon-Fri noon-2pm and 6:30-10:30pm, Sat 6:30-10:30pm. €€€* –

Hot Tip: Take exclusive to new heights at the private chef's table. Available by special request only, it's an 8-course, culinary tour de force.

Van Vlaanderen

Weteringschans 175, Canal Belt, 622-8292 • Classic

The Draw: Chef Philippart's contemporary spins on French-Belgian classics have set a standard for culinary excellence, earning a Michelin star along the way.

The Scene: It's where sophisticated diners come looking for a rarified gastronomic experience and informed servers are happy to oblige, but the spotlight remains firmly focused on the food. Patrons excuse the bare décor and instead come for some of this city's finest cuisine. *Tue-Thu from 6:30pm, Fri-Sat from 7pm. €€€* –

Hot Tip: Bas, the sommelier, is one of the city's best. Trust him.

Yamazato

The Okura Hotel, Ferdinand Bolstraat 333, De Pijp, 678-7111 • Classic

The Draw: It might be Europe's finest Japanese restaurant. The traditional dishes prepared with Zen-like artistry have earned a Michelin star.

The Scene: Tokyo meets Holland. Japanese businessmen and local gourmands dine at the superb sushi bar or retire to tables, enjoying selections from the classic menu. A minimalist Eastern interior and great selection of sake are the perfect complements to Akira Oshima's creations, fueling the Buddhist-like devotion of loyal diners. *Daily noon-2pm and 6-9:30pm. €€€* –

Hot Tip: Request a table overlooking the scenic Japanese garden.

Gay Scenes

#37–39: Amsterdam is known for being a gay-friendly destination where alternative and straight crowds readily mix without much attitude. Nevertheless, dedicated gay bars, mostly focused on Warmoesstraat and Reguliersdwarsstraat, do exist, and they are loud, proud, and draw the best crowds.

Arc
Reguliersdwarsstraat 44, Rembrandtplein, 689-7070 • Cool

The Draw: Come dinnertime, this trendy cafe turns into a design restaurant, bar, and nightclub.

The Scene: Young, hip, mainly male patrons spill out into the street, sipping smart cocktails and greeting passing friends and colleagues, lending a neighborhood pub feel to this popular and stylish meeting spot. *Sun-Thu 10am-1am, Fri-Sat 10am-3am.* ≡

Hot Tip: Don't miss Arc's popular cocktail "hour"; 5-7pm nightly and all night Wednesday, but eat elsewhere. The food here isn't great.

Soho
Reguliersdwarsstraat 36, Rembrandtplein, 422-3312 • Hip

The Draw: One of the city's most popular gay scenes, it has swank and very handsome crowds.

The Scene: Not for the claustrophobic. This bar, featuring acres of wood and comfortable seats (think English pub décor) has a-great looking clientele, but gets packed like no other. On weekends, DJs add a clubby party feel to the slightly cruisy ambience. *Sun-Thu 8pm-3am, Fri-Sat 8pm-4am.* ≡

Hot Tip: Happy hour features two-for-one drinks from midnight until 1am nightly.

De Trut
Bilderdijkstraat 165, West, (no phone) • Hip

The Draw: De Trut, "The Bitch," is a very popular dance party, and a Sunday night spent here grooving and flirting is a gay Amsterdam tradition.

The Scene: Don't expect design décor. Come for the exclusively gay and lesbian crowd, great DJs, inexpensive drinks, unpretentious and high-energy vibe, international visitors, locals, and serious flirting. *Sun 11pm-4am.* ⊂≡

Hot Tip: Be in the line-up by 10:30pm: It's that busy, and once it's full, it's full.

Guided Tours

Best

#40–42: Amsterdam's beauty is on the surface, but its true glory is often hidden where you least expect it. From contemporary architecture to historic spots to the Red Light District, you'll feel like an insider, not a tourist, on these expert-led tours that take you where the crowds can't follow.

Architectour

Various locations, 625-9123 • Cool

The Draw: See Amsterdam's famous buildings through architectural historian Caroline van Raamsdonk's keen eye.

The Scene: Caroline is energetic, knowledgeable, humorous, and passionate about architecture. Her excursions are the perfect introduction to the city's modern landmarks and neighborhoods. €€€€+

Hot Tip: Caroline's extensive network of contacts allows her to bring you to private buildings that are off-limits to other guides.

ARTTRA Cultural Agency

Tweede Boomdwarsstraat 4, Jordaan, 625-9303 • Classic

The Draw: Knowledgeable guides tailor each tour to your interests, ensuring that you see what you want to see when you want to see it—particularly good if you're interested in this city's rich artistic legacy.

The Scene: All of the guides are art historians, making this the perfect tour for those wanting a bit of scholarly insight into Amsterdam's storied art world. €€€€+

Hot Tip: Nobody said it had to be a walking tour. Consider making it a canal tour by arranging for a boat to speed you through your itinerary.

Yellow Bike Tours

Nieuwezijds Kolk 29, Nieuwe Zijde, 620-6940 • Classic

The Draw: Experience Amsterdam and its surroundings the way that the locals do—from the comfort of a classic bicycle.

The Scene: Sticking to the safe and extensive cycling paths, informed and enthusiastic guides give international visitors a comprehensive overview of the city's highlights. *Daily 8:30am-5:30pm.* €€

Hot Tip: For the more adventurous, Yellow Bikes also offers a country village tour that will give you a taste of Dutch villages.

Historic Sites

#43–45: An 800-year-old city has a lot of stories to tell. Head to the top historic sites for a glimpse into Amsterdam's rich, glorious, and sometimes darkly fascinating past.

Amsterdam Historical Museum • Amsterdams Historisch Museum

Nieuwezijds Voorburgwal 357, Nieuwe Zijde, 523-1822 • Classic

The Draw: Everything you ever wanted to know about Amsterdam's history under one roof.

The Scene: Housed in a 14th-century orphanage and organized according to topics like crime and punishment, the Golden Age, and children, the exhibitions emphasize the human side of Amsterdam, bringing this city's past to life. *Mon-Fri 10am-5pm, Sat-Sun 11am-5pm.* €

Hot Tip: Take a stroll through the Civic Guard Gallery, one of the city's most unique laneways.

Anne Frank House • Anne Frank Huis

Prinsengracht 267, Jordaan, 556-7105 • Classic

The Draw: The one time hiding place of Amsterdam's most famous citizen is now a museum centered on the intact secret annex where Anne hid during World War II.

The Scene: Visitors from all over the world come to pay their respects and to celebrate the spirit of Anne Frank. Her original diary is on display, and context is given through the presentation of short films, documents, and photographs. *Apr-Aug 9am-9pm, Sept-Mar 9am-7pm.* €

Hot Tip: Be there when the doors open to beat the summer crowds.

Begijnhof

Entry from Gedempte Begijnensloot, Nieuwe Zijde, 622-1918 • Classic

The Draw: This courtyard garden is an oasis of peace and tranquility in the heart of the city.

The Scene: Steps from the retail madness of the Kalverstraat and still in use as a refuge for single women, the Begijnhof houses two churches and the city's oldest house, Het Houten Huis (The Wooden House). *Daily 9am-5pm.*

Hot Tip: The Engelse Kerk (English Church) is one of very few Protestant churches that hold Sunday services in English.

Hot-Shot Chefs

#46–48: Whether they're serving up creations from their latest seasonal menus or playing to the cameras, the city's big-name chefs keep crowds buzzing with some of Europe's most inventive dishes and avant-garde attitudes.

Fifteen Amsterdam*

Jollemanhof 9, Eastern Harbor, 0900-343-8336 • Cool

The Draw: Mega-star Jamie Oliver's international reputation packs the house at his first restaurant outside the UK.

The Scene: The highly skilled Ben van Beurten stands in for Jamie, the seasonal four-course menu changes weekly, the design-meets-the-street décor works, the beautiful young professionals keep showing up, and the proceeds help to transform unemployed youth into skilled chefs. What's not to like? *Mon-Sat 6pm-1am, Sun 3pm-1am. €€ (set menu)* ≡

Hot Tip: Come early for cocktails—it's a fun spot to watch the evening heat up.

Le Garage

Ruysdaelstraat 54-56, Zuid, 679-7176 • Cool

The Draw: It's not the newest place in town, but Dutch A-list celebrities continue to hold court at chef-cum-television star Joop Braakhekke's smart French-style rotisserie.

The Scene: Imagine Paris the Dutch way: bustling waiters, red plush seats, lots of brass, and a great steak frites. An abundance of mirrors and high-wattage lights conveniently allow you to sneak glimpses of the beautiful people sitting three tables away. *Mon-Fri noon-2pm and 6-11pm, Sat-Sun 6-11pm. €€* ≡

Hot Tip: Come on Thursday for lunch or dinner, when the local who's who meet for their weekly see-and-be-seen sessions.

Lute Restaurant

Oude Molen 5, Ouderkerk aan de Amstel, 472-2462 • Cool

The Draw: From the food to the stylish chef-owner to the Marcel Wanders-appointed dining room and cosmopolitan guests, this place is sexy.

The Scene: International style mavens and local fashionistas pack the industrial design space to dine on edible wonders. In the décor, in the prime ingredients that make up the dishes, and even in the parking lot with its parade of luxury cars, no expense has been spared, making nights at Lute smart, exclusive affairs. *Mon-Fri noon-2pm and 6-10pm, Sat-Sun 6-10pm. €€* ≡

Hot Tip: Show up in style. Arrange for a water taxi to transport you from the city center to the pastoral, canal-side village location.

Hotel Bars

#49–51: While every hotel has its own version of a lobby bar, a select few stand out as places where more than tourists gather. Whether you're looking for a great view, great drinks, or simply a good place to check out the scene, these spots make the grade.

Bar Americain

Leidsekade 97, Canal Belt, 556-3000 • Classic

The Draw: Fine cocktails and great people-watching are complemented by the comfort of an Art-Deco classic.

The Scene: Bar Americain courts the pre- and post-dinner crowds who watch the bustling Leidseplein from the wide front window. In summer the hotel's international guests lounge on the terrace. *Daily 5pm-1am.* ≡

Hot Tip: Be sure to try some "borrel hapjes." Holland's equivalent to pretzels and peanuts, they're omnipresent in the Netherlands' classic cocktail bars.

Ciel Bleu Bar*

The Okura Hotel, Ferdinand Bolstraat 333, De Pijp, 678-7111 • Classic

The Draw: Enjoy your drinks with a panoramic view of the Amsterdam skyline that stretches from the city's southern edge to the harbor in the North.

The Scene: On the 23rd floor of the Okura Hotel, beside the Michelin star restaurant of the same name, this international cocktail bar attracts a mature clientele as well as the city's business crowd. *Daily 6pm-1am.* ≡

Hot Tip: Time your visit to see the sun set over the city: around 10pm in the summer and as early as 4:30pm in the winter, or after-work to enjoy the best crowds.

College Bar & Lounge*

The College Hotel, Roelof Hartstraat 1, Museumplein, 571-1511 • Cool

The Draw: Sophisticated, fashionable locals join the stylish hotel guests drinking designer cocktails in a warm design space.

The Scene: Dark, rich colors, black oak floors, a fireplace, and intimate corners give this bar real sex appeal. Not to be upstaged, groups of beautiful guests dress to fit in, making this bar the stylish 30-somethings' current weekend watering hole of choice. *Daily 9am-1am.* ≡

Hot Tip: In a coveted seat beside the fireplace, order a "Dutch College Swinger," the lounge's signature drink, with champagne, raspberry liqueur, and blackberries.

Italian Eateries

#52–54: The Dutch taste for hearty comfort food and *gezelling* (cozy) spaces has helped make Italian restaurants a popular choice with locals. Choose old-world charm and classic dishes, or up-to-the-minute, minimalist décor with new spins on this beloved cuisine.

Hostaria

2e Egelantiersdwarsstraat 9, Jordaan, 626-0028 • Classic

The Draw: Hostaria offers the sights, the sounds, and the tastes of Italy the way you—and Sophia Loren—might imagine it.

The Scene: Cramped, very informal, and high energy, yet somehow still cozy, this place welcomes a cross section of Amsterdam, who come to dine on traditional Italian dishes. Seafood options stand out, as do well-executed home-style classics like pigeon and vitella tonato. *Tue-Sun 6:30-10pm.* € =

Hot Tip: Sit near the open kitchen to experience the chef's frantic showmanship.

Restaurant Bice

Stadhouderskade 7, Museumplein, 589-8870 • Cool

The Draw: Big-name Italian dining with a reputation for quality and style.

The Scene: With views of a busy street and a canal, Bice is in the thick of the action, but the light, airy, and elegant eatery is a peaceful oasis of calm perfection. Well-prepared dishes and staff who are smart and efficient ensure that the international Bice standard is intact. *Mon-Sat 6:30-10:30pm, lunch by appointment only, closes in summer for vacation, call for dates.* €€ =

Hot Tip: Ask for the corner table with a view toward the Leidseplein. Grand architecture, a canal, and a bustling street scene will be your reward.

Segugio

Utrechtsestraat 96a, Rembrandtplein, 330-1503 • Classic

The Draw: Chefs Adriano Paolini and Simone Ambrosin render fine Italian dining at its very best.

The Scene: Simple and elegant dishes presented by informed, professional servers who are never intrusive. What more could you ask for? How about an updated, sophisticated-classic décor and a noise level that's just right for private conversation? *Mon-Sat 6-11pm.* €€ =

Hot Tip: Order one of the delicious risottos; they're the stuff of local dining legend.

Jazz Scenes

#55–57: Laid-back, creative, and sometimes quirky, jazz provides the perfect soundtrack for a visit to Amsterdam—but we're not talking easy listening. While the standards can be found, this is also a town that has its share of avant-garde audio explorations.

Bimhuis
Piet Heinkade 3, Eastern Harbor, 788-2188 • Cool

The Draw: Catch a concert in an architectural showpiece and sneak a peek at the future of jazz.

The Scene: Designed by Danish firm 3xNielsen, the new Bimhuis is one of Europe's premier spots to hear fresh developments in jazz and world music. A selection of mainstream music is also on the agenda, but Amsterdam's sophisticated jazz cognoscenti demand the challenging stuff and the Bimhuis delivers nightly. *Most performances start at 9pm.* C≡

Hot Tip: Choose your concerts wisely or come with a very open mind—sometimes the future can be very edgy.

Cristofori Salon
Prinsengracht 581-583, Jordaan, 624-4969 • Classic

The Draw: This is the perfect Sunday evening venue for unwinding to the sounds of live jazz.

The Scene: Local fans and a handful of lucky visitors crowd the loft of a 17th-century tobacco warehouse, listening to smooth sounds and basking in the quaint glory of Europe's old-world salon culture. *Sundays at 8:30pm.* C≡

Hot Tip: Check the online agenda (cristofori.nl) and book well in advance—the size of the room and popularity of the performances mean that the locals will have snapped up tickets before you arrive.

Jazzcafé Alto
Korte Leidsedwarsstraat 115, Canal Belt, 626-3249 • Classic

The Draw: Amsterdam's oldest jazz joint is home to nightly jams that showcase local and visiting artists.

The Scene: Top mainstream musicians play to a mixed-bag crowd of locals and visitors. The friendly vibe and cozy dark room are everything a neighborhood jazz bar should be, and the opportunity to catch outstanding performers elevates Alto's reputation to that of Amsterdam's most reliable jazz spot. *Sun-Thu 9pm-3am, Fri-Sat 9pm-4am.* ≡

Hot Tip: Go on a Wednesday to catch local sax legend Hans Dulfer.

Late-Night Scenes

#58–60: Amsterdam isn't a late-night party capital like Paris or Athens. But that doesn't mean there isn't fun to be found if you know where to look. Amsterdam won't shut down until you're good and ready.

Bourbon Street Blues Club

Leidsekruisstraat 6-8, Canal Belt, 623-3440 • Classic

The Draw: This is one of the few places that has energetic live music long into the morning hours.

The Scene: Local and visiting night-owls of all stripes—but who all share a love for live tunes—dance, drink, and party. Every genre of music including Latin, funk, and soul gets its moment in the spotlight. *Fri-Sat 10pm-5am with live music 11pm-4am, Sun-Thu 10pm-4am with live music 10:30pm-3am.* C≣

Hot Tip: If the Rolling Stones have a concert in Amsterdam, drop by to catch an up-close glimpse of Mick and Keith; Bourbon Street is a favorite cool-down spot for visiting big-name rockers.

't Kalfje*

Prinsenstraat 5, Jordaan, 626-3370 • Classic

The Draw: A bustling pub and grill, it has a full menu offered into the dawn.

The Scene: In a word—authentic. Nighthawks polish the bar with their elbows and dig into hearty grub. The hungry post-club crowd and the occasional red-eyed tourist join in the mix. *Mon-Thu 4pm-3am, Fri-Sun 4pm-4am.* ≣

Hot Tip: The best thing about the food is that—the steaks, ribs, and daily specials are decent—you can get it at 2am. Drinking is the activity of choice.

Youll Lady's Dancing

Amstel 178, Rembrandtplein, 421-0900 • Hip

The Draw: When most other clubs are cleaning up and shutting down, this serious dance spot with a mostly gay and lesbian clientele is just heating up.

The Scene: They come to dance: An unpretentious, youthful, and good-looking crowd grooves and flirts all night to the sounds of classic and current club hits. *Fri-Sat 10pm-5am.* C≣

Hot Tip: Come between 1am and 2am to avoid lining up until sunup.

Live Music

#61–63: From the blues to Latin, soul, funk, jazz-fusion, worldbeat, alternative rock, and everything in between, you can catch it all on any given night.

De Badcuyp*
Eerste Sweelinckstraat 10, De Pijp, 675-9669 • Hip

The Draw: A full roster of events in one of Amsterdam's liveliest neighborhoods brings fun crowds.

The Scene: In this former city bath-cum-cultural spot, local hipsters dance to the sounds of live jazz, worldbeat, Latin, funk, and soul. Dance parties, salsa evenings, and a very casual on-site cafe make this newcomer an instant local favorite. *Most programs start between 9 and 10pm, call for specifics.* ≡

Hot Tip: Drop by on Sundays (2:30-5:30pm) when bebop, funk, and soul jam sessions take place.

Bitterzoet
Spuistraat 2, Nieuwe Zijde, 521-3001 • Hip

The Draw: Surprising tunes and a reliably good-looking, vibrant, friendly, and casual all-ages crowd keep it at the top of its game.

The Scene: High-energy, but low-attitude locals groove to music that runs the gamut from mainstream rock to experimental jazz in this space that moonlights as a dance bar and cinema. *Sun-Thu 8pm-3am, Fri-Sat 8pm-4am.* ©≡

Hot Tip: Come on Thursday nights to hear resident DJs team up with local bands.

Sugar Factory
Lijnbaansgracht 238, Canal Belt, 627-0008 • Hip

The Draw: Groove all night to smooth and funky live jazz—sometimes with DJ accompaniment.

The Scene: A seriously hip crowd. The city's artiest and funkiest scenesters gather to watch spontaneous—and often edgy—art programs, and stick around to chill the night away to progressive, electronic-inspired, beat-heavy tunes. *Thu-Sun; times vary so call ahead.* ©≡

Hot Tip: Try to catch one of the regular performances by local favorites the New Cool Collective.

Best

Lunch Spots

#64–66: Unless it's a weekend, tradition dictates that most locals will opt for a simple lunch eaten on the go—think hearty buns, a sandwich, or fries with mayonnaise—but lengthier business lunches are growing in popularity and the trendy crowd has embraced the leisurely mid-day meal.

EspressoBar Puccini

Staalstraat 21, Oude Zijde, 620-8458 • Cool

The Draw: Excellent lunches in a casual setting.

The Scene: Small, with a limited number of seats inside and fewer still outside, Puccini might not look like much, but the food is tops. Hearty soups and sandwiches hold their own against some of the best salads in town, and the casual atmosphere and staff are favored by the city's hip crowd. *Mon-Fri 8:30am-6pm, Sat-Sun 10am-6pm.* €€ ▢

Hot Tip: Don't smuggle in chocolates from equally noteworthy Puccini Bomboni just doors away. Though they share a name, that's where the harmony ends.

Het Land van Walem

Keizersgracht 449, Canal Belt, 625-3544 • Hip

The Draw: This contemporary classic spot packs 'em in, offering consistently fine food in a bright and stylish room, complete with current fashion and design magazines on hand.

The Scene: The fashionable, creative class lunch on smart sandwiches and salads, attracted by the restaurant's stylish façade (designed by De Stijl architect Gerrit Rietveld) and Scandinavian-chic interior. *Daily 10am-10:30pm, Fri-Sat cafe until 1am.* € ≡

Hot Tip: Don't despair if you can't get a table canal-side. There's a second terrace nestled away in the rear garden.

Quartier Sud

Olympiaplein 176, Zuid, 675-3990 • Classic

The Draw: An all-day dinner menu and rotating cast of influentials makes this Amsterdam's powerlunch champ.

The Scene: The décor (plush red and black accented by dark woods) and menu (prime cuts and chops) take their inspiration from a traditional gentlemen's club. Expect the best in personal attention; having refined their practice on the city's top movers and shakers, the servers go the extra mile. *Mon-Fri 10:30am-10:30pm.* €€ ▭

Hot Tip: Bet on the house: The award-winning house wines win rave reviews and local accolades.

Of-the-Moment Dining

#67–69: In the A-list world—where restaurants are only as hot as their clientele—fashion and design are just as important as the menu. Who knows what the scene will be next year? All the more reason to head to the current hot spots, so you can have that "been there, done that," cachet.

College*

The College Hotel, Roelof Hartstraat 1, Museumplein, 571-1511 • Cool

The Draw: Hot-shot chef Schilo van Coevorden pays homage to classic Dutch dishes while giving them a very contemporary update.

The Scene: Amsterdam's most up-to-the-minute crowd flocks to this temple devoted to all things Dutch: From the chairs and lights to the locally sourced ingredients and the gorgeous, tall blond at the next table, everything's home-grown. Dishes like gurnard with licorice, citrus, and butterhead lettuce draws flocks of ardent foodies—so be sure to book ahead. *Mon-Sat noon-2pm and 7-10pm, Sun noon-2pm.* €€ (set menu) =

Hot Tip: The attached College Bar & Lounge is one of Amsterdam's hottest watering holes—and a great place to start the night with a cocktail.

Envy

Prinsengracht 381, Jordaan, 344-6407 • Cool

The Draw: Italian tapas—what will they think of next?—and the wow-factor in design give guests something to talk about even before they sit down at the communal tables.

The Scene: The best of the city's who's who and generally fabulous dine shoulder to shoulder, in an elegant chrome and black space. *Sun-Thu 5pm-1am, Fri-Sat 5pm-3am.* €€€ ▯=

Hot Tip: There are only two seatings nightly, with a strict reservation policy.

Herrie

Utrechtsestraat 30a, Canal Belt, 622-0838 • Cool

The Draw: Take your pick: Hyper-flavorful French-inspired cuisine, a high-wattage celebrity chef, a revolving cast of very stylish locals, or a smart design décor.

The Scene: The contemporary French fare is big, bold, robust, and adventurous, and the same can be said of superstar chef Herman den Blijker. The cigar chomping, shaven-headed mountain of a man's man wouldn't look out of place leading a motorcycle gang, but looks can be deceiving, and Herman expresses his gentle side in his elegantly crafted, painstakingly prepared cuisine, albeit vicariously since he leaves the actual cooking to a very capable stand-in. *Mon-Sat 6pm-late.* €€ =

Hot Tip: Amsterdam may be casual, but Herrie is not. This is a great place to dress up to fit in.

On-the-Water

#70–72: It's not called "Venice of the North" because of its beer—it's the water. And a complete Amsterdam experience demands you commandeer a spot on one of the many boats that cruise the canals and rivers daily.

Holland International Boat Tours

Locations vary, 622-7788 • Classic

The Draw: Discover the city's historical sights from a public tour boat.

The Scene: A kitsch classic. Narrated tours of the city's famous canals provide a great introduction to Amsterdam and give seasoned visitors a new, water-level perspective. *Daily, Apr-Oct 10am-10pm; Nov-Mar 10am-6pm, sailings every 30 min.* €€

Hot Tip: If you're looking for a fast way to pack in the city's sites, try the "100 Highlights" cruise which departs several times an hour, no reservation needed.

Paradis Private Boat Tours

Locations vary, 684-9338 • Cool

The Draw: Enjoy custom tours of Amsterdam's most romantic canals in an elegant wooden saloon boat.

The Scene: Slender and sleek, the teak and mahogany boats aren't the only way to see the canals, but they're definitely the chicest. Whether you're looking for a lift to the opera or a leisurely, romantic cruise, sip some champagne while you ride in style. *Available with one-hour notice.* €€€€+

Hot Tip: Let your imagination run wild. From onboard musicians to custom catered dinners, anything can be arranged.

SupperClub Cruise*

Departure locations vary nightly, 344-6404 • Cool

The Draw: The place to be on Holland's North Sea is a smart dinner lounge-dance spot with an award-winning contemporary interior.

The Scene: When the popular SupperClub Lounge concept takes to the sea, it's "All aboard!" for the local scenesters and cool tourists alike. Some enjoy the views from the deck while others sip drinks at the sleek black "Bar Noir." Either way, lounging on the 100-person bed in the all-white "La Salle Neige" remains the activity of choice for Amsterdam's trendsetting crowd. *Sailing at 8pm sharp, Fri-Sat.* €€ (set menu) ▤

Hot Tip: Very carefully note the departure location—it can change from one night to the next—and arrive early because once it sails, it's "Bon voyage, baby!"

Only-in-Amsterdam

#73–75: Amsterdam isn't all hash, hookers, and houseboats, although that might be enough. There's a lot of other only-here activities to fill your nights and days, from the quirky to the eternally classic.

Bierbrouwerij 't IJ

Funenkade 7, Plantage, 622-8325 • Classic

The Draw: It's a double dose of Dutch culture with the city's finest microbrewery and a location next to a windmill.

The Scene: The windmill is striking, so take a good look—then head to the crowded and smoky tasting house next door, where very friendly locals enjoy the brewery's small but highly regarded selection of beers. *Wed-Sun 3-8pm.* ≡

Hot Tip: Be here when the doors open if you want to grab a coveted seat indoors or outside on the small garden terrace.

Blauw aan de Wal

Oudezijds Achterburgwal 99, Oude Zijde, 330-2257 • Cool

The Draw: Providing the perfect illustration of the Dutch "live and let live" attitude, this gorgeous oasis of wining and dining tranquility is located in the heart of the garish Red Light District.

The Scene: It's a shock to tourists, but—arguably—Amsterdam's most uniquely situated and charming restaurant is hidden down a graffiti blighted alleyway, itself bordered by sex shops. Moneyed locals just shrug, dine on delicate Mediterranean bites, sip fine wines, and smile smugly, knowing that few out-of-towners will find this diamond in the rough. *Mon-Sat 6:30pm-late.* €€ ≡

Hot Tip: The alleyway that leads to the restaurant is directly opposite the infamous Casa Rosso sex show theater.

Café Nol

Westerstraat 109, Jordaan, 624-5380 • Classic

The Draw: Check out the kitschiest, come-one-come-all, anything-goes experience you're likely to find in the city.

The Scene: Love it or hate it, Nol has to be seen to be believed. Faux crystal chandeliers, hideous potted plants, neon lighting, and red carpeting add up to Amsterdam's most garish drinking experience, but that doesn't deter the crowd (irony-loving hipsters and occasional celebrities included) who sing along to the campy, old-time accordion tunes. *Sun-Thu 9pm-3am, Fri-Sat 9pm-4am.* ≡

Hot Tip: It gets odder still on Thursdays with "Tjerk" playing live music.

Outdoor Markets

#76–78: Shopping at outdoor markets is part of the European experience, and Amsterdam is no exception. Browse these outdoor labyrinths where you'll find anything from the perfect Amsterdam keepsake to delicacies to nibble while you look.

Albert Cuypmarkt
Albert Cuypstraat, De Pijp • Hip

The Draw: Amsterdam's largest public market.

The Scene: Located in one of the hippest neighborhoods, this warren of booths contains everything from fine cheeses, clothes, and cosmetics, to chocolates and prepared foods. It's the perfect place to try cavity-inducing Dutch treats like poffertjes (small pancakes slathered in icing sugar) or stroopwaffels (hot, thin waffles coated in syrup). *Mon-Sat 9:30am-5pm, weather permitting.*

Hot Tip: To find a diamond in the rough, come early, especially on Saturdays when the market is at its busiest. For people-watching, anytime is great.

Flower Market • Bloemenmarkt
The Singel canal between the Koningsplein and the Muntplein, Rembrandtplein • Classic

The Draw: Browse and buy all things floral at the city's historic flower market.

The Scene: While tourists stop to buy bulbs for their gardens or to stare in astonishment at the vast array of *bloemen* (flowers), Amsterdammers pick up fresh cut flowers for their homes. Best of all, it floats: Cross the Singel to get a good view of the system of barges keeping the whole thing above water. *Daily 9am-8pm.*

Hot Tip: Don't mess with customs! Most bulbs have import restrictions, so ask before you buy.

Waterlooplein Market
Waterlooplein (at Mr. Visserplein), Oude Zijde • Hip

The Draw: Here's your chance to stumble upon a must-have find.

The Scene: Selling everything from clothing, collector's items, accessories, household items, music and books, to vintage items, this outdoor market with a hipster, flea-market ambience is a browser's paradise, popular with locals and tourists alike. *Mon-Sat 9am-5pm.*

Hot Tip: Leisurely browsers should avoid Saturday mornings when the crowds are thickest, but those looking to people-watch will be well-pleased.

Restaurant-Lounges

#79–81: Amsterdammers love nothing better than to *tafel*—or "table"—the night away. They show up early for drinks, stick around for a leisurely dinner, and let the night slowly unfold.

Bar Ça*

Marie Heinekenplein 30-31, De Pijp, 470-4144 • Hip

The Draw: Inspired tapas and Spanish libations will satiate your hottest Mediterranean fantasies.

The Scene: It's Las Ramblas, only taller and blonder: buzzing, sultry, warm, and great-looking by candlelight—both the room and the stylish and youthful crowd. Locals linger inside on plush, low-slung couches or outside on the bustling patio. *Sun-Thu 3pm-1am, Fri-Sat 3pm-3am.* € ▤

Hot Tip: Quench your thirst with Bar Ça's signature "cavas"; great with tapas, the sparkling Spanish wine is a Catalonian specialty.

Rain*

Rembrandtplein 44, Rembrandtplein, 626-7078 • Cool

The Draw: Superb cocktails, delicious global-fusion cuisine, mellow tunes, and a contemporary décor: What's not to love?

The Scene: From the fashionable locals to the spicy, Asian-influenced cuisine and sultry worldbeat tunes, Rain is hot. Exquisitely crafted drinks and occasional live music performances push this spot, with a modern, chic interior, high on the list of stylish dining-lounging favorites. *Sun-Thu 6pm-2am, Fri-Sat 6pm-4am.* €€ ▤

Hot Tip: Rain is one of the few places where you can order bottle service.

Vakzuid*

Olympisch Stadion 35, Zuid, 570-8400 • Cool

The Draw: Cool dining and lounging is made even better by a location in the 1928 Summer Olympics stadium.

The Scene: A multi-use space popular with Amsterdam's moneyed and creative 30-somethings for everything from casual meetings, post work drinks, and dinner, to dancing and DJs. Inside, wooden accents bring style and warmth to the industrial space, while outside, the massive terrace and waterfront views bring an urban beach feel to the party. *Mon-Thu 10am-1am, Fri 10am-3am, Sat 4pm-3am, Sun 3-10pm.* €€ ▤

Hot Tip: Ask your hostess for a complimentary blanket if you want to enjoy the terrace when the mercury starts to drop.

Romantic Dining

#82–84: Whether your definition of romance includes dining in a candlelit garden or chilling on a plush daybed, there's a place in Amsterdam that agrees with your aesthetics.

Nomads
Rozengracht 133, Jordaan, 344-6401 • Hip

The Draw: **1001 Arabian Nights meets Blade Runner.** Style setters dine reclining on sexy divans, sharing plates of delicious North African finger foods.

The Scene: Hipsters cozy up to their companions and sip chic cocktails. DJs, belly dancers, rose-water foot massages, and apple-scented tobacco smoked out of hookahs round out the wondrous sensory feast. *Tue-Thu 7pm-1am, Fri-Sat 7pm-3am, Sun 7pm-1am.* €€ (set menu) –

Hot Tip: Call ahead to request one of six semi-private "chambers," There is no additional cost, and they hold up to six people.

Le Pêcheur
Reguliersdwarsstraat 32, Rembrandtplein, 624-3121 • Classic

The Draw: Traditional seafood and attentive servers draw 30- and 40-somethings looking for a touch of elegance.

The Scene: Delicious dishes, flowers, white tablecloths, and candlelight set a sophisticated tone, but the real attraction is the courtyard terrace. With views of elegant canal house gardens, it can't be beat for old-world charm. *Mon-Fri noon-3pm and 5:30-11pm, Sat 5:30-11pm.* €€ –

Hot Tip: Start with the oysters. They're delivered twice daily.

Voorbij Het Einde
Sumatrakade 613, Eastern Harbor, 419-1143 • Cool

The Draw: A suave contemporary setting is enhanced by views of the River IJ, and a small but adventurous and noteworthy seafood-based menu.

The Scene: Amsterdam's jet set crowd makes the pilgrimage (about 10 minutes by cab from the city center) to Java Island, where glass, stainless steel, earth tones, and gray slate create a modern décor. Thoughtfully paired wines and a professional approach to service complement Tony Philippi's 7-course extravaganzas. *Wed-Sat 6:30-11pm, lunch by appointment Wed-Fri.* €€ –

Hot Tip: Ask for a river view table or one in the garden-side glass atrium.

Best

See-and-Be-Seen Clubs

#85–87: The who's who will be different—think European football stars and Dutch television personalities—but the rules are the same. Go early, dress well, bring a gorgeous date, and slip the concierge a tip to skip lines.

Jimmy Woo

Korte Leidsedwarsstraat 18, Canal Belt, 626-3150 • Cool

The Draw: It's Amsterdam's most exclusive club.

The Scene: Opium den-style meets the 21st century. You'll find the city's hottest club crowd, from visiting soccer players to international A-listers, mixed with beautiful hopefuls swaying to the music or oh-so-casually lounging. *Wed-Thu 11pm-3am, Fri-Sat 11pm-4am, Sun 11pm-3am.* C ≡

Hot Tip: Confucius says: Have your concierge get you on the guest list. All other paths will only lead to frustration.

The Mansion* (formerly Vossius)

Hobbemastraat 2, Museumplein, 616-6664 • Cool

The Draw: Gorgeous club. Gorgeous people.

The Scene: With ostrich leather embossed walls—some of which are accented with real gold leaf—and ceiling paintings inspired by the Sistine Chapel, the only thing more flashy than the room is the clientele. It's a regular pit-stop on Amsterdam's design-dining circuit and you can count on a trendsetting, head-turning crowd. *Tue-Thu 6pm-1am, Fri-Sat 6pm-3am.* C ≡

Hot Tip: Come for "Jazz and Cocktails" on the first and third Sundays of each month. It's a chilled-out but very stylish live music session.

Onassis

Westerdoksdijk 40, West, 330-0456 • Cool

The Draw: A super-stylish crowd comes for waterside cocktails.

The Scene: Arriving by boat or sports car, Amsterdam's current and moneyed set looks even more attractive with the designer bar and the River IJ as backdrops. Dancing late into the night adds a touch of Ibiza beach party ambience to the affair. *Sun-Thu noon-1am, Fri-Sat noon-3am.* ≡

Hot Tip: A beach party vibe doesn't mean shorts and flip-flops. It's calculatedly casual here, with hours spent prepping to look thrown together.

Best Sex-in-the-City

#88–90: Amsterdam. Sex. Amsterdam. Sex. The two are linked in the minds of travelers, and with good reason. It's a liberal city, to say the least. If you're looking for something adventurous or even downright shocking, look no further.

Erotic Museum
Oudezijds Achterburgwal 54, Oude Zijde, 624-7303 • Hip

The Draw: An interesting exhibition of erotic art and artifacts that's more informative than shocking.

The Scene: Couples, small groups, and individuals—mostly from abroad—peruse surprisingly educational displays that include prostitute fashions throughout history, and a mockup of a Red Light District window. *Sun-Thu 11am-1am, Fri-Sat 11am-2am.* €

Hot Tip: Beatles fans will appreciate the collection of original John Lennon sketches penned during the famous Amsterdam bed-in.

Marlies Dekkers
Cornelis Schuytstraat, Zuid, 471-4146 • Cool

The Draw: Shop for award-winning contemporary lingerie in a setting that oozes style and sex.

The Scene: Fashion designer Marlies Dekkers' boutique is a temple to sophisticated sensuality. The plush room, decorated with decadent red fabrics, black wood, and crystal chandeliers, sets the perfect mood for trying on fabulous little nothings. *Mon noon-6pm, Tue-Wed and Fri 10am-6pm, Thu 10am-7pm, Sat 10am-5pm.*

Hot Tip: Dress him up! Dekkers makes a very chic men's line, too.

Theater Casa Rosso
Oudezijds Achterburgwal 106-108, Oude Zijde, 627-8954 • Classic

The Draw: The spectacle with the classiest reputation among the handful of only-in-Amsterdam live sex-shows.

The Scene: Seeing is believing. While performers—both solo and in pairs of various combinations—strut their stuff in repeating one-hour shows, stag parties, visiting businessmen, and more couples than you might expect watch wide-eyed. *Sun-Thu 8pm-2am, Fri-Sat 8pm-3am.* ℂ ≡

Hot Tip: Avoid aisle seats or risk becoming part of the grand finale.

Tables with a View

#91–93: Amsterdam's charms are the perfect backdrop to a fine meal. It's not just the canals that draw the eye. From the quaint skyline to the harbor, it's a beautiful city just waiting for you to discover the perfect vantage point.

De Belhamel

Brouwersgracht 60, Jordaan, 622-1095 • Classic

The Draw: Dine al fresco, waterside, at the junction of two scenic canals.

The Scene: Amsterdammers showing off their city to out-of-town guests and international visitors looking for up-close views of the city's legendary waterways pack Belhamel's canal-side tables to capacity. *Daily noon-4pm and 6-10pm.* €€ ≡

Hot Tip: The window-side table at the front of the house and those on a small balcony provide the best canal views from inside should the weather work against your open-air dining plans.

Ciel Bleu*

The Okura Hotel, Ferdinand Bolstraat 333, De Pijp, 678-7111 • Classic

The Draw: Located on the 23rd floor of The Okura Hotel and serving Michelin-star-anointed dishes, Ciel Bleu takes Amsterdam dining to new heights.

The Scene: The sweeping view fails to upstage Onno Kokmeijer's elegant French cuisine, but it comes darn close. Discerning business diners share the space with hopeful romantics as candlelight, flower arrangements, and thoughtful wine pairings provide an elevated experience. *Daily 6:30-10pm.* €€€ ▭

Hot Tip: Not all of the tables have a view, so be sure to request one when you make your reservation.

11*

Oosterdokskade 3-5, Eastern Harbor, 625-5999 • Hip

The Draw: The city's best harbor view also has a lively, artsy scene.

The Scene: 11 has everything a hipster could want: Screens showing video installation art, an industrial-design décor, a large bar, and a late-night metamorphosis into a trendy dance venue means that the 20- to 30-somethings come in droves. *Daily 11am-4pm and 6-10pm. Dancing Thu-Sat until 4am.* € ≡

Hot Tip: It's a bit out of the way, so if you're coming for the "drinks only" terrace, call ahead to make sure it's open—located twelve stories above street level, occasional high winds make it a no-go.

Tastes of the Exotic

#94–96: At the height of the Golden Age, dishes from the Netherlands' overseas colonies (particularly Indonesia and, to a lesser extent, South Africa) began appearing on Dutch tables. More recently, North African and Turkish immigrants have added their delicious cuisines to the United Nations of Dutch dining.

Bazar
Albert Cuypstraat 182, De Pijp, 675-0544 • Hip

The Draw: Forget buzzing. The 20- to 30-something crowd roars at this very popular and colorful spot located in a former church.

The Scene: Istanbul as a fashion designer might imagine it. With delicious dishes, a trendy crowd, and a vaulted ceiling—painted sky blue and adorned with Hebrew and Arabic script—it's the ideal introduction to the vibrant world of Eastern dining. *Sun-Thu 8am-11pm, Fri-Sat 8am-2am.* € ≡

Hot Tip: Let your server recommend the perfect Turkish beer.

Pygma-Lion
Nieuwe Spiegelstraat 5a, Canal Belt, 420-7022 • Cool

The Draw: Walking on the wild side means mouth-watering modern interpretations of traditional African dishes like ostrich and zebra.

The Scene: The eye-catching presentation and streamlined interior attract adventurous diners and African expats looking for a taste of home. The Malaysian, Indian, and Portuguese items that fill the long menu pair perfectly with the wide selection of South African wines. *Tue-Sun 6-11pm.* € ≡

Hot Tip: If you're new to South African cuisine, try Bobotie, a curry-based dish, or potjiekos, an antelope stew.

Tempo Doeloe
Utrechtsestraat 75, Canal Belt, 625-6718 • Classic

The Draw: In a city teeming with Indonesian restaurants, Tempo Doeloe's spicy delicacies shine above the rest.

The Scene: Chef Ghebrial's rijstafel "rice table" and comprehensive wine list are so popular that he keeps the door locked rather than devote a staff member to turning people away. The somewhat tired décor doesn't deter Amsterdam's elite or visitors like Gwyneth Paltrow and husband Chris Martin, who knew enough to book ahead. *Mon-Sat 6-11pm.* €€ –

Hot Tip: The uninitiated should opt for the "Ricetable Istemewa," the tasting menu consisting of twenty-four small dishes. It's the perfect way to explore Indonesian cuisine.

Best

Terraces

#97–99: A sunny afternoon is the ultimate time to be in Amsterdam, even for locals. When the temperatures rise, the streets are packed with people jockeying for every park bench or patio seat. Stake some prime real estate on one of these great terraces, order a drink or a few, and experience the city's laid-back culture at its best.

Café de Jaren*
Nieuwe Doelenstraat 20-22, Oude Zijde, 625-5771 • Hip

The Draw: One of the city's hippest grand cafes, de Jaren also has one of the best waterside terraces for lounging away an afternoon or evening.

The Scene: Spacious. With high ceilings, stylishly tiled floors, and an international reading table, de Jaren was voted "Dutch Café of the Year" a while back and nothing has changed. The large, vine-covered terrace, at water level, makes this a prime sunny day destination. *Restaurant daily 10am-10:30pm; cafe Sun-Thu 10am-1am, Fri-Sat 10am-2am.* € ≡

Hot Tip: Watching what you eat? The well-stocked salad bar is one of the city's very few.

La Terrasse
Hotel de l'Europe, Nieuwe Doelenstraat 2-8, Oude Zijde, 531-1705 • Classic

The Draw: This waterside patio offers views of the Amstel River, the Muntplein, and the Rokin, and may well be the city's best vantage point.

The Scene: Celebrating locals and visitors with padded wallets come for the stellar setting. And the menu? Comprised of well-rendered classic dishes—fish, chops, and steaks—it's no slouch either. *Easter–mid-Oct noon-10pm, weather permitting.* €€ ≡

Hot Tip: They have no indoor seating. Head elsewhere when the weather turns poor or ask for your reservation to be transferred to Excelsior, the hotel's fine dining room.

Werck
Prinsengracht 277, Jordaan, 627-4079 • Cool

The Draw: A contemporary-cool rooftop and garden lounge, it rewards with outstanding views and a cool vibe.

The Scene: The nearly 400-year-old Westerkerk looms high over this industrial space, making it appear as though it's about to be crushed by history. But don't be fooled. The location and sleek all-white daybeds give this popular fair-weather spot a secure future. *May-Oct Sun-Thu noon-1am, Fri-Sat noon-3am; Oct-May Sun-Thu 4pm-1am, Fri-Sat noon-3am.* ≡

Hot Tip: Play to its strengths. Drink and lounge here before searching out more noteworthy gastronomic destinations.

EXPERIENCE AMSTERDAM

Every city has a thousand faces. Which one you see depends on your angle. We've crafted three in-depth itineraries, *Cool* (p.50), *Hip* (p.78), and *Classic* (p.104), to help you discover some of the best ways to view Amsterdam, and experience it as well. They're packed with hot restaurants, smart clubs, and fashionable fun—planned for Thursday to Saturday (since a city this fabulous demands a three-day weekend). Whichever one—or ones—you choose, it will keep you buzzing for three perfect, high-energy days. Sleep is purely optional—just the way Amsterdammers like it.

Cool Amsterdam

Amsterdam prides itself as much on sense as style. Even at its most Euro-glam, you'll find something substantial behind its trends, whether in the thoughtful lines of a contemporary design, or the exotic ingredient that makes a dish sublime. Beautiful people, chilled cocktails, and sexy lounges may be the set dressing of the sleek-chic Amsterdam scene, but this city knows that the core of cool is tangible. From the laid-back vibe of the hottest clubs to the liberal attitude of the cafes, this itinerary will keep you out on the town enjoying Amsterdam's urban savvy from morning until deep into the dawn. Immerse yourself in metropolitan hedonism—hit the edgiest galleries, design-dine at the A-list hot spots, and sleep in luxurious boutique hotels that have the world's style-setters buzzing. Amsterdam for aesthetes is a non-stop affair, so get moving: You don't want to miss a beat.

Note: Venues in bold are described in detail in the listings that follow the itinerary. Venues followed by an * asterisk are those we recommend as both a restaurant and a destination bar.

Cool Amsterdam:
The Perfect Plan (3 Nights and Days)

Hotel: **The College Hotel**

Perfect Plan Highlights

Thursday

Afternoon	**Paradis Private Boat Tours**
Cocktails	**Profloekaal Janvier, College Bar and Lounge***
Dinner	**Envy, The Mansion*, Le Garage**
Nighttime	**En Pluche, Bar Bep**
Late-night	**NL Lounge**

Friday

Breakfast	**Brasserie de Joffers**
Morning	**Architectour**
Lunch	**College*, CaffePC**
Afternoon	**shopping, Gassan Diamonds, Christie's, Loods 6**
Cocktails	**Vibing, Arc**
Dinner	**Lute, SupperClub*, Herrie**
Nighttime	**Vakzuid* SupperClub Cruise***
Late-night	**Onassis, Rain*, Escape**

Saturday

Breakfast	**'t Buffet van Odette**
Morning	**FOAM, Cobra Museum**
Lunch	**EspressoBar Puccini, Tomo Sushi**
Afternoon	**ARCAM, Platform 21, shopping, Koan Float spa**
Cocktails	**Joia, Vuong, Werck**
Dinner	**Voorbij Het Einde, Fifteen* Ams., Pygma-Lion**
Nighttime	**Jimmy Woo, Panama**
Late-night	**Zebra Lounge, Bubbles**

Morning After

Brunch	**Brasserie van Baerle**

5pm Start your Amsterdam weekend by experiencing this city's gorgeous canals in the most chic way. From the privacy of your own beautiful, wooden runabout operated by **Paradis Private Boat Tours**, you'll enjoy perfect sightseeing with a little romance. From beer and pretzels to champagne and caviar, they'll provide anything and everything.

7pm Once on land, if the sun is still shining, a cool drink on the terrace of **Profloekaal Janvier** may be in order. Or consider joining the stylish business crowd in the **College Bar & Lounge***.

8:30pm Dinner Join the city's most stylish at **Envy**, the black and chrome design space serving tapas-sized Italian bites, or go east to **The Mansion***—it offers gorgeous Asian fusion cuisine, a crowd of Dutch A-listers, and an interior inspired by the Sistine Chapel. Alternatively, at **Le Garage**, Joop Braakhekke (Holland's first celebrity chef) continues to impress with his French bistro-inspired cuisine.

11pm Pay a visit to the cozy, and very plush, **En Pluche**, where Amsterdam's elite lounges on

…d black sofas; or …ar **Bep**, the retro '70s …nd lounge hotspot.

If your idea of a good time is an intimate space with a stylish, local crowd, head to the **NL Lounge**, where the décor, patrons, and tunes are strictly sexy.

Friday

9am Breakfast Follow in the footsteps of Amsterdam's chic locals to **Brasserie de Joffers**, the spot with mouth-watering breakfasts that are rumored to have tempted royalty to drop in for a bite.

10am Hook up with Caroline of **Architectour** for a private peek behind some of Amsterdam's closed doors. She'll share her expertise—she's an architect and historian—and lead you on a customized tour of the city's most noteworthy buildings. Alternatively, choose a museum from another itinerary. We love both the Stedelijk CS for contemporary art, or the Rembrandt House.

Noon Lunch Head back to the hotel and **College*** restaurant where super-chef Schilo van Coevorden dishes out his critically acclaimed contemporary Dutch fare, or eat at **CaffePC**, the "let's do lunch" spot for Amsterdam's ladies of leisure.

1:45pm Stroll over to PC Hooftstraat, Amsterdam's high-end shopping corridor. It caters to the deep-pocketed, style-conscious set. Filippa K carries sleek clothing from Sweden, while the dramatically designed Shoebaloo stocks sexy footwear.

3:15pm The "City of Diamonds" has 24 diamond polishing factories, and although most give tours, they vary in quality. At **Gassan Diamonds** you'll witness polishing and cutting and best of all, you won't get pushy, hard-sell tactics. Be sure to check out the Otazu line: The local celebrity designer has made pieces for Britney and Madonna. Then drop by **Christie's Auction House**. Even if you're not in the market for a Giacometti, a visit here is like a trip to a private museum.

Alternatively, if it wasn't covered on your morning tour, catch a glimpse of the future wandering the Eastern Harbor area, where you'll find the coolest modern architecture and galleries featuring radical art and design. At **Loods 6** you'll see exhibitions from four of Europe's trendiest collectives, including Quarantine and Transit, alongside design shops like Pol's Potten. Should you prefer your art on a grander scale, walk through the neighborhood to view futuristic structures like the undulating Red Bridge (better known as the Python) and the contemporary canal houses.

6pm Chill out at **Vibing**, a cocktail lounge with two stylish rooms— one high energy, and the other mellow. Although **Arc** is considered a gay bar, its eye-catching, space-age décor attracts a mixed crowd. But if you're headed to **Lute Restaurant** later, plan to arrive early to enjoy the high-style after-work pre-dinner cocktail scene.

8pm Dinner If you're at **Lute Restaurant** in the nearby village of Oudekerk aan de Amstel, stay. Peter Lute's acclaimed modern cuisine is presented in a room designed by superstar Dutch designer Marcel Wanders, raising the cool factor through the roof. And never mind Lute's out-of-the-way location—the restaurant shuttles diners to and from Amsterdam in an antique canal boat. If it's city life you're after, go to **SupperClub***; it's the grand-daddy of Amsterdam's lounge-restaurant scene. Or hit **Herrie**. Loosely translated as "commotion," Herrie has been generating a buzz since opening its stylish doors.

10pm Take a break at **Vakzuid***, the industrial design lounge and restaurant in the 1928 Olympics' stadium. The crowd is gorgeous and the terrace is a favorite among the city's stylish business set. An alternative is the **SupperClub Cruise***, which pulls the same smart crowd as its landlocked sibling. The nautical version of Amsterdam's legendary lounge and restaurant makes a post-dinner docking to pick up the dancing set.

1am Party like Ari at **Onassis**, a waterside design lounge-bar-restaurant, or drop into **Rain*** for excellent cocktails and dancing. The sophisticated purple and black room has quickly become one of this city's see-and-be-seen spaces.

3am Wrap it up by getting down: Drop by the stylish **Escape deLux** for progressive dance beats and a fashionable crowd that parties until sunrise.

Saturday

9am Breakfast Kick-start your day with a mouthwatering traditional Dutch breakfast at the local canal side favorite **'t Buffet van Odette en Yvette**.

10am Visit **FOAM Photography Museum** to view famous photos by the likes of Annie Leibovitz and Henri Cartier-Bresson.

11am Earn some art world cool-cachet with a 15-20 minute cab ride to **Cobra Museum of Modern Art**, the gorgeous space dedicated to works from the only modern art movement to have originated in Amsterdam.

12:30pm Lunch Head back into the city, grab a canal-view seat at **EspressoBar Puccini**, and lunch on some of the city's finest sandwiches, salads, and soups. Or head to **Tomo Sushi**, serving some of Amsterdam's best in a sleek and stark, minimalist-inspired room.

1:30pm Drop into **ARCAM Amsterdam Centre for Architecture**, to view exhibitions on housing, urban development, and philosophy of design.

3pm **Platform 21 Amsterdam Design Center** is the self-styled Dutch design think tank, and the exhibition space hosts displays on everything from fashion to street culture to industrial design.

4pm Head over to the bustling Negen Straatjes (Nine Streets), Amsterdam's finest location for boutique shops. Check out Mendo for art and design books; Analik, the boutique from the playful Dutch fashion designer of the same name; and **Van Ravenstein**, Amsterdam's only shop selling creations from fashion gods Viktor & Rolf. If shopping doesn't appeal, indulge at **Koan Float and Massage Center** spa and linger in sound- and lightproof chambers—filled with saline water, they create the effect of weightlessness.

6pm The jungle décor at **Joia** packs in a trendy crowd, as do the cocktails at **Vuong**, the Asian fusion lounge. In great weather, head to the industrial, canalside **Werck**. Nestled under the Westerkerk, the rooftop is a popular meeting place for the afterwork crowd.

8pm Dinner Dine at **Voorbij Het Einde**. The contemporary restaurant dishes out mouth-watering seafood to Amsterdam's most stylish foodies. Fans of chef Jamie Oliver will want to visit **Fifteen Amsterdam***, the Brit's first venture outside England. Or head to **Pygma-Lion** for an aromatic South African feast.

11pm Tip your concierge to get you on the guest list at Amsterdam's A-list dance spot **Jimmy Woo**. To party with the big boys—as well as some of the world's hottest DJs—head to **Panama**, where you'll find three bars and two dance floors.

1am Continue your urban safari at **Zebra Lounge**, where exotic, beautiful locals and visiting guests sip equally exotic cocktails in the comfort of private booths. For something a little more mellow but no less fabulous, drop into **Bubbles & Wines** to sip premium wine and champagne by the glass or bottle.

The Morning After
Dress up and wind down with a brunch at **Brasserie van Baerle**, the city's classy-cool breakfast hot spot. You'll need a reservation.

Cool Amsterdam:
The Key Neighborhoods

The **Eastern Harbor** is a largely residential area that is quickly emerging as a destination for shopping by day and wining and dining by night. It's home to much of Amsterdam's groundbreaking modern architecture, as well as a steadily growing number of contemporary galleries, studios, and one-of-a-kind boutiques.

The **Jordaan** is centered around the charming Negen Straatjes and the postcard-perfect canals. It's home to numerous studios and galleries, unique shops, and some of the most sophisticated dining and nightlife that this city has to offer.

The **Museumplein** boasts three of the world's best art museums—the Stedelijk, the Van Gogh, and the Rijksmuseum—but it's PC Hooftstraat, the Netherlands' chicest shopping street, that draws the stylish masses to the area. The neighborhood is also home to the Vondelpark, which is enormously popular with the "old money" set whose houses overlook the park itself.

The **Nieuwe Zijde**, or "New Side" to English speakers, is anchored by the Dam Square and the surrounding historical monuments, and it's the commercial hub of the city. Shopping—in international chain stores as well as in boutique shops—remains the daytime activity of choice, while a wealth of restaurants, cafes, pubs, and lounges makes this area a popular night-on-the-town option.

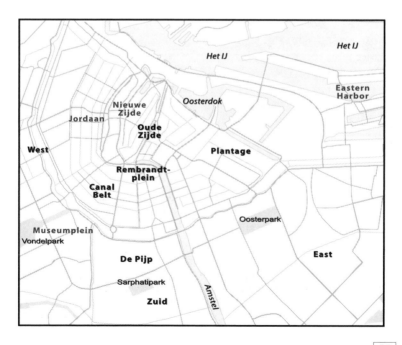

Cool Amsterdam:
The Shopping Blocks

Eastern Harbor

The Eastern Harbor is progressive in the extreme. That translates into a small but stimulating and edgy shopping scene with lots of high design.

J.C. Creations Couture lingerie. Tindalstraat 150 (Panamakade), 419-7220

Jos Art Galerie Futuristic modern and contemporary art. KNSMlaan 291 (Messinastr.), 418-7003

Keet in Huis Upmarket goods for the pre-teen set. KNSMlaan 297 (Messinastr.), 419-5958

De Ode Custom-made items (bookshelves, bike trailers, and planters) that convert into coffins. Levantkade 51 (Verbindingsdam), 419-0882

Pol's Potten Contemporary furnishings, accessories, and gadgetry. KNSMlaan 39 (Verbindingsdam), 419-3541

Sissyboy Homeland Clothing and accessory collections from a local, trendy chain. KNSMlaan 19 (Verbindingsdam), 419-1559

Negen Straatjes (Nine Streets)

Nine Streets has smart shops and an endless supply of stylish surprises.

Hester van Eeghen Designer leather. Hartenstraat 37 (Keizersgracht), 626-9212

Mendo High-concept bookstore/gallery. Berenstraat (Prinsengracht), 612-1216

Skins Cosmetics Luxe lines for both sexes. Runstraat 9 (Keizersgracht), 528-6922

Van Ravenstein Big-name Belgian designers as well as Viktor & Rolf. (p.77) Keizersgracht 359 (Huidenstraat), 639-0067

De Vlieger Contemporary art in various media from the world's emerging talents. Huidenstraat 13 (Herengracht), 625-7030

PC Hooftstraat

With one big-name luxury boutique after another (and a host of Holland-only stores), PC has the hallmarks of international style, as well as local cool cachet.

Caroline Biss Bohemian-chic prêt-à-porter collections from the Belgian fashion house. PC Hooftstraat 95 (Van de Veldestr.), 673-8137

Leeser Women's fashions from a popular Dutch designer. PC Hooftstraat 117 (Van Baerlestr.), 679-5020

Oger High-end menswear: casuals, business wear, and the finest bespoke garments. PC Hooftstraat 75-81 (Van de Veldestr.), 676-8695

Shoebaloo Great shoes in a chic shop. PC Hooftstraat 80 (Honthorststr.), 671-2210

Cool Amsterdam: The Hotels

Bilderberg Jan Luyken • Museumplein • Modern (62 rms)
Since Amsterdam is the perfect mix of old and new, staying here might be an ideal and surprising option. The three 19th-century houses that make up the hotel have retained many of their original characteristics, but beyond the traditional lobby, the hotel and guest rooms have benefited from a contemporary makeover that is certain to please discerning interior design fans. Decorated in muted colors like cream and chocolate, and accented with modern but warm furnishings—think dark wood four-poster beds alongside contemporary lighting—guest rooms are cozy retreats (OK, they're on the small side, but still comfortable—ask for one with a balcony for a bit more space). PC Hooftstraat, Amsterdam's high-end shopping district, is just steps away, and the Leidseplein's legendary nightlife and cafes are around the corner. In the hotel, a smart-looking lounge/bar anchors a social scene, and secretarial services can be arranged. If it's solitude you're after, you can book the tiny, private on-site spa room that includes a whirlpool, solarium, sun bed, and Turkish steam bath.
€€ Jan Luykenstraat 58 (PC Hooftstr.), 573-0730, janluyken.nl

Breaks and Butlers • Oude Zijde • Trendy (1 rm)
This elegant, contemporary ground-floor apartment is a serious contender for the title of Amsterdam's most stylish home away from home. The building dates back to the 17th century and has views of two canals as well as the historic Zuiderkerk (South Church), but that's where the nostalgia ends. This place is up-to-the-minute gorgeous, and if the hospitality game doesn't work out, the owners will surely have a future in interior design. Heated wooden floors, a luxurious slate bath with a separate shower and boutique products, designer linens, eiderdown duvets, bottled water and chocolates, fresh flowers, and a full butler service on request are just a few of the touches that make this one of the city's best properties. At 600 square feet—divided almost equally between the large bedroom and the great room that includes a full kitchen, dining area, and den—it is as big as it is beautiful. And of course, it has amenities like an office area with high speed internet, 2 flat-screen televisions—one in the den and one in the bedroom—a private bar complete with soft drinks, beer, and wine, and an attractively appointed kitchen, making this perfect for stays both long and short.
€€€ Groenburgwal 1 (Raamgracht), 638-9944, breaksandbutlers.nl

The College Hotel • Museumplein • Trendy (40 rms)
Like so much of Amsterdam, the chic College Hotel toes the line between history and the future by updating an authentically classic space with an up-to-the-minute design. A former school renovated with exposed brick, mood lighting, rich earth-tone fabrics, and touches of Asian-inspired glamour, this newcomer to the city's style scene has already made a sophisticated splash. Rooms are generously appointed, if understated—in the common areas, architectural accents provide most of the grand flourishes—creating a tranquil mood. Amenities like spacious, bliss-inducing bathrooms, flat-screen televisions, and optional in-room spa treatments ensure that luxury trumps simplicity. The

hotel's restaurant, also named College* (see p.63), has super-chef Schilo van Coeverden whipping up contemporary Dutch dishes. The College Bar & Lounge* (see p.70) draws sophisticated and stylish upmarket hotel guests and equally fashionable locals. Try to book room 101 or the split-level 206; both are especially spacious and have views of the bustling street scene outside. €€ Roelof Hartstraat 1 (Balthasar Floriszstr.), 571-1511, thecollegehotel.com

EnSuite Apartment • Jordaan • Trendy (1 rm)
Situated on one of the city's storied canals, the smartly decorated apartment is located in a house that dates back to 1675, but that's where the history lesson ends. The large space is very contemporary in style, and the black and white color scheme of the furnishings, floors, and striped walls gives it a very modern look. A generously-sized sitting room overlooks the Keizersgracht canal and boasts all the amenities you'd expect, including a flat-screen television, a CD player, and a comfortable sofa and chairs facing a gas fireplace. The spacious bedroom overlooks the courtyard garden at the rear of the home, and has a television of its own, as well as a washbasin and an electronically adjustable double bed. The bathroom has a separate bath and shower, and there's a fully equipped kitchen. While breakfasts aren't provided, the apartment's superb location gives guests instant access to plenty of options. Excellent dining—and shopping and lounging—can be found steps from the front door in the nearby Nine Streets, and few of the city's top attractions are more than 15 minutes away on foot. €€ Keizersgracht 320 (Berenstr.), 421-1887, ensuite-logies.nl

Hotel Dylan Amsterdam (formerly Blakes Amsterdam) • Jordaan • Trendy (41 rms)
Anouska Hempel's signature style continues to reign supreme at this 17th-century theater and alms house-cum-boutique hotel, situated on the Keizersgracht, one of Amsterdam's most coveted canal addresses. The labyrinthine compound includes 33 rooms and eight suites, a lounge, an eponymous destination restaurant (see p.63), and a health club. Common areas look stunning, decorated in a contemporary pan-Asian motif that continues in the guest rooms, each of them uniquely appointed—black and blue lacquered wood in the Kimono rooms, and ginger and turmeric fabrics and mahogany floors in La Carmona rooms, for example. It must be said that the detail in the rooms, like the service, seems to have slipped a bit with the new management (beware of the leaking showers). Nevertheless, the Hotel Dylan Amsterdam continues to offer fashion-minded travelers and the occasional A-list movie star a handsome canal-side residence in close proximity to the city's best attractions, as well as conveniences like a fleet of retro-cool Swedish Kronan bikes, and staff that are well informed, well connected, and reliably discreet. Book a "Klassbol" room in bold red and white stripes and with four-poster beds, or let yourself be surprised with any room in the old building since they all have tranquil courtyard views. €€€€ Keizersgracht 384 (Berenstr.), 530-2010, dylanamsterdam.com

Lute Suites • Ouderkerk aan de Amstel • Trendy (7 rms)
When a hotel that's located 20 minutes from the city center still makes the cut as one of Amsterdam's top hotels, you know they're doing something right—although at Lute, they don't just do some things right, they do everything to spectacular perfection. The hotel's seven luxurious, spacious, and bright suites have private entrances that make them feel more like townhouses than hotel rooms, and each was uniquely designed by Marcel Wanders. Furniture and

accessories from Moooi and Capellini, Bisazza mosaics, and Boffi bathroom fixtures feature into the spaces—some split level—making them some of the best-looking rooms to have graced the pages of the glossy design mags. But the hotel doesn't place form above function. Kitchenettes, as well as high-tech conveniences like flat-screen televisions, DVD players, and wireless internet, are on hand to ensure that you feel right at home—if your home happened to look half as fabulous—and delicious breakfasts can be delivered to your front door. Macrame banisters, Swarovski accents, screens of metal flowers, and lime green floorboards reveal Wanders' penchant for whimsical flourishes, and while each space is different, suite five with its suspended balcony, inlaid floor, panoramic Amstel River views, and giant "wetroom" is a favorite of the designer as well as many of the hotel's chic international guests. When it comes to lunch and dinner, you'll want to see-and-be-seen in the on site Lute Restaurant (see p.66)—a favorite with the stylish local who's who. €€€ Amsteldijk Zuid 54-58 (Arnsteldijk), 472-2462, lutesuites.com

Miauw Suites • Jordaan • Modern (3 rms)

Local fashion designer and all-around trendsetter Analik has a great eye for style. She's already enjoyed tremendous success with the Miauw hotel she designed in Antwerp. It's no surprise then that the Amsterdam branch of her luxury suites should prove just as popular. Located in the beautiful Negen Straatjes (Nine Streets), and nestled among some of the best shopping and dining Amsterdam has to offer, the three large suites are as gorgeous as they are practical. Composed of a living room, separate bedroom, bathroom, and full open kitchen, each is massive by most hotel standards—on average 750 square feet—making them suited to long stays as well as short visits. Rooms are modern and brightly decorated with a mix of vintage and contemporary, and there's an emphasis on warmth and comfort that, thankfully, doesn't compromise the design ethos. Creature comforts include low-cost phone lines, widescreen televisions, and combination DVD/CD players. For the business-minded, all rooms have a workstation with an iMac and complimentary high-speed wireless and ethernet access. All-natural bath and skin care products are provided, and limited concierge duties can be performed by the staff of the Analik boutique—located underneath the suites, the shop does triple duty as a concept store, gallery, and exhibition space catering to the same style-savvy guests who might spend the night. For those who wish to stay longer, weekly and monthly rates can be negotiated. €€ Hartenstraat 36 (Keizersgracht), 422-0561, miauw.com

NH Amsterdam Centre • Museumplein • Modern (230 rms)

Located at the southern end of the city center canal belt, the hotel is just steps from the buzzing Leidseplein as well as many of the city's top tourist draws: The Vondelpark—Amsterdam's equivalent to New York's Central Park—the Museumplein with its array of cultural attractions, and PC Hooftstraat, the Netherlands' premier destination when it comes to shopping for international designer clothing, are all just a five-minute walk away. The public spaces as well as the guest rooms have been renovated and the results are dramatic: The hotel's atmosphere is surprisingly more tasteful and modern than what you'd expect from a large chain, with contemporary (albeit mass-produced) art gracing the walls, hip furniture in chocolate and gray, and throw rugs accenting dark wooden floors. That sense of international urban sophistication is bolstered by the attractive, international 30-somethings who frequent the hotel, along with trendy locals who stop in to dine at Amsterdam's outpost of Restaurant Bice (see p.67), the internationally acclaimed Italian eatery. You won't find big-name designer furniture in the hallways or boutique hotel prices. You will find all of the amenities that you'd expect from a chain hotel, including a helpful concierge, 24-hour room service, conference area, wireless internet, and a large buffet-style breakfast. Some rooms overlook the canal, but note that from the fifth floor, an overhang blocks the water. Lower rooms allow the view, but can be noisier. €€ Stadhouderskade 7 (Vondelstr.), 685-1351, nh-hotels.com

The Okura Hotel • De Pijp • Modern (315 rms)

A member of The Leading Hotels of the World, the five-star Okura has the deep-seated low-key elegance and comfort this group has come to represent. Clean-lined, stylish rooms are decorated with modern but comfortable furniture in a soft palette of tan, blue, and white. Bathrooms have heated mirrors (to prevent fogging) and separate showers with rain heads. The spacious rooms also have flat-screen TVs in both the main area and the bath, along with a large desk and leather chair for working, should the need arise. The Okura also has a nicely appointed health club and spa, with Japanese massage. Two Michelin-star restaurants are on site: Yamazato (see p.123) and Ciel Bleu (see p.116). Most rooms have sweeping city views (we like to look over the Amstel Canal), but ask for one with a view from the bathroom window as well. And for the techno-savvy, take note: The concierge here will rent you a GPS device with maps of the city to get you anywhere you need to go. €€€€ Ferdinand Bolstraat 333 (Jozef Israelskade), 678-7111, okura.nl

Cool Amsterdam:
The Restaurants

Altmann Restaurant & Bar • De Pijp • Fusion
London, New York, and Paris: Every cool city has a must-do bistro and Amsterdam's version holds its own against the best of them. The black, cream, and white interior is a stylish backdrop for chef Mohammed Mahraoui's colorful global cuisine and the attractive 30-something crowd that packs the tables, especially on weekend nights. Reliably gracious service keeps Altmann popular with locals, as do complex and inventive dishes that treat the eye as well as the palate. Reserve in advance to score a coveted VIP table or prepare for a cramped evening. *Tue-Fri noon-2pm and 6pm-midnight, Sat-Mon 6pm-midnight.* €€ ≡ Amsteldijk 25 (2e Jan v.d. Heijdenstr.), 662-7777, altmann.nl

Beddington's • Canal Belt • Fusion
From the stark cobalt and white décor, to service that's formal yet leisurely, and dishes that are lauded equally for their ambition and execution, Beddington's is a gorgeous experience for those with advanced palates. The cuisine features adventurous combinations of ingredients drawn from the four corners of the globe, and the sophisticated wine pairings are well suited to the bold flavors of chef-owner Jean Beddington's elegant creations. Factor in the stylish who's-who crowd and an unwavering commitment to quality, and you have one of the city's premier culinary extravaganzas. *Tue-Sat from 5:30pm.* €€ (set menu) ≡ Utrechtsedwarsstraat 141 (Amstel), 620-7393, beddington.nl

Blauw aan de Wal • Oude Zijde • French
Best Only-in-Amsterdam Experiences Opening a sophisticated bistro in a graffiti-filled alley in the middle of the Red Light District might seem shocking to American sensibilities, but you can find some surprising gems nestled among the legendary seedy shops. Chic locals enjoy the crisp table linens, minimalist décor, tranquil garden tables, rare non-smoking dining area, extensive wine list, and delicate Mediterranean cuisine. It's a stylish oasis popular with a trendy 30-ish crowd, and a case study in Amsterdam's famous "live and let live" attitude. *Mon-Sat 6:30pm-late.* €€ ≡ Oudezijds Achterburgwal 99 (Barndesteeg), 330-2257

Blender • Zuid • Mediterranean
It's so high wattage—both the interior and the crowd—you'll think you're in a nightclub. Theatrical lighting, bold geometric graphics, chic chairs, acres of shiny surfaces, and more chrome than you'd see at a Hell's Angels rally, all add up to a first-rate glam-dining experience. Light fish and meat dishes with distinctive Mediterranean touches mean that the meals are just as appealing as the décor, while the large grappa, digestive, and cigar selections reflect the sophisticated-cool tastes of the urban crowd. A summer-only terrace offers an outdoor dining option. *Tue-Sat 6pm-1am; kitchen until 11pm.* €€ ≡ v.d. Palmkade 16 (Jacob Catskade), 486-9860, blender.to

Bond • Zuid • Mediterranean
With its glamorous décor (more Goldfinger than 007), this '60s-inspired space draws a sexy international crowd. Mirrors, plush materials, and acres of gold

lls to the furniture coverings—form the backdrop for din-
are well-executed and delicious, if a little less adventurous
namesake. Steaks, fish dishes, and the omnipresent pasta
bulk of the menu that's bolstered by memorable desserts and
on-Sat noon-10:30pm, bar until 1am, Fri-Sat bar until 2am.
raat 128b (Dufaystr.), 676-4647, restaurantbond.nl

b..   ers • Zuid • Continental
The ..   als-to-visitor ratio and friendliness of the crowd make this slightly
out-of-the-way spot a hit for breakfast or lunch, popular at any time of the day.
They serve what are arguably the city's tastiest breakfasts to some of
Amsterdam's best-dressed, earning a loyal following. Even the Prince is rumored
to drop in for a bite on occasion. If the tables are full, ask to share; the friend
you make could be your ticket to Amsterdam society. *Mon-Fri 8am-10pm, Sat-
Sun 9am-6pm.* € ▭ Williamsparkweg 163 (Cornelis Schuytstr.), 673-0360

Brasserie Harkema* • Nieuwe Zijde • French
The after-work crowd arrives early for cocktails and stays for dinner, often packing
the room with gorgeous locals of all ages. The menu is decadent, some it very good
while other dishes are merely well-presented. Nonetheless, you're not really here for
the food. Harkema makes for a fun evening out. Service can be slow, so don't make
this your "before concert" option, and ask for a balcony/platform table as they have
the best view. *See Cool Nightlife, p.69. Daily 11am-1am.* €€ ▭ Nes 67
(Grimburgwal), 428-2222, brasserieharkema.nl

Brasserie van Baerle • Zuid • French
Best Brunches Amsterdam's coolest brunch date is a reservation-only affair. Sure
the restaurant is ground zero for professional lunches and formal elegant dinners, but on Sundays, things really heat up. Order from the same extensive wine
list, but dine on gourmet breakfasts of smoked salmon and caviar blinis.
Champagne and orange juice flow like water, giving this hot spot, complete with
a shaded garden terrace, a glorious Left-Bank cosmopolitan edge on the competition. *Mon-Sat noon-11pm, Sun 10am-11pm; brunch Sun 10am-1pm.* €€
▭ Van Baerlestraat 158 (Ruysdaelstr.), 679-1532, brasserievanbaerle.nl

't Buffet van Odette en Yvette • Jordaan • Dutch
To experience an Amsterdam breakfast through the eyes of a stylish local, head
to this canal-side favorite where you'll be joined by a cross-section of the city.
Forget bacon and eggs—you're in Holland, remember? Instead follow the lead
of the locals and order a gourmet roll adorned with such toppings as goat cheese
with walnuts and honey, or smoked salmon with cream cheese and spring
onions. Felling less adventurous? Yogurt with muesli, croissants and omelets
round out the menu. *Mon-Fri 8:30am-5:30pm, Sat 10am-5pm, Sun noon-5pm.*
€ ▭ Herengracht 309 (Oude Spiegelstr.), 423-6034, buffet-amsterdam.nl

CaffePC • Museumplein • Continental

For a quick breakfast, lunch, or dinner, you can't beat this small but stylish cafe located in the heart of Amsterdam's international designer boutique district. Surrounded by all those trendy shops, and with a smart but simple black and orange décor, CaffePC attracts flashy chic shoppers as well as locals doing lunch. Open for breakfast, it's also a great choice for those looking for a casual but stylish pre-museum meal; the Van Gogh and Rijksmuseum are just steps away. *Sun-Wed 8am-8pm, Thu 8am-midnight, Fri-Sat 8am-9pm.* € ▤ PC Hooftstraat 87 (v.d. Veldestr.), 673-4752

Chang-I • Zuid • Asian

Chang-I is a pan-Asian post-modern hot spot, and from the décor—silk curtains, Buddha-head statues, and colonial influenced furniture—to the see-and-be-seen trendsetters, it makes a stylish impact. Designed by the crew responsible for Jimmy Woo, the space has the goods to back up its reputation for both flash and substance. Dishes like market fish with bok choy and ginger-soy, and wok-cooked tenderloin skillfully combine Eastern and Western flavors, while the convenient location behind the Concertgebouw, Amsterdam's premier concert hall, makes this a great choice for pre-theater dining. *Mon-Sat 5-10:30pm.* €€ ▤ Jan Willem Brouwersstraat 7 (Alexander Boersstr.), 470-1700, chang-i.nl

Cinema Paradiso • Jordaan • Italian

Best Always-Trendy Tables With a name inspired by Italian cinema, a rotating cast of Euro-glam diners, and an entryway with red carpet, this spot will tempt you to thank the Academy before sitting down. Have a drink at the bar—they don't take reservations, and you're bound to wait—and try to spot the members of whichever carb-loading football team is in town. Service can be indifferent or arrogant unless you really are a star, so try to dress the part and relax, taking solace in the fact that the eye candy, yummy cocktails, and flashy crimson and gold accented room will tide you over until your meal arrives. *Tue-Sun 6-11pm.* € ▤ Westerstraat 184-186 (Tichelstr.), 623-7344, cinemaparadiso.info

College* • Museumplein • New Dutch

Best of-the-Moment Dining The first term reports are in so let's review the grades handed out at Schilo van Coevorden's newest project. The "New Dutch" cuisine gets an A+ for inventiveness, consistency, and respect for traditions. A+ also for the interior. Located in a former school gymnasium, the room is a tasteful combination of old and new Holland—think delft blue porcelain juxtaposed against Dutch design furniture. And an A+ for the crowd, made up of the city's stylish leisure class and business set. The only failing mark? Scoring a table. The long wait for a summer dinner reservation is positively F-. *See Cool Nightlife, College Bar & Lounge, p.70. Mon-Sat noon-2pm and 7-10pm, Sun noon-2pm.* €€ (set menu) ▤ The College Hotel, Roelof Hartstraat 1 (Balthasar Floriszstr.), 571-1511, thecollegehotel.com

The Dylan (formerly Blakes Amsterdam) • Jordaan • Fusion (G)

Best Always-Trendy Tables The name has changed but Anouska Hempel's fingerprints remain, giving this culinary hotspot its signature style. Exposed brick and geometric accents in black, white, and cream bring a Zen-like tranquility, while Schilo van Coevorden's East-meets-West dishes turn some heads of their own. Creations like fillet of veal baked with shanso pepper, udon noodles, and black bean sauce have bold Asian influences, while the chic factor is universal, extending from stylish locals to visiting A-list celebrities staying at the eponymous hotel. *Daily noon-2pm and 6:30-10:30pm; tea 3-5pm.* €€€ ▬ Hotel Dylan Amsterdam, Keizersgracht 384 (Berenstr.), 530-2010, dylanamsterdam.com

Envy • Jordaan • Italian

Best-of-the-Moment Dining This is one of the city's newest hedonist hot spots, featuring an oh-so-cool wall of 26 back-lit fridges, a bustling open kitchen, and a sleek black seating area. The only obvious Italian touches are on the plates, where micro-sized portions (meant for sharing) of charcuterie, cheeses, risottos, and pastas have been attracting the city's chic since opening the doors in 2005. Gloat at securing a reservation, ogle your hot dining companions, and give your friends a reason to be jealous. *Sun-Thu 5pm-1am, Fri-Sat 5pm-3am.* €€€ ▬ Prinsengracht 381 (Reestr.), 344-6407, envy.nl

EspressoBar Puccini • Oude Zijde • Deli

Best Lunch Spots If you're headed to Puccini there's one Dutch word you need to know—*lekker*. Delicious. *Lekker* sandwiches, *lekker* soups, and very *lekker* salads make this informal spot the perfect pit stop after a morning of shopping or strolling. The few outdoor tables offer people-watching and canal views, but the interior is so small that virtually every table is a window seat anyway. Show off your insider knowledge and reserve a seat for dinner if you're headed to a show at the Muziektheater—they stay open until 8pm to accommodate theater goers, and it's the only time the space feels less than ultra-casual. *Lekker* indeed. *Mon-Fri 8:30am-6pm, Sat-Sun 10am-6pm.* €€ ▬ Staalstraat 21 (Zwanenburgwal), 620-8458

Fifteen Amsterdam* • Eastern Harbor • French

Best Hot-Shot Chefs It's celebrity chef Jamie Oliver's first project outside London—and his hit "feel-good" television show about unemployed Dutch youth learning the cooking trade at Fifteen made this restaurant a success from day one. Both in front of the camera and behind the stove, chef Ben van Beurten holds his own with creations that are heavy on organic ingredients for a set 4-course menu. Designer Marcel Wanders has added signature touches, confirming the restaurant's credibility with the style-set. Come for drinks before the dining scene heats up around 8pm—and ask to be seated on one of the raised areas that allows for the best people-watching. *See Cool Nightlife, p.70. Mon-Sat 6pm-1am, Sun 3pm-1am.* €€ (set menu) ▬ Jollemanhof 9 (Kattenburgerstr.), 0900-343-8336, fifteen.nl

Le Garage • Zuid • French

Best Hot-Shot Chefs Holland's first celebrity chef, Joop Braakhekke, has the flashy restaurant, over-the-top personality, and Dutch A-list friends to match. Enticing fish and meat dishes in the French bistro style are bound to please, but that's only half of the attraction. Everyone from international football stars (and tennis ace Richard Krajicek) to glamorous society types drops in after 8pm for a bite, reassured that if all else fails, they can resort to admiring themselves—the plush red interior features more mirrors than a Coney Island funhouse. *Mon-Fri noon-2pm and 6-11pm, Sun 6-11pm.* €€ ≡ Ruysdaelstraat 54-56 (Pieter de Hoochstr.), 679-7176, restaurantlegarage.nl

Gorgeous • De Pijp • French

Gorgeous? More like understated-stylish and chic. Nevertheless, this cool neighborhood bistro serves appealing dishes to attractive 30-something locals who are casually but smartly dressed. The rich brown and pink décor looks trendy and cheerful, and the same can be said of the crowd. On weekend evenings the room fills and buzzes with couples on dates as well as groups of friends who come for the chef's seasonal menu, for the very local, cozy vibe, and to check out this new addition to the city's culinary scene. *Tue-Fri noon-2pm and 8pm-late, Sat 8pm-late.* €€ ≡ 2e v.d. Helststraat 16 (Van Ostadestr.), 379-1400, gorgeousrestaurant.nl

Herrie • Canal Belt • French

Best of-the-Moment Dining Star-chef Herman den Blijker's handful of successful restaurants and hit search-for-a-new-chef television show ensured that his first foray into Amsterdam's culinary scene would be successful—even if he merely "supervises" the show's eventual winner. The cream and golden décor suggests a touch of opulence, and neither the fare nor the casually chic crowd disappoints. French dishes characterized by vibrant flavors make up the bulk of the menu, while the local see-and-be-seen set fills the tables to capacity hoping to catch glimpses of Herman's who's-who circle of friends. Not a celebrity? Don't worry; everyone gets a warm welcome, fine service, and a personal visit from the man himself, making everyone feel oh-so-special. *Mon-Sat 6pm-late.* €€ ≡ Utrechtsestraat 30a (Keizersgracht), 622-0838

Incanto • Rembrandtplein • Italian

Canal views, pale tables, stark white walls, and comfortable, retro-chic chairs welcome a well-dressed crowd that shows up to dine on well-executed classics. The popular risottos, roast venison, guinea fowl, and daily fish selection are all highly regarded among local foodies, as are the well-matched wines. *Daily 11am-11pm.* €€ ≡ Amstel 2 (Muntplein), 423-3681, restaurant-incanto.nl

Jean-Jean • Jordaan • French

Who says good looks and attitude have to go hand in hand? Stark white walls and Gispen chairs make this bistro a hit among locals expecting great food and a splash of style, while eschewing elitism and glitz. Locally sourced ingredients—organic where possible—are inventively blended to create a small but wholly recommendable menu, and you can count on the service to be friendly and attentive ... at its worst. Feeling indecisive? Try the three-course "surprise" menu which ensures special attention. *Sun-Thu 6pm-1am, Fri-Sat 6pm-2am.* €€ ≡ 1e Anjeliersdwarsstraat 14 (Anjeliersstr.), 627-7153, jean-jean.nl

Letting • Jordaan • Continental

This lesser-known spot, with a simply styled interior, tiny terrace, and chalkboard specials, is perfect at any time of the day, but it's the all-day every-day champagne breakfast that makes it special and attracts those in the know. Come lunchtime, a stylish crowd of all ages makes the scene, noshing on sandwiches and soups, popping in for a borrel—a glass of beer served with savory snacks—and sipping coffee while munching on delicious tarts and pies. Call ahead to guarantee a Saturday-morning table. *Sun-Mon 8am-5:30pm, Tue-Sat 8am-9pm.* € ≡ Prinsenstraat 3 (Keizersgracht), 627-9393

Lute Restaurant • Ouderkerk aan de Amstel • Fusion (G)

Best Hot-Shot Chefs Executive chef Peter Lute creates magnificent dishes for a sophisticated, style-conscious, 30-plus crowd that comes as much for the scene as the food. The room was made over by Moooi chief Marcel Wanders, and the results are dramatic. Industrial elements like concrete floors are warmed with shag rugs, accent lighting, and gorgeous furniture, and the atmosphere toes the chic line between cold and cozy. The canal-side location also makes it a great spot to arrive by water taxi. Inventiveness and style also define the tasting menu. *Mon-Fri noon-2pm and 6-10pm, Sat-Sun 6-10pm.* €€ ≡ Oude Molen 5 (Amsteldijk), 472-2462, luterestaurant.nl

The Mansion* (formerly Vossius) • Museumplein • Asian

One of the city's hottest nightspots is also a favorite for A-list dining. *See Cool Nightlife, p.71, for details. Tue-Thu 6pm-1am, Fri-Sat 6pm-3am.* €€€ ≡ Hobbemastraat 2 (Stadhouderskade), 616-6664, the-mansion.nl

Nana Gentile • Nieuwe Zijde • Italian

The cool gray and black décor borders on being cold, but everything else in this small Italian eatery is hot enough to warm the heart of even hardened foodies. The meals are consistently delicious, the service prompt and personal, and the atmosphere refined and serene. The menu changes often, but the stylish local crowd remains the same, returning time and time again for owner-chef John Crucianelli's thoughtful interpretations of hits like veal scaloppine with lemon, capers, white wine, and garlic. *Tue-Wed and Sun 6-10pm, Fri-Sat 6-10:30pm.* €€ ≡ Nieuwezijds Voorburgwal 289 (Paliesstr.), 420-0202, nanagentile.nl

De Ondeugd* • De Pijp • Fusion

A local favorite in a neighborhood with many great restaurants, De Ondeugd (Dutch for "the naughty") has all of the components for a perfect evening Dutch-style—warm service, a good-looking crowd, a mellow atmosphere, and just the right design touches to strike a balance between coziness and glam. Two rooms, one in black and white, and one in soft pastels with acres of sheer fabrics, create the perfect setting for enjoying the chef's fusion creations. Come late to mingle with the handsome crowd that hangs out sipping concoctions from the bar and noshing on decadent desserts like the chocolate fondue. See *Cool Nightlife, p.72. Sun-Thu 6pm-1am, Fri-Sat 6pm-3am, kitchen daily until 11pm.* € ≡ Ferdinand Bolstraat 13-15 (Daniël Stalpertstr.), 672-0651, ondeugd.nl

Pont 13 • West • French

Situated on a renovated, antique ferry, Pont 13 has simple industrial-chic flourishes, and every table boasts water views. Nevertheless, the eye-catching setting remains a side attraction. The stylish and loyal fans really come for the consistently delicious, hearty, and uncomplicated French fare that's earned the accolades of Amsterdam's most finicky food critics. You can count on a great steak frites, but regulars know to trust the chef with more subtle treats like partridge with pancetta in a light mustard sauce, or roasted chicken with spinach, fennel, and olive tapenade. A fine bar scene and terrace add to the appeal, making it a popular option for a lazy Sunday afternoon. *Tue-Sat from 6pm, Sun from 1pm.* € B≡ Stavangerweg 891 (Tasmanstr.), 770-2722, pont13.nl

COOL (vertical sidebar text)

Proeflokaal Janvier • Canal Belt • Fusion

Under a different name, Proeflokaal Janvier was merely a great pla__
the warm summer sun (the large terrace ranks among this city's best) __
new name and a new chef, the wooden former church appears born again. Pau__
Kelder's menu—stylized takes on French classics along with a touch of international flourishes—is noteworthy for delivering surprising and bold flavors as well as
stealing the limelight from that superb patio scene, but in case you're wondering;
yes it's still here and it's still packed with hipsters. *Tue-Sun 6-10pm.* € ▤
Amstelveld 12 (Prinsengracht), 626-1199, proeflokaaljanvier.nl

Pygma-Lion • Canal Belt • South African

Best Tastes of the Exotic For design fans with exotic tastes, Pygma-Lion is not to be
missed. The interior, in earth tones and dark wood, is as handsome as the stylish
crowd, but that's where familiarity ends. The menu reads like a casting call for The
Crocodile Hunter, and true to form, crocodile is featured along with minced zebra,
antelope, and smoked ostrich, all skillfully prepared. Exotic and aromatic dishes
paired with a great wine selection—all of it South African—make this a perfect
adventure-dining experience. *Tue-Sun 6-11pm.* € ▤ Nieuwe Spiegelstraat 5a
(Herengracht), 420-7022, pygma-lion.com

Rain* • Rembrandtplein • Fusion

Best Restaurant-Lounges One of the city's newest all-in-one concept spaces pulls a
great-looking crowd with vibe-y beats and a purple and black sleek-chic décor.
"Global cuisine" dishes artfully marry the best of Eastern and Western traditions—like crab risotto with avocado ice cream, claw tempura, and lemongrass
bubbles—while DJs and decadent cocktails mean that diners are happy to hang
out dancing and lounging post-meal. *See Cool Nightlife, p.72. Sun-Thu
6pm-2am, Fri-Sat 6pm-4am.* €€ ▤ Rembrandtplein 44 (Utrechtsestr.),
626-7078, rain-amsterdam.com

Restaurant Bice • Museumplein • Italian

Best Italian Eateries Renowned for fine cuisine, top service, and an equally distinguished crowd, this stalwart of the Bice brand will satisfy Italian gourmands of
the highest order. The interior is subdued yet contemporary, with light woods
and crisp linens setting an elegant tone. A chic 30-plus crowd—visitors as well
as locals—makes the scene, and, in keeping with the Bice tradition, the large
antipasti menu and comprehensive selection of fish and meat main courses are
all traditionally prepared. *Mon-Sat 6:30-10:30pm, lunch by appointment only.*
€€ ▤ NH Amsterdam Hotel, Stadhouderskade 7 (Vondelstr.), 589-8870, bice.nl

Stout • Jordaan • International

This two-story room is known for friendly servers and a casual approach to delicious
design-dining. Style might set the mood—the black-and-white décor is very au
courant—but the main attraction here, aside from the attractive 30-something
locals, is Asian-influenced Dutch, and inventive plates incorporating wild game are
the norm; opt for a two-person sharing "plateau." *Sun-Thu noon-10pm, Fri-Sat
noon-11pm, bar until 1am.* € ⓑ▤ Haarlemmerstraat 73 (Herenmarkt), 616-3664,
restaurantstout.nl

SupperClub* • Nieuwe Zijde • Fusion

Best Always-Trendy Tables Pioneering, trendsetting, ultra-chic ... and over 10 years
old? Yep. The hyper-designed nexus of Amsterdam's lounge-restaurant scene, and

the darling of the *Wallpaper* magazine set, remains a sight to behold. Eating dinner while reclining on all-white daybeds as DJs and performance artists entertain is a seminal Amsterdam-moderne experience that will always feel louche. The crowd may be predominantly made up of jet-set visitors nowadays—bad girl Pink was the latest in a long line of A-listers—but it remains a must-see-and-do. *See Cool Nightlife, p.72. Sun-Thu 8pm-1am, Fri-Sat 8pm-3am, private lounge open nightly from 7pm.* €€ (set menu) ≡ Jonge Roelensteeg 21 (Nieuwezijds Voorburgwal), 344-6400, supperclub.nl

SupperClub Cruise* • Various Locations • Fusion
Best On-the-Water Like its landlocked sibling, the seafaring version of SupperClub is a design décor hotspot featuring exquisite five-course set-menu meals, delicious drinks, decadent lounging, and a chic 20- and 30-something crowd. On-board attractions include resident DJs, a sleek black bar, and open-air dancing on the ship's deck, but the undisputed showcase is the massive white daybed that you share with 99 other scenesters. Theme parties add extra cachet to the cool-factor and the annual New Year's Eve cruise is a popular event that sells out long in advance. *See Cool Nightlife, p.72. Fri and Sat sailing at 8pm.* €€ (set menu) ≡ Departure locations vary nightly, 344-6404, supperclubcruise.nl

Tomo Sushi • Rembrandtplein • Sushi
A resounding "domo arigato" to the folks behind this sushi joint—one of Amsterdam's best. They care as much about the décor and atmosphere as they do the food, and that pays dividends with the style-conscious locals. Design-cool round stools and chairs complement the stark white and gray walls, giving the space a somber but stylized ambience that's bolstered with candles and groovy tunes. Sushi has pride of place on the small-ish menu, but regulars have made a meal of the highly regarded grilled skewers of ingredients like enoki and quail egg. *Daily 5:30-10:30pm.* €€€ ≡ Reguliersdwarsstraat 131 (Openhartsteeg), 528-5208

Vakzuid* • Zuid • Fusion
Best Restaurant-Lounges "Swifter, higher, stronger" is so passé. It's strictly "cooler, sleeker, tastier" at this restaurant-lounge-club located in the city's 1928 Olympic Stadium. The trendy industrial décor and Amsterdam's largest lounge terrace attract young-professional locals for after-work drinks, and that same crowd sticks around, making an evening out of dining and lounging. Dine on chef Andy Tan's Asian-French creations outside with views of the river—take a blanket if it's cool—or inside in the sleek-chic space featuring views of the playing field. *See Cool Nightlife, p.72. Mon-Thu 10am-1am, Fri 10am-3am, Sat 4pm-3am, Sun 3-10pm.* €€ ≡ Olympisch Stadion 35 (Stadionplein), 570-8400, vakzuid.nl

Voorbij Het Einde • Eastern Harbor • French (G)
Best Romantic Dining With glass ceilings and walls, stainless steel accents, and earth tone surfaces—slate gray and clay red—this is one great-looking modern space. It's no easy feat then that the real attraction is on the plates. The set menus, ranging in size between three and seven courses, provide one of the city's finest gastronomic experiences, and they've earned the restaurant a cult-like adoration among the well-heeled and well-dressed set. Discreet professional service, valet parking, and consistently perfect dishes create an air of distinction, making this an excellent place to celebrate a special occasion. *Wed-Sat 6:30-11pm, lunch by appointment Wed-Fri.* €€ ▭ Sumatrakade 613 (Javakade), 419-1143, voorbijheteinde.nl

Cool Amsterdam:
The Nightlife

Arc • Rembrandtplein • Lounge

Best Gay Scenes Designer furniture, contemporary lighting, funky DJ music, flavorful cocktails, and more good-looking 20- and 30-somethings than you can shake a martini at, add up to the city's coolest gay bar-lounge—and a surprisingly mixed crowd. You can eat better elsewhere, so drop in for pre-clubbing or late-night drinks, and since you probably won't find space inside, be content to people-watch from the terrace that overflows into the street in all but the worst of weather. The place to come at cocktail time—between 5 and 7 nightly, and all evening Wednesdays. *Sun-Thu 10am-1am, Fri-Sat 10am-3am.* ▤ Reguliersdwarstraat 44 (Geel Vinksteeg), 689-7070, bararc.com

Bar Bep • Nieuwe Zijde • Bar/Restaurant

Steps from the Dam Square at the geographic center of the city, this small spot provides a metropolitan beginning or end to any night of clubbing, lounging, and drinking. Concrete, the folks responsible for the SupperClub design, have created the interior, and the results, a mix of stone, plaster, and wood contrasted with nightclub lighting, are electric. Stick around long enough and a small dancing scene breaks out, but most smart locals warm up here before parting for hotter dance climes. *Mon-Thu 5pm-1am, Fri 5pm-3am, Sat 4pm-3am, Sun 4pm-1am.* ▤ Nieuwezijds Voorburgwal 260 (Korte Lijnesteeg), 626-5649

Bimhuis • Eastern Harbor • Performance

Best Jazz Scenes Located in a building where the stellar architecture is as much a draw as the music inside, Bimhuis is a premier spots for jazz lovers. The facility hosts more than 250 concerts each year, ranging from free jam sessions to touring legends. Tickets can be hard to come by, but don't despair if a show is sold out: Unclaimed tickets are sold first-come first-served beginning a half-hour before the concert. Plan on lining up early if this is your only option. *Most concerts begin at 9pm, call to confirm.* ▣▤ Piet Heinkade 3 (Vemenplein), 788-2188, bimhuis.nl

Brasserie Harkema* • Nieuwe Zijde • Bar/Restaurant

Popular spot for after-work cocktails. *See Cool Restaurants, p.62, for details. Daily 11am-1am.* ▤ Nes 67 (Grimburgwal), 428-2222, brasserieharkema.nl

Bubbles & Wines • Nieuwe Zijde • Wine Bar

You only need to know one thing to fit in here and that's *proost*—Dutch for "bottom's up." Amsterdam's trendiest champagne and wine bar serves up 180 wines by the bottle and over 50 by the glass in a slick-looking designer space. Tables made from dark woods with red accents provide the perfect resting spot for your drink of choice, and whether you perch on the high bar stools, or sit on the gray couches, you'll have the perfect vantage point for checking out the style- conscious young professionals who drop in for drinks and gourmet snacks, both after work and late into the evening. *Mon-Sat 3:30pm-1am.* ▤ Nes 37 (Pieter Jacobszstr.), 422-3318, bubblesandwines.com

Club More • Jordaan • Nightclub

A long bar complete with backlit fridges, and a dance space blessed with minimal-modern design by Concrete—the same firm responsible for the SupperClub—provide the perfect backdrop for the mixed 20s and 30s crowd that turns out for big-name DJs and the casual-cool local vibe. Urban genres like reggae, hip-hop, dancehall, and R&B get heavy rotation as do house and disco, so check the agenda before heading out to this dance spot, or simply show up confident that a hot-looking, ready-to-boogie crowd will magically appear. *Thu-Sun; times vary according to events.* Ⓒ☰ Rozengracht 133 (Ankoleienstr.), 528-7459, expectmore.nl

College Bar & Lounge* • Museumplein • Hotel Bar

Best Hotel Bars A chic interior combined with great drinks and a moneyed, professional, and stylish crowd puts College at the top of its class. Traditional touches like candelabras and a fireplace give the lounge a sophisticated air while modern design elements like embossed wall coverings and chic lighting ensure that the space is firmly of-the-moment cool. The after-work crowd mingles seamlessly with the jet-set guests staying at the College Hotel, and come weekends, the dressed-up regulars rule the room. *See Cool Restaurants, p.63. Daily 9am-1am.* ☰ The College Hotel, Roelof Hartstraat 1 (Balthasar Floriszstr.), 571-1511, thecollegehotel.com

En Pluche • Zuid • Lounge

En Pluche is plush. The warm and velvety red interior, delicious cocktails, tasty and creative "street" finger foods, and fashionable crowd mean space is at a premium, making things extra cozy when the gorgeous locals spill onto your lap. You can make a meal of the mini-bites, but regulars, including fashionistas and entertainers, know to settle into a cushy sofa and plan the rest of the night over drinks. Pit stops at En Pluche, either before or after dinner at Le Garage—it's next door—are an Amsterdam celebrity tradition. *Tue-Sat 6pm-2am.* ☰ Ruysdaelstraat 48 (Pieter de Hoochstr.), 471-4695, enpluche.nl

Escape deLux • Rembrandtplein • Nightclub

Best Dance Clubs With tiny tables, a blue backlit bar area, and a door policy that favors those younger than 35, this trendy international club is as good looking as it is reliably fun. The student scene is noticeably absent, meaning cocktails are the drink of choice, stylish trumps casual, and "your place or mine" means swanky apartments instead of dorm rooms. When not shaking it on the dance floor, partiers get some conceptual comic relief by peeking through the windows to watch the scene in the adjoining dance club, Escape proper. *Thu 11pm-4am, Fri-Sat 11pm-7am, Sun 11pm-4am.* Ⓒ☰ Rembrandtplein 11 (Halvemaansteeg), 622-1111

Fifteen Amsterdam* • Eastern Harbor • Restaurant/Lounge

Celebrity chef Jamie Oliver's place draws a chic crowd for sophisticated cocktails and meals. *See Cool Restaurants, p.64, for details. Mon-Sat 6pm-1am, Sun 3pm-1am.* ☰ Jollemanhof 9 (Kattenburgerstr.), 0900-343-8336, fifteen.nl

Jimmy Woo • Canal Belt • Nightclub

Best See-and-Be-Seen Clubs This is Amsterdam's hands-down, no-holds-barred, reigning A-list champion. Make it past the ruthless and legendary door girl and enter into a world where opium den decor meets Blade Runner chic. Lanterns, Asian art, lounge sofas, and an outrageous lighting scheme—think George Bush Sr.'s "thousand points of light" gone clubbing—have attracted a global who's who clientele. The cast of *Ocean's Twelve*, Britney Spears, the Red Hot Chili Peppers, Will Smith, and virtually every European football star that's passed through Amsterdam have graced the dance floor or hung out sipping gorgeously crafted cocktails. Have your concierge get you on the guest list, show up early, and dress your best: When getting in is this hard, imagine what it takes to stand out from the crowd. *Wed-Thu 11pm-3am, Fri-Sat 11pm-4am, Sun 11pm-3am.* C⊜ Korte Leidsedwarsstraat 18 (Leidsestr.), 626-3150, jimmywoo.com

Joia • Canal Belt • Lounge

Sip excellent cocktails at this seen-to-be-believed spot where a décor inspired by a Moulin Rouge brothel and an Asian casino is only the tip of the iceberg in the medley of styles adorning this space. A large glass wall partitions guests from a jungle-like garden, Grandma's floral chairs pair up with design couches and stools to provide seating areas, and lanterns hang from what can best be described as a characteristically out-of-place wooden ceiling. The trendy and great-looking mid-20's-plus crowd eats elsewhere and comes for the tropical Latin music and barman Salvatore's liquid creations that are Leidseplein area legends. *Tue-Thu 6pm-1am, Fri-Sat 6pm-3am, Sun 6pm-1am.* ⊜ Korte Leidesedwarsstraat 45 (Leidsestr.), 626-6769, tao-group.nl

The Mansion* (formerly Vossius) • Museumplein • Cocktail Bar

Best See-and-Be-Seen Clubs When this spot was known as Vossius, it was the place for A-list see-and-be-seen dining and lounging. Nothing has changed. The restaurant—along with the four bars and dance floor—has benefited from a gorgeous redesign, and the modern-Baroque style sets a tone of grace and sophistication. Sexy Asian tapas enliven the tables, while chandeliers, velvet chairs, creamy tapestries, and a ceiling inspired by the Sistine Chapel provide the perfect backdrop. *See Cool Restaurants, p.66. Tue-Thu 6pm-1am, Fri-Sat 6pm-3am.* C⊜ Hobbemastraat 2 (Stadhouderskade), 616-6664, the-mansion.nl

NL Lounge • Nieuwe Zijde • Lounge

For well-dressed trendy 30-plus locals and their foreign doppelgangers, this big and bold club with an exclusive door policy offers a mellow vibe and looks good doing it. The bar and the seating areas, both in plush reds and black, seem to stretch into the distance, with plenty of low-slung plush couches to lounge on. Up-tempo music, good-looking and skillful bar staff, and a balanced guy-girl ratio also help to make this scene a friendly favorite with the cool artsy-media set. *Sun-Thu 10pm-3am, Sat-Sun 10pm-4am.* ⊜ Nieuwezijds Voorburgwal 169 (Nieuwezijds Armsteeg), 622-7510, clubnl.nl

Onassis • West • Lounge

Best See-and-Be-Seen Clubs If the first things that come to mind are "money," "hedonism," and "water," you're on the right track. This new see-and-be-seen spot has waterfront views, an excellent terrace, a design décor featuring Vitra furniture, and a handsome crowd that's equally upscale. Those in the know eat elsewhere and show up late to dance to DJ'd tunes, sip delicious cocktails, and simply hang out looking fabulous. Come by boat to make a grand entrance. *Sun-Thu noon-1am, Fri-Sat noon-3am.* ⊜ Westerdoksdijk 40 (Berentszstr.), 330-0456, onassisamsterdam.nl

De Ondeugd* • De Pijp • Bar/Restaurant
Fashionable dining spot that draws a late-night crowd to the bar for cocktails and a bite to eat. *See Cool Restaurants, p.66, for details. Sun-Thu 6pm-1am, Fri-Sat 6pm-3am, kitchen daily until 11pm.* ☰ Ferdinand Bolstraat 13-15 (Daniël Stalpertstr.), 672-0651, ondeugd.nl

Panama • Eastern Harbor • Nightclub
Best Dance Clubs Offering one-stop shopping for all of your drinking, dining, and lounging needs, Panama is also a topflight international dance club featuring two dance rooms, exciting play lists, and big name DJs that bring even the most worldly crowds to their feet. The resident DJs are more than capable, but try to time your visit with a performance by a superstar spinner like Dutch DJ-god Tiësto or British heavyweight Jon Digweed. Once you've worked up a sweat, cruise the three large bars or chill out on the balcony, enjoying the view of the eternally young, high-energy crowd below. *Thu-Sun; times and prices vary according to events.* ©☰ Oostelijke Handelskade 4 (Piet Heinkade), 311-8686, panama.nl

Rain* • Rembrandtplein • Restaurant/Lounge
Best Restaurant-Lounges An all-in-one space that draws diners and loungers to its chic interior in equal numbers. *See Cool Restaurants, p.67, for details. Sun-Thu 6pm-2am, Fri-Sat 6pm-4am.* ☰ Rembrandtplein 44 (Utrechtsestr.), 626-7078, rain-amsterdam.com

SupperClub* • Nieuwe Zijde • Restaurant/Lounge
One of Amsterdam's most famous (and chicest) nightlife and dining spots always delivers a memorable experience. *See Cool Restaurants, p.67, for details. Sun-Thu 8pm-1am, Fri-Sat 8pm-3am; private lounge open nightly from 7pm.* ☰ Jonge Roelensteeg 21 (Nieuwezijds Voorburgwal), 344-6400, supperclub.nl

SupperClub Cruise* • Various Locations • Restaurant/Lounge
Best On-the-Water Upping the ante on SupperClub's cool factor, the cruise takes the hyper-chic scene onto the canals. *See Cool Restaurants, p.68, for details. Fri and Sat sailing at 8pm sharp.* ©☰ Departure locations vary nightly, 344-6404, supperclubcruise.nl

Vakzuid* • Zuid • Lounge/Nightclub
Best Restaurant-Lounges With a restaurant, lounge, bar, and club, this all-in-one spot in the Olympic stadium is a world-class, gold medal contender. The DJs keep the crowd hopping, the cocktails are well-executed, the cool industrial design décor in dark rich colors looks as great as the guests, and the large outdoor terrace—blankets provided in cooler weather—ensures that the scene is hot outdoors as well as inside this large space. If you're headed here for nightlife, save it for weekends when the young professionals who dine here during the week roll up their sleeves and get down to some serious partying. *See Cool Restaurants, p.68. Mon-Thu 10am-1am, Fri 10am-3am, Sat 4pm-3am, Sun 3-10pm.* ☰ Olympisch Stadion 35 (Stadionplein), 570-8400, vakzuid.nl

Vibing • Canal Belt • Cocktail Bar
This Amsterdam rarity—a true cocktail lounge with an attractive modern design—is blessed with talented DJs that play chilled-out groovy tunes at a level that allows conversation with attractive 20- and 30-something locals who stop in before or after clubbing. Come early and score a comfy sofa or choose from

the "Egg Chair Lounge," where white design elements go hand in hand with the purple-hued mood lighting, or the "Chill Area," where soft lighting takes the edge off your post-club vibe. *Tue-Thu 7pm-1am, Sat-Sun 7pm-3am, Sun 7pm-1am.* ▤ Raamstraat 27 (Raamplein), 624-4411, vibing.nl

Vuong • Canal Belt • Lounge

Following the adage "don't mess with success," the folks behind the ultra-successful dance club Jimmy Woo have again looked to Asia for ultra-modern inspiration, only this time they've created a lounge and the theme is colonial Vietnamese meets modern-chic. The black walls, black furniture, and black flooring all look magnificent by candlelight, as does the trendy-sexy crowd that skips the first-floor restaurant and heads upstairs for pre-clubbing cocktails and DJ'd tunes. Come dancing time, do like the locals and head to Jimmy Woo to continue the pan-Asian vibe—it's right across the street. *Sun-Thu 9pm-1am, Fri-Sat 9pm-3am.* ▤ Korte Leidsedwarsstraat 51 (Leidsestr.), 530-5577, vuong.nl

Werck • Jordaan • Lounge

Best Terraces High ceilings, a large open staircase, and a design theme where earth tones set the mood and wood and metal contrast artfully, making Werck one of Amsterdam's most industrial-chic hangouts. You can't go wrong with any seat indoors, but the coveted ones are outside where light-colored couches offer open-air drinking and dining in the shadow of the historical Westerkerk, one of the city's most attractive churches. Be sure to drop in before clubbing or on a sunny weekend afternoon when the space, and fashionable 30-something crowd, looks its best. *May-Oct Sun-Thu noon-1am, Fri-Sat noon-3am; Oct-May Sun-Thu 4pm-1am, Fri-Sat noon-3am.* ▤ Prinsengracht 277 (Westermarkt), 627-4079, werck.nl

Xtra-Cold Amsterdam • Rembrandtplein • Bar/Lounge

This sleek lounge is really two spots in one—a heated section and a much cooler area. Decorated in luscious red with white accents it offers the perfect mix of style and comfort. First, there's the the main attraction of the ice bar itself. From the walls to the tables, and from the animal-pelt covered benches to the glasses, everything is crafted from frozen aqua. Everyone gets complimentary use of a down jacket, and this optional uniform gives the place an egalitarian air. But make no mistake about it; a second draw is that this is a meet-market located in what was surely once a meat freezer, giving the whole scene a touch of irony. What, you'll wonder, is hidden under all those puffy parkas? *Sun-Thu 11am-1am, Fri-Sat 11am-3am.* ⓒ▤ Amstel 194-196 (Amstelstr.), 320-5700, xtracold.nl

Zebra Lounge • Canal Belt • Lounge/Nightclub

Yes, it's next door to the über-hot Jimmy Woo and, no, the celebrity factor barely registers here, but consider this: Even with the mellow door policy, Zebra is full of beautiful, stylish locals and visitors who know how to make a scene. Several bars serving great cocktails make this a great lounge party space, but regulars count on champagne, enjoyed by the bottle from the luxury of private booths, to add a touch of cool sophistication. It used to be the city's only strip bar—why is stripping a no-no while everything else seems permissible?—but now the poles are gone and the heavenly bodies stick to the dance floor or zebra-themed sofas. *Mon-Sun noon-late.* ⓒ▤ Korte Leidsedwarsstraat 14 (Leidsestr.), 612-6153

Cool Amsterdam:
The Attractions

ARCAM (Amsterdam Centre for Architecture) • Oude Zijde • Visitors' Center
Housed in a waterfront building designed by René van Zuuk, ARCAM is the best
one-stop place to get some perspective on the city's famous bricks and mortar.
Displays on architecture, housing, innovative building techniques, philosophy of
design, and urban development issues make for a full agenda of rotating exhibitions—as well as a fascinating glimpse into the future of European cities.
Evenings see symposiums, lectures by visiting luminaries such as distinguished
architects, and cultural events that add a human dimension to the program.
Excellent self-published maps and guidebooks to Amsterdam's stand-out buildings are also for sale in ARCAM's shop. *Tue-Sat 1am-5pm and evenings for special programming.* Prins Hendrikkade 600 (Schippersstr.), 620-4878, arcam.nl

Architectour • Various • Guided Tour
Best Guided Tours With over 25 years on the Amsterdam scene, high-energy archi-
tect-architectural historian Caroline van Raamsdonk knows the landscape, the
buildings, and the people behind them. Whether you customize a tour with her
or ask her to show you highlights, tours—which can be conducted on bicycle—
are eye-opening, informative, and deeply insightful glimpses into Amsterdam's
landmarks. Best of all: Her relationships within the city allow you to see behind
the scenes in private buildings like the residential Walvis and the fabulously
ornate Scheepvaarthuis, where she's the only guide allowed access.
By appointment. €€€€+ 625-9123, email: architectour@wish.net

Christie's Auction House • Zuid • Auction House
Amsterdam's branch of the auction house is known for offering lots of Asian art,
maritime-themed items, and perhaps surprisingly—given the absence of a
Dutch viticulture industry—fine and rare wines. The foremost Northern
European saleroom for fine and decorative arts is a great place to pick up a sou-
venir-treasure of your visit to the Netherlands, and browsing pre-sale exhibitions
will offer a brief but worthwhile diversion for high-end art fans. *Mon-Fri 9am-
5:30pm.* Cornelis Schuytstraat 57 (Willemsparkweg), 575-5255, christies.com

Cobra Museum of Modern Art • Amstelveen • Art Museum
Dedicated to showing works from the little-known Cobra artists, this modern art
museum gives visitors a glimpse into the Netherlands' most significant art
movement in the post-Golden Age. The name is an acronym—the movement
had roots in Copenhagen, Brussels, and Amsterdam—as well as a reference to
the pioneering artists' goals: to strike out at convention with the venom of a
deadly snake. In addition to the permanent Cobra collection, the museum shows
installation art, photography, and mixed media, making this venue, slightly outside the city proper, an insider must-do for fans of contemporary visual arts.
Tue-Sun 11am-5pm, closed Dec 25, Jan 1, and Apr 30. €- Sandbergplein 1
(Amstelveen), 547-5050, cobra-museum.nl

FOAM Photography Museum • Canal Belt • Art Museum

This medium-sized museum, located in two large canal houses, hosts exhibitions of the world's most famous photographers along with small-scale shows from emerging talents from Holland and abroad. Amsterdam's art cognoscenti—particularly the edgier, more stylish—turn out to view historical works, documentary photography, applied works, and contemporary collections organized according to themes like "American Street Photography in the 1960s" and "Made in Britain." Retrospectives of big-name artists like Henri-Cartier Bresson, Garry Winogrand, and Boris Mikhailov are also top draws. *Sat-Wed 10am-5pm, Thu-Fri 10am-9pm.* € Keizersgracht 609 (Vijzelstr.), 551-6500, foam.nl

The Frozen Fountain • Canal Belt • Store

Best Dutch Design So many shops in Amsterdam sell gorgeous products, so it was no easy feat that the Frozen Fountain placed first in a recent local survey of best places to shop for modern design pieces. Boasting "stores within stores'" it carries lines like Vitra, Moooi, and Studio Job, as well as pieces from designer Piet Hein Eek, and specializes in furnishings and accessories that showcase gorgeous Dutch craftsmanship. An in-house gallery hosts exhibitions from up-and-coming artists and designers. *Mon 1-6pm, Tue-Fri 10am-6pm, Sat 10am-5pm.* Prinsengracht 645 (Leidsestr.), 622-9375, frozenfountain.nl

Gassan Diamonds • Oude Zijde • Guided Tour/Store

The 24 diamond-cutting shops in this city make it a global epicenter for the industry, and while the quality of the gems is—presumably—uniformly high, there's a huge difference in the quality of experiences that visitors get when they show up for a look around. Come to the surprisingly fascinating Gassan and you'll witness cutting and polishing, learn about the diamond industry, and gain insight into the life of Amsterdam's Jews during World War II. Best of all, you'll avoid any annoying sales pitches. Of course, if you want to buy, there is plenty to choose from. *Daily 9am-5pm.* Nieuwe Uilenburgerstraat 173-175 (Houtkopersburgwal), 622-5333, gassandiamonds.com

Jacobus Toet • Museumplein • Store

Dedicated to helping you celebrate the hedonistic good-life, this specialty boutique offers the absolute finest Cuban and Dominican cigars, Russian blinis, foie gras, champagnes, cognacs, and caviars. Once you've picked up some Iranian beluga, a Faberge serving dish, some fine bubbly, a nice terrine, and a post-meal Cohiba, head to the steps-away Vondelpark for the ritziest picnic this side of heaven. *Tue-Wed 10am-6pm, Thu 10am-9pm, Fri-Sat 10am-6pm, Sun noon-5pm.* Hobbemastraat 4 (PC Hooftstr.), 679-9162, jacobus-toet.nl

Koan Float and Massage Centre • Jordaan • Spa

True day spas are as scarce as mountains in Holland—you just won't find them—so if you're after some serious R&R, try "koan floating," and mellow out the way this city's see-and-be-seen crowd does. Lying in enclosed light and soundproof chambers, patrons float in a warm saline bath, experience the feeling of weightlessness, and escape from the stress of the day-to-day world. And if that sounds like it might be a little too metaphysical for your tastes, you're not entirely alone: Traditionalists drop in for a massage; many techniques, including Shiatsu, can be arranged. *Daily 9:30am-11pm by appointment only.* €€€€ Herengracht 321 (Raamsteeg), 555-0333, koan-float.com

Loods 6 • Eastern Harbor • Art Gallery

Best Contemporary Art Spaces A one-stop, contemporary art and design wonderland, Loods 6 is a multidisciplinary space with galleries, installations, design shops, over 50 private ateliers and studios, and a staging ground where four of Amsterdam's heavyweight art collectives exhibit their latest works. Exhibitions are diverse—multimedia, photography, graphic arts, installation works; everything makes the cut—and die-hard contemporary art fans often find must-have pieces in the many studios. Look for the soon-to-be-installed permanent exhibition on the area's development—it's a hotbed of architecture and an outstanding example of modern urban planning—or rest your feet at the on-site cafe; With sweeping harbor views and Sunday afternoon high tea, it's the perfect time-out from your Amsterdam art immersion. *Mon-Fri 9am-5pm, weekends and evenings for events.* KNSMlaan 143 (Levantkade), 418-2020, loods6.nl

Marlies Dekkers • Zuid • Store

Best Sex-in-the-City Given Amsterdam's reputation for openness when it comes to sexuality, it's fitting that what is surely one of the world's sexiest and most chic lingerie shops should open its doors here. Of course it helps that Marlies Dekkers, one of Europe's foremost designers in the field, is Dutch, but having shown her contemporary collections on runways and in modern art exhibitions around the globe, she waited until 2005 to open a dedicated shop. The cobalt and black floors and walls, coupled with plush red carpeting, create a sexy atmosphere, while a gorgeous fireplace and small lounge area set the mood for romance before you even leave the shop. *Mon noon-6pm, Tue-Wed 10am-6pm, Thu 10am-7pm, Fri 10am-6pm, Sat 10am-5pm.* Cornelis Schuytstraat (Van Breestr.), 471-4146, marliesdekkers.nl

Paradis Private Boat Tours • Various • Guided Tours

Best On-the-Water Of the countless ways to enjoy Amsterdam from the water, it would be hard to think of one more sophisticated and refined than touring the city's famous canals in the comfort of an elegant, antique wooden runabout. Customize your trip to take in Amsterdam's most romantic sights, eat dinner on board while the sun sets, or simply let the captain guide you to the highlight attractions while you relax with a bottle of champagne and a plate of canapés; it's Amsterdam at its stylish and waterborne best. *Available with one-hour notice.* €€€€+ 684-9338, privateboattours.nl

Platform 21 Amsterdam Design Center • Zuid • Art Gallery

Best Dutch Design Located in a renovated church, and focused on promoting innovation in the field of design, Platform 21 is part exhibition space, part showroom, and part lecture hall. Themes like "Design in Developing Countries" explore practical issues facing our world, while events like the Streetlab: Streetfashion Festival, or graphic art retrospectives, focus on aesthetics. Lectures from visiting luminaries such as Rem Koolhaas on heady subjects like "Design in the Creative Economy" add a slightly less populist feel to the proceedings. *Agenda varies according to exhibition calendar.* Prinses Irenestraat 19 (Beethovenstr.), 344-9449, platform21.com

Puccini Bomboni • Oude Zijde • Store

Amsterdam has so many designers, artists, and boutique shops that it should come as no surprise that the city is home to a world-class artisan chocolatier.

Purists opt for heavenly takes on the standards, like Gianduja, Caramel, and Milk-Almond, while those with adventurous palates gravitate towards truffles featuring unlikely flavors—unless you're up-to-the-minute on chocolate trends—like Tea, Tamarind, and Lemon Grass. *Staalstraat location (there is also a Singel location) Sun-Mon noon-6pm and Tue-Sat 9am-6pm.* Staalstraat 17 (Kloveniersburgwal), 626-5474, puccinibomboni.com

Soap Treatment Store • Nieuwe Zijde • Spa

The central location, professional staff, and boutique products from Murad make Soap the destination of choice for Amsterdam's manicured crowd. Factor in a high design décor—pale wooden floors and a white-on-white color scheme—and Soap becomes a must-do for jet-lagged visitors looking for a boost. Few places in town offer the same selection of services—facials, massages, detoxifying wraps, manicures, pedicures, waxing, and a small range of gentlemen-only treatments—and only Soap does it with such gracious style. If only they had a pool. *Tue-Sat 10am-10pm, Sun 10am-6pm.* €€€€ Spuistraat 281 (Palelsstraat), 428-9660, soapcompany.com

Van Ravenstein • Jordaan • Store

Shop in the footsteps of Amsterdam's most fashionable society at this woman's chic-boutique; it's the only one in Amsterdam that carries the collections of local fashion madmen Viktor & Rolf. Factor in the extensive collections from other designers like Balenciaga and Belgians Ann Demeulemeester and Dries van Noten, and this Nine Streets–situated gem is a must for fans of international couture. *Mon 1-6pm, Tue-Wed 11am-6pm, Thu 11am-7pm, Fri 11am-6pm, Sat 10:30am-5:30pm.* Keizersgracht 359 (Huidenstr.), 639-0067

Wonderwood • Oude Zijde • Store

The name suggests that this boutique and gallery specializes in wonderful designs—furniture, art, and decorative items—made from wood, but what it doesn't reveal is that the shop is like a modern design museum. Icons of contemporary design appear in the form of antique pieces from the likes of Alvar Aalto and Charles and Ray Eames, while reissued classics like pieces from Hein Stolle, many of which appear in the Stedelijk Museum CS's permanent collection, promise gorgeous surprises. *Wed-Sat noon-6pm or by appointment.* Rusland 3 (Oudezijdsachterburgwal), 625-3738, wonderwood.nl

Hip Amsterdam

Think back to the first rumors you heard about this city. They're all true! Hot bodies, a high-energy party scene, and a relaxed vibe give Amsterdam a hip reputation, and this itinerary places you in the heart of the spontaneous action. Welcome to the edgy art scene, all-night dance events, word-of-mouth-only restaurants, funky hotels, and über-chilled lounge spaces where high style meets easy-going, and where casual-cool is a way of life.

*Note: Venues in bold are described in detail in the listings that follow the itinerary. Venues followed by an * asterisk are those we recommend as both a restaurant and a destination bar.*

Hip Amsterdam:
The Perfect Plan (3 Nights and Days)

Perfect Plan Highlights

Thursday

Lunch	**Royal Café de Kroon***
Afternoon	**Albert Cuypmarkt**
	Heineken Experience
Cocktails	**Pilsvogel, Helden**
Dinner	**Mamouche, Bazar**
Nighttime	**Bar Ça*, Chocolate Bar**
Late-night	**Escape, Weber, Bitterzoet**
	Suzy Wong, Lux

Friday

Breakfast	**Latei**
Morning	**Canal cruise, De Appel**
Lunch	**Het Land, Hein**
Afternoon	**Huis Marseille, Droog**
	Erotic Museum
Cocktails	**Café Hoppe, Café 't Schuim***
Dinner	**Café Morlang, Herengracht***
Nighttime	**Odeon*, Lime, Melkweg**
Late-night	**Magazijn, Youll Lady's**

Saturday

Breakfast	**Nielsen**
Morning	**MacBike**
Lunch	**Kanis & Meiland, Snel**
Afternoon	**Stedelijk Museum CS,**
	Kalverstraat, shopping
Cocktails	**Arena:toDrink*, 11***
Dinner	**Arena:toDine*, 11***
Nighttime	**Arena:toNight*, 11***
Late-night	**Odessa*, Diep,**
	Sugar Factory

Day After

Morning	**Wolvenstraat***
Afternoon	**De Badcuyp***

Hotel: **The Lloyd Hotel and Cultural Embassy**

Thursday

1pm Lunch Grab a bite overlooking the lively Rembrandtplein at **Royal Café de Kroon***. The over-the-top interior, great fair-weather terrace, and attractive crowd make it an instant crowd-pleaser. Or opt for a seat at **Caffe Esprit**. The outdoor seats are among the city's best for people-watching.

3pm Dive into Amsterdam with a visit to its funkiest neighborhood, De Pijp, home to the **Albert Cuypmarkt**. The city's largest open-air market, it sells everything from clothing to antiques to delicious snacks like creamy chocolates and hot waffles.

4pm After browsing, head to the **Heineken Experience**. The former brewery houses exhibits and the Bottle Ride, which traces the company's history and illustrates the art of brewing. And yes, you get a couple—small—free beers along the way.

6pm Continue your sampling of Dutch brews at any one of the area's many popular bars—the best ones, like **Pilsvogel** and **Helden**, are generally packed with friendly locals, have large patios, and are buzzing after-work singles scenes.

HIP

8pm Dinner Stay in De Pijp for a taste of the exotic. At **Mamouche**, both the patrons and the sleek black décor look sexy by candlelight, creating a romantic backdrop for the mouthwatering Middle Eastern-inspired cuisine. And at the buzzing and casual **Bazar**, Turkish dishes are served in a handsome setting complete with North African advertisements and a soaring ceiling.

10pm As the destination of choice for hipster bar hoppers, De Pijp boasts more than its share of great watering holes. Get your sexy Latin vibe on at **Bar Ça***. "Cavas," a sparkling Spanish wine and the house specialty, is the perfect companion to Latin tunes and excellent tapas. Or head over to **Chocolate Bar**, where a sexy crowd mingles over drinks in a space that looks good enough to eat. For an equally eye-catching scene, cruise into **18 Twintig***, one of De Pijp's most happening bars and lounges.

Midnight For dancing until the wee hours, check out **Escape** on the busy Rembrandtplein, lounge at **Weber**, or try **Bitterzoet** to catch live music.

2am Glam it up a notch and head to **Suzy Wong**, where the plush black and red interior provides a sultry backdrop for delicious cocktails and gorgeous patrons. Or chill to mellow tunes at **Lux**; the very popular and laid-back

space attracts creative locals and visitors in equal numbers.

Friday

9am Breakfast You'll need lots of energy today, so start at **Latei** in the heart of Amsterdam's Chinatown. The cafe has baked treats and breakfasts that rival any in the city.

10am It wouldn't be a true Amsterdam experience without a canal cruise, so head to Holland International (see p.131) to earn your sea legs. Most tours will show you classic Amsterdam sights, but hipsters take note: You can also do a tour of contemporary Amsterdam, which takes in many of the city's exciting new structures from a unique, waterside perspective.

11:45am Contemporary arts 101. Drop in at **De Appel Centre for Contemporary Art** to view tomorrow's art trends, then pay a visit to **Lambiek Comics Shop** for the latest graphic novels.

1:15pm Lunch For great soups and sandwiches, and to dine alongside a trendy crowd of all ages, stop in at the always-busy **Het Land van Walem**. Drop by **Hein** to let the eponymous chef please you with the signature hearty fare.

3pm Continue your exploration of Amsterdam's art scene with a walk to the small but stimulating

Huis Marseille to check out their latest exhibition of international photography. For Dutch design, wander over to the gallery and showroom **Droog Design**. Works from top designers like Tejo Remy and Marcel Wanders share space with exhibitions from the globe's hottest up-and-comers.

5pm Drop into **Kadinsky**, the most stylish of the famous "coffeeshops," or give your city visit some context by checking out the **Erotic Museum** or the **Hash Marihuana & Hemp Museum**—both of which are higher on the information scale and lower on the titillation scale than you'd expect.

6pm Head to **Café Hoppe**, where your Amsterdam indoctrination continues with a cool-down drink. Open since 1670, this timeless brown bar caters to the younger, hipper set. Or take part in the after-work scene at **Café 't Schuim***. It's a great spot to grab a beer while brushing up on your Dutch since the staff is friendly and the crowd approachable.

8pm Dinner **Café Morlang** serves international cuisine, and the modern interior has Baroque influences, creating an attractive background. Or go to **Herengracht***, where exposed brick, original art, and a buzzing crowd dines on modern bistro fare, then retires to the lounge. For a dining event, get a reservation at **Saskia's Huiskamer**; the local crowd sits at a long communal table, but they're always happy to make room for a visitor.

10pm **Odeon*** is a popular dance scene that goes late. Try to score the private lounge—complete with your own dedicated bartender. Lounge into the wee hours sipping cocktails at **Lime** or check out the DJs at **Melkweg**—many of the world's most popular performers make appearances.

1am With a reputation for no-nonsense dancing and a welcoming vibe, **Club Magazijn** is worth a visit, as is **Youll Lady's Dancing**; the crowd is predominantly gay but as long as you love to dance, you'll fit right in.

Saturday

9am Breakfast Start your day with an Amsterdam ritual—a trip to **Nielsen**. Mellow tunes, excellent coffee, and king-sized breakfasts are the hallmarks of this sunny spot that's a hit with Jordaan's eclectic locals.

10am Walk to **MacBike Bike Rentals**, rent a two-wheeler, and head toward the city's futuristic Eastern Harbor. You'll pass by iconic architecture like Renzo Piano's Nemo, the Walvis, and the modernist housing on Borneo and Java—two of the harbor's small islands. Hop off to browse galleries and shops.

Noon Lunch Stay in the Eastern Harbor, where the mellow **Kanis & Meiland** serves soups, salads, and sandwiches on a waterside patio, while indoors the regulars shoot pool. Nearby at **Snel**, in the Lloyd Hotel, locals mingle with guests in an arty scene.

1pm Get back on your bike and head downtown, checking out the **Stedelijk Museum CS** in the Post CS building along the way. With temporary exhibitions, it's the interim home of Amsterdam's contemporary art museum.

2pm If you still have energy to burn, pedal your way along the scenic grand canals of the Jordaan and cruise your way through the lush Vondelpark. The urban oasis is Amsterdam's equivalent to New York's Central Park. Alternatively, work off your lunch at stylish and chic **Splash Healthclub**, where many visiting celebrities go to pump up and wind down. If it's retail therapy you're after, get a hipster dose on the Kalverstraat, which has excellent stores including the cheap-chic H&M, Puma, and local favorites Mexx and the upscale Sissy Boy.

6pm Unwind in one of the city's after-creative-work social spots, **Arena:toDrink***. Or head to the venerable **11***, where, weather permitting, drinks are served on the 12th-story rooftop terrace, offering harbor views.

8pm Dinner If you're already at **11***, stick around, enjoy the sunset, and order some modern bistro dishes that are just as appealing

as the growing crowd around you. **Arena:toDine*** serves contemporary international food as well as modernized Dutch classics to a hip, pre-clubbing crowd.

10pm Whether or not you ate at **11***, you'll want to see the room when it's packed with a fun dance crowd. **Arena:toNight*** offers two floors of dancing in an unusual venue—a renovated chapel.

1am If it's a more intimate affair that you're after, hit **Odessa***, a lounge spot located on a former Russian trawler. Likewise **Diep** boasts a loyal following of regulars, and is a sure bet for an evening of chilled-out lounging.

3am Visit **Sugar Factory** for a late-night sweet time. The vibe, part art house, part dance club, and fully stylish, lasts until morning, attracting the city's creative party-going set.

The Day After

Start your day at **Wolvenstraat***. The nighttime lounge vibe carries over into the morning, attracting clubbers, loungers, and all-around hard-partiers with its low-key design atmosphere, unhurried pace, and funky tunes.

On Sunday afternoon, it must be **De Badcuyp***, a rocking experience. Sunday night belongs to **De Trut**, where partying is a gay Amsterdam tradition.

Hip Amsterdam:
The Key Neighborhoods

The **Eastern Harbor** is a new and largely residential area that's characterized by artistry, youthfulness, and spontaneity, with modern architecture, galleries, ateliers, restaurants, lounges, clubs, and edgier cultural venues.

The **Jordaan** has scenic canals and historic waterside pubs alongside edgy galleries and casually stylish restaurants, dance clubs, and bars. Boutiques, vintage shops, and a laid-back atmosphere add to the hip quotient.

The **Museumplein** is the home of Amsterdam's main art museums. It also has excellent dining, shopping, open air concerts and festivals—and the leafy Vondelpark, Amsterdam's beloved urban park.

Nieuwe Zijde, the city's "New Side," is anchored by the Dam Square and contains countless trendy dining, lounging, drinking, dancing, and shopping options—the latter being concentrated on Kalverstraat, the area's commercial epicenter.

De Pijp has some of Amsterdam's most buzzing restaurants, happening bar scenes, and trendiest cafes. The heart of this cultural melting pot is the Albert Cuypmarket, and while relatively few tourists venture into the area, those who do are guaranteed to find large crowds of the casually stylish locals who live nearby.

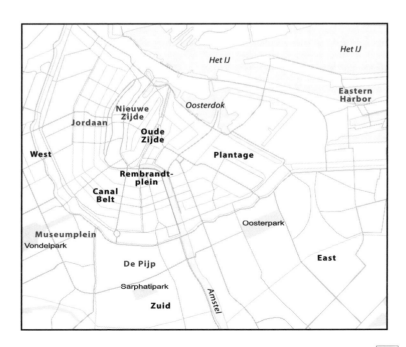

Hip Amsterdam:
The Shopping Blocks

Negen Straatjes (Nine Streets)

The Nine Streets have bohemian roots that run deep, despite their classic front.

Analik Homegrown designer with seasonal collections of unique fashions aimed at youthful and stylish women. Hartenstraat 36 (Keizersgracht), 422-0561

Claire V Colorful, funky, fair-trade-produced handbags and accessories. Prinsengracht 234 (Reestr.), 421-9000

Daniele Allesandrini Men's and women's fashions from the only non-Italian outpost of the urban-chic label. Hartenstraat 20 (Keizersgracht), 638-1744

Donna Fierra Women's fashions from hard-to-find European collections. Huidenstraat 18 (Keizersgracht), 428-9250

Laura Dolls Stylish vintage European clothing and textiles from the 1920s to the 1970s. Wolvenstraat 7 (Herengracht), 624-9066

Spuistraat

Spuistraat shopping means urban and trendy, with a nod to European styles.

Athenaeum Nieuwscentrum International magazines and independent publications. Spui 14-16 (Nieuwezijds Voorburgwal), 624-2972

Björn Borg Colorful and trendy streetwise sportswear from bags to underwear. Spuistraat 137 (Magna Plaza), 626-2153

Dom A funky decorating shop with an ever-changing selection of trendy products. Spuistraat 281 (Roskamsteeg), 428-5544

Innerspace Smartshop Natural and legal (in Holland anyway) marijuana seeds, magic mushrooms, and other highs. Spuistraat 108 (Mosterdpotsteeg), 624-3338

Utrechtsestraat

Utrechtsestraat is where Amsterdam's laid-back, urban scenesters come to mix.

Angel Basics A collection of designers (French Connection, Corinne Aarrut, Indian Rose, Betsey Johnson). Utrechtsestraat 132 (Utrechtsedwarsstr.), 624-1348

Concerto The record shop for music lovers with excellent indie, jazz, and world-beat collections. Utrechtsestraat 52-60 (Keizersgracht), 623-5228

Infini Men's and women's Euro-urban fashions from smaller labels (J-wear, Kudo, Peter Werth, Rehash, Ecchimosi). Utrechtsestraat 68 (Kerkstr.), 626-2664

Jan Quirky, unique items for your home and office. Utrechtsestraat 74 (Kerkstr.), 626-4301

Hip Amsterdam:
The Hotels

Hotel Arena • Plantage • Trendy (127 rms)
Even though it's a little removed from the city center, this cavernous 1890s orphanage-turned-youth hostel-turned-design hotel is a popular hipster destination packed with on-site facilities. The bustling restaurant and cafe complete with a garden terrace attracts locals as well as guests (see p.87), and there's a dance club (see p.93) located in a former church that rocks late into the night. Most of the rooms combine ornamental elements from the original building with wood floors and a Scandinavian-style design, but try to score one of the six rooms where pieces from Holland's top designers like Marcel Wanders and his colleagues at Moooi set the mood with furniture straight from the Milan Fair. Of course, all of the requisite amenities are on hand, including high-speed internet in every room, and whimsical touches like complimentary PlayStation 2s. € 's-Gravesandestraat 51 (Mauritskade), 850-2400, hotelarena.nl

Hotel V • De Pijp • Trendy (24 rms)
Hotel V's motto is "Design without attitude," and sure enough, this is a great-looking hotel with a youthful, welcoming, and chilled-out vibe. In the lobby, funky music, trendy magazines, and a stylish fireplace create a cozy and hip setting that continues into each of the 24 guest rooms, where stylish simplicity trumps extravagance. Bright and simple rooms with white walls and pale wooden furnishings evoke images of Scandinavian summers, and rooms with black and gunmetal gray accents provide a moodier, but equally hip backdrop that looks even better with the addition of fresh-cut flowers. Free wireless throughout the hotel makes this feel like a home away from home, and there's a free-to-use G5 on hand just steps from the courtyard garden where you can dine during fairer weather. The culture of the Museumplein is a 15-minute walk away, and closer by, in De Pijp, you'll find one of the city's hippest residential neighborhoods, with great dining and lounges that buzz with stylish 20- to 40-somethings. And here's a secret about checking in: Rooms facing the courtyard are not only much quieter, they also have small balconies overlooking the gardens; book one if you can. € Victorieplein 42 (Vrijheidslaan), 662-3233, hotelv.nl

The Lloyd Hotel and Cultural Embassy • Eastern Harbor • Trendy (116 rms)
This historic structure once housed a migrant hotel and later, a prison, but an interior redesign by Dutch powerhouse architects MVRDV has given the building new life as a light and airy meeting place for globetrotting hipsters looking for something truly new and different. Guest rooms—sometimes quirkily designed—range in luxury from one to five stars according to size, style, and amenities. Tiny one-star rooms are positively hostel-like and guests staying in those share a common bathroom, while five-star rooms are massive and feature flourishes that range from the practical to the bizarrely extravagant. The outstanding room 221 has both a grand piano and a bed designed to accommodate eight adults, while room 608 is a large and gorgeous industrial loft with exposed post-and-beam work and hammocks. Rooms in the two-, three-, and four-star categories offer a similar range of surprises—like shower heads in the middle of

the guest room—but are distinguished more by the amount of space they offer than amenities. The décor in all of the rooms is from a who's who of contemporary Dutch design, with textiles, accessories, and furnishings that come from some of this country's oldest firms. A packed agenda of edgy cultural activities ensures that ultra-hip local Amsterdammers frequent the hotel's public spaces; library; quality restaurant, Snel (see p.92), and bar; and performance and gallery spaces where the artistically inclined show off their talents in organized exhibitions and impromptu events. Also, the owners' connections run deep: If there is an off-site cultural event you want to attend, or a mover and shaker you'd like to be introduced to, just ask. €€ Oostelijke Handelskade 34 (Lloydplein), 561-3636, lloydhotel.com

NL Hotel • Museumplein • Trendy (10 rms)

Perfectly located between the nightlife of the city center and the culture of the Museumplein, the NL is an excellent home base for exploration of restaurants, museums, lounges, galleries, and dance clubs. The hotel's owners worked with an award-winning local designer, and the resulting combinations of materials and decorations make each room come alive with vibrant color and low-key style. Comfortable beds are largely covered in white, while patterned textiles decorate head boards and furnishings, and Eastern ornaments evoke a vaguely Zen-like atmosphere. Common areas feature modern lighting fixtures, fresh-cut flowers, and plenty of glass and black wood. However, the NL isn't about to put style before substance: Plenty of personal touches ensure that your stay will be a comfortable one. All rooms feature flat-screen cable televisions, hairdryers, and electronic safes, and high-speed wireless internet access is complimentary throughout the hotel. There's no front desk staff present in the evenings—instead guests let themselves in and out—which adds an "apartment" feel to the lodgings. However, in the morning, guests congregate in a sparkling breakfast area. Rooms 5, 6, 9, and 10 have classic canal views; room 6 stands out as a favorite as it's the only room with a small terrace. € Nassaukade 368 (Derde Helmersstr.), 689-0030, nl-hotel.com

Wolvenstraat 23 • Jordaan • Trendy (1 rm)

For instant, insider hip status and privacy that you can't get at a hotel, the suite at Wolventstraat is second to none: It's situated in the trendy Nine Streets area, and the décor is contemporary boudoir chic. The suite—actually a walk up apartment with its own entrance—is dominated by a great room, characterized by wooden floors, shaggy designer throw rugs, a large sitting area, and a black and red canopy bed replete with numerous plush pillows that sits in an alcove and is further set off from the main space by a beaded curtain. A collection of drinks, snacks, CDs, and DVDs will help you to feel at home, as will the large contemporary bathroom, full kitchen, and small terrace that overlooks the gardens of Amsterdam's storied canal houses. Countless bars, cultural attractions, and boutique shops are just steps from the front door, and there's a cool scene just downstairs: the suite is affiliated with Wolvenstraat* (see p.92), one of the city's hippest restaurant-lounges, where you'll find drinks, chilled music, and a great vibe any time of the day. Make your reservation early enough, and the well-connected restaurant staff can make sure you're on the guest lists at the city's top clubs and art events. Note: Currently, there is no phone for reservations. Book online at the very long web address below. € Wolvenstraat 23 (Keizersgracht), (no phone), apartments-for-rent.nl/amsterdam/apartments/?ar=centrum&loc=4

Hip Amsterdam:
The Restaurants

Arena:toDine* • Plantage • Continental
Employing clean and subdued design elements with natural materials, Dutch interior designer Ronald Hoofd has created an atmosphere that reflects the stylish yet unpretentious vibe of the 20- and 30-something crowd. Mosaic tile walls, stark white chairs, and black and white walls set the mood, while the mix of international fare and contemporized, traditional Dutch dishes, served in small or large portions, provides the perfect fuel for weekend evenings of dancing in the hotel's equally hip adjacent club, Arena:toNight* (see p.93). *Daily 6-10:30pm.* € ≡ Arena Hotel, 's-Gravesandestraat 51 (Mauritskade), 850-2460, hotelarena.nl

De Badcuyp* • De Pijp • Cafe
Check out Amsterdam's hottest jazz scene while having a bite from the limited but good cafe menu. *See Hip Nightlife, p.93, for details. Most programs start between 9 and 10pm; call for specifics; cafe Tue-Sun 6-10pm.* € ⃞≡ Eerste Sweelinckstraat 10 (Albert Cuypstr.), 675-9669

Balthazar's Keuken • Jordaan • Mediterranean
Always crowded to overflowing, the room has a pleasant high-energy buzz. The décor, best described as shabby-chic, incorporates classical elements that add a touch of distinction. From the open, black-and-white tiled kitchen, the duo in charge produce consistently delicious and creative three-course menus—your only options being fish, meat, or vegetarian. But the regular guests trust their hosts, knowing that their meal is in good hands. *Wed-Fri 6-11pm.* € (set menu) ≡ Elandsgracht 108 (Looiersdwarsstr.), 420-2114, balthazarskeuken.nl

Bar Ça* • De Pijp • Spanish
Best Restaurant-Lounges Check out sparkling Spanish "cavas" to start your night, then head to the formal dining room, or stick to tapas at the bar. *See Hip Nightlife, p.93, for details. Sun-Thu 3pm-1am, Fri-Sat 3pm-3am.* € ≡ Marie Heinekenplein 30-31 (Ferdinand Bolstr.), 470-4144, bar-ca.com

Bazar • De Pijp • North African
Best Tastes of the Exotic Decorated with Arabic signs and Turkish mosaics, this former church with vaulted ceilings attracts the 20- to 30-something-year-old hipster crowd. Since it's always packed, the volume can reach high levels, so forget about intimate conversation. Come around 8pm, opt for a table on the balcony, order some tasty North African tapas—like merguez lamb, saffron grilled salmon, couscous, and kebabs—and take in the buzzing scene below. *Sun-Thu 8am-11pm, Fri-Sat 8am-2am.* € ≡ Albert Cuypstraat 182 (1e v.d. Helststr.), 675-0544

Café de Jaren* • Oude Zijde • Cafe
This casual spot attracts students and media-types with its lively atmosphere, hearty fare, and great patio drinking scene. *See Hip Nightlife, p.94, for details. Daily 10am-10:30pm; café Sun-Thu until 1am, Fri-Sat until 2am.* € ≡ Nieuwe Doelenstraat 20-22 (Binnengasthuisstr.), 625-5771, cafe-de-jaren.nl

Café Morlang • Canal Belt • Continental

Hungry hipsters flock to this smart canal-side cafe designed by Concrete, the same architects responsible for the upscale SupperClub. Embossed walls hint at Baroque grandeur, marbled cafeteria-type tables toe the line between shabby and chic, and an attractive crowd completes the scene. Upstairs, comfortable couches add a relaxed touch, while downstairs things tend to be more vibrant. Great salads and a noteworthy tomato-basil soup are consistently popular. Drop in for dinner when the lights are dim and the décor really shines. *Daily 11am-1am.* € ▤ Keizersgracht 451 (Leidsestr.), 625-2681, morlang.nl

Café 't Schuim* • Nieuwe Zijde • Cafe

The scene here is hottest for after-work cocktails, but don't hesitate to order a bite to eat. *See Hip Nightlife, p.94, for details. Sun-Wed 11am-1am, Thu-Sat 11am-3am.* € Ⓑ▤ Spuistraat 189 (Wijdestr.), 638-9357

Caffe Esprit • Nieuwe Zijde • Cafe

Instant salvation for those who start each day in need of a latte fix and a great place to grab lunch while shopping. This minimal-moderne cafe never fails to attract a smart-looking crowd. Delicious pastas and salads are on hand for the hungry while homemade brownies, cheesecakes, carrot cakes, and scones—all highly recommended—provide the ideal mid-shopping pick-me-up. Best of all, the cafe's sizable terrace, set back from the traffic on the Spui Square, offers a perfect vantage point for people-watching. *Mon-Wed and Fri-Sat 10am-6pm, Thu 10am-10pm, Sun noon-6pm.* €– ▤ Spui 10 (Voetboogstr.), 622-1967

Coffee & Jazz • Canal Belt • Indonesian

You could stop here for coffee—the omnipresent jazz tunes make this a nice java joint—or you could come for lunch and earn your insider stripes. This small cafe should be very well-known for its tiny but tasty Indonesian menu, but it somehow remains the obscure domain of locals and their privileged confidants. Order satay (kebab with peanut sauce). *Tue-Thu 9am-8pm, Sat 10am-4pm.* € ▤ Utrechtsestraat 113 (Herengracht), 624-5851

18 Twintig* • De Pijp • Continental

Bright, spacious, colorful, airy with a decent bar, flatscreen monitors, groovy tunes, recessed fireplaces … what's not to like? Well, the good looks are only veneer-deep—design on a budget trumps pricey big name pieces—and the friendly, good-looking staff can be slow on a good day. But you're not here to rush in and out, so grab a seat and savor the food, delicious drinks, and attractive crowd that builds the buzzing scene. Come late to enjoy the dinner rush, then linger into the late evening when guests come to sip drinks, nosh from a dedicated snack menu, and listen to DJ'd tunes. *See Hip Nightlife, p.95. Daily noon-11pm.* € ▤ Ferdinand Bolstraat 18-20 (Marie Heinekenplein), 470-0651, 18twintig.nl

11* • Eastern Harbor • Continental

Best Tables with a View For an Amsterdam high that can't be bought at the city's legendary coffeeshops, head to the 11th floor of the Post CS building—just east of Centraal Station—where you'll find this hipster hideaway. This open industrial space features a large bar, a drinks-only terrace, video screens that air art project films, a dance floor, and best of all, huge banks of windows that offer some of Amsterdam's finest harbor-front views. Casually stylish regulars come to enjoy the scenery and modern bistro fare, knowing better than to pop in for a quick lunch or dinner; it's busy at both times and the waiters are here to enjoy the mellow vibe too. *See Hip Nightlife, p.95. Daily 11am-4pm and 6-10pm, dancing Thu-Sat until 4am.* € ≡ Oosterdokskade 3-5 (De Ruyterkade), 625-5999

Hein • Jordaan • Continental
Informal, familiar, homey, and buzzing are the, uhm, buzzwords at this tiny, hip spot with memorable breakfasts and lunches served in a forgettable décor. The menu contains enough pleasant surprises—chicken crepes, stuffed Turkish bread, and peanut chicken soup—to satisfy almost everyone, but if you don't see your heart's desire, just ask. If they have the ingredients on hand, chances are they'll whip it up. Only a lucky few score an outdoor table, but indoors or out, everyone feels like part of the very local family. *Daily 8:30am-3pm.* € ─ Berenstraat 20 (Keizersgracht), 623-1048

Helden • De Pijp • Continental
The white-apron-wearing staff, exposed brick, chilled music, and smart international menu will have you thinking you've landed in a funky New York bistro, but the coterie of tall blondes speaking Dutch will remind you that you're still in Amsterdam. Busy for after-work drinks, dinner, and lounging and nibbling into the wee hours of morning, this popular eatery is at its best from mid-afternoon onwards, when the casually stylish regulars show up and take their seats on the street-front terrace. *Sun-Thu 11am-1am, Fri-Sat 11am-3am.* € ≡ 1e v.d. Helststraat 42 (Quellijnstr.), 673-3332

Herengracht* • Canal Belt • Continental
The servers aren't the best, but the funky décor and tasty menu ensure that young professionals show up for post-work drinks and dinner. Exposed brick walls, an over-the-top chandelier, art by local artist Donkersloot, and velvet wall-coverings complement contemporary furniture, creating a sophisticated bistro. Always crowded, and sometimes smoky; come on a Thursday or Friday for dinner when it's most lively. *See Hip Nightlife, p.96. Daily 10am-10:30pm.* €€ ≡ Herengracht 435 (Leidsestr.), 616-2482, deherengracht.nl

Het Land van Walem • Canal Belt • Continental
Best Lunch Spots From the historically hot (style icon Gerrit Rietveld designed the façade) to the current cool (the latest design magazines lying around), Walem is home base for casually trendy Amsterdammers of all ages. The small menu, made up of mostly soups, salads, and sandwiches, and the bustling scene provide the perfect midday fix, and the two terraces—one canal side and one garden—allow for fine people-watching when the weather turns fair. *Daily 10am-10:30pm; Fri-Sat cafe until 1am.* € ≡ Keizersgracht 449 (Leidsestr.), 625-3544, cafewalem.nl

Kanis & Meiland • Eastern Harbor • Cafe
Kanis is serious about creating a low-key atmosphere for its patrons, and after settling into these inviting, relaxed surroundings, you're bound to add a chilled-out vibe of your own. Enjoy your meal—complete with views of the river IJ as well as some of Amsterdam's hottest modern architecture—and do like the locals do; hang out and read magazines, play board games, listen to music, shoot a game of pool, or get to know some of the friendly and approachable regulars. *Daily 10am-1am.* € ≡ Levantkade 127 (Piraeusplein), 418-2439

Latei • Oude Zijde • Cafe

Hipsters of all ages drop into this so-garish-it's-fun spot where you'll find baked goods and meals made from Grandma's secret recipes. Have some coffee with apple pie or fill yourself with tasty couscous—several variations are on the tiny dinner menu—while admiring the garage sale-meets-flea market interior. Should you spy a must-have gem hidden amid the tacky clutter, pony up! It's all for sale. Tables, chairs, lamps, paintings, mirrors, and probably even the plate you're eating off of can be yours for a price. Come for breakfast and watch the seedy neighborhood slowly wake up. *Mon-Wed 8am-6pm, Thu-Fri 8am-10pm, Sat 9am-10pm, Sun 11am-6pm.* €– ▤ Zeedijk 143 (Nieuwmarkt), 625-7485

Local • Jordaan • Continental

You're bound to meet Amsterdammers at this aptly named restaurant since it has only two tables, each communal and 25 ft. long. Better-dressed 20-somethings and young-ish professionals appreciate the modern décor, highly recommended mixed drinks, and comforting fare. All main courses are invariably delicious grilled skewers of meats and fish, so vegetarians beware; outside of a dinner salad and grilled vegetables, there's not much here for you. The music can be loudish, and sitting shoulder to shoulder with strangers (even attractive stylish ones) isn't for everyone, though it's a great way for solo travelers to rub shoulders with the locals. *Daily 6pm-midnight.* € ▯▤ Westerstraat 136 (Prinsengracht), 423-4039, local-amsterdam.nl

Mamouche • De Pijp • Moroccan

When the cool winter rains leave the locals dreaming of warmer climes, De Pijp's stylish slice of North Africa is a welcome ray of sunshine. Dark and minimal design elements play off Eastern flourishes like brass lamps, fresh roses, candles, and Moroccan lounge music, creating an atmosphere that is warm and cozy. The kitchen dishes out French-influenced Moroccan and Tunisian plates that are carefully prepared. No matter what the season, dinners at Mamouche are stylish, crowded affairs popular with 30-something locals. Weather permitting, ask for a seat on the minuscule terrace. *Daily 6:30-10pm.* €€ ▤ Quellijnstraat 104 (1e v.d. Helststr.), 673-6361, restaurantmamouche.nl

Nielsen • Jordaan • Coffeehouse

Friendly servers, big breakfasts and lunches, and a great location—in the boutique-lined Nine Streets—make this small, three-story cafe a hit. Factor in the difficulty of tracking down a solid North American-style breakfast outside of hotels and this place can't be beat. The eggs, toast, fruit, juice, and coffee is the perfect jumpstart to any morning, while sandwiches and salads ranging in size from simply large to enormous fit the bill for lunch. *Tue-Sat 8:30am-3:30pm, Sun 9am-3:30pm.* €– ▤ Berenstraat 19 (Keizersgracht), 330-6006

NOA • Jordaan • Asian

Noodles of Amsterdam. Or is it Noodles of Asia? Either way, head over to this hip lounge and restaurant just steps away from the Leidseplein's tourist throngs. Glass tables, white floors, low-slung chairs, and earth-tone fabrics—on the walls and furniture—provide the ideal backdrop for a chilled-out dining experience. Whether you're in for skillfully mixed drinks and lounging or dining on the eponymous noodles, stake your claim to a spot near the fireplace and let the warm vibes wash over you. *Tue 6pm-midnight, Wed 6pm-1am; Thu-Sat 1pm-1am, Sun 1pm-midnight.* € ▤ Leidsegracht 84 (Prinsengracht), 626-0802, tao-group.nl

Nomads • Jordaan • North African
Best Romantic Dining Get decadent and sheikh it, playboy! There are no tables here—attractive patrons dine reclined on large beds, low-slung divans, and pillows. Add to that the DJ'd music, gyrating belly dancers, and award-winning modern-classic décor, and you have all the makings for an excellent night of lounging. The food, served tapas style, is a flavorful interpretation of traditional North African and Middle Eastern dishes, but that's just a side attraction at this sensory feast. If you really fancy yourself the Queen of Sheba, ask the staff for an after-dinner water pipe. Filled with flavored tobacco, it completes the otherworldly experience. *Tue-Thu 7pm-1am, Fri-Sat 7pm-3am, Sun 7pm-1am.* €€ (set menu) ⎕ Rozengracht 133 (Hazenstr.), 344-6401, restaurantnomads.nl

Odeon* • Canal Belt • Continental
In addition to being a restaurant, Odeon is a dance club, and lucky diners are allowed to bypass the late-night line up. Even if you don't want to stick around late, Edwin Takens' Burgundy-influenced, seasonal 4-course menus are worth a reservation. *See Hip Nightlife, p.97, for details. Tue-Sun 6:30-10:30pm.* €€ ⎕ Singel 460 (Koningsplein), 521-8555, odeontheater.nl

Palladium • Canal Belt • Cafe
The lunch menu has excellent salads and sandwiches, but the stars come out at night, even though the dinner menu suffers slightly from a lack of originality. Gispen chairs and a chocolate and white décor compete for attention with the clubby clientele and the staff who are legendary for their funkier-than-thou aloofness. Style might have the edge on substance, but you can't deny it: The crowd looks sexy, and Palladium stands out as a place to see-and-be-seen. *Sun-Thu 10am-1am, Fri-Sat 10am-2am.* € Ⓑ≣ Kleine Gartmansplantsoen 7 (Leidsestr.), 620-5536

Resto-Bar Knus* • Rembrandtplein • Fusion
Located in a three-story, 16th-century house with artwork from emerging artists adorning the walls, this popular restaurant and lounge is a destination any night of the week. A sense of adventure and whimsy defines the constantly evolving fusion menu, and the regulars show up for playful treats like "Bloody Mary soup" and pear popsicles with a shot of vodka for dipping. Attentive but informal and friendly servers and a location that's perfectly suited to a night on the town make this spot very popular with the locals. *Daily, 6pm-1am.* € Ⓑ≣ Reguliersdwarsstraat 23 (Sint Jorisstr.), 427-7828, restobarknus.nl

Royal Café de Kroon* • Rembrandtplein • Cafe
De Kroon means "the crown," and that's a fitting name for this gem, which serves upscale cafe fare. It dates back to 1898, but the lounge atmosphere and crowd are strictly modern-day hip, and the food is only part of the attraction. Contemporized Louis XVI furniture, insects mounted in shadow boxes, and embossed walls set the tone for dining, drinking, and lounging. DJs spin Latin, club, and soul on weekends. Afternoon or night, take your seat on the covered terrace for a view of the Rembrandtplein. *See Hip Nightlife, p.97. Sun-Thu noon-1am, Fri-Sat noon-3am.* € ≣ Rembrandtplein 17 (Halvemaansteeg), 625-2011

Saskia's Huiskamer • De Pijp • Dutch
Best Dutch Dining A gorgeous secretary, a young neurologist clad in Diesel jeans, and a trendy retail clerk walk into a restaurant. What sounds like the beginning of a bar

joke is actually the type of crowd you'll meet at Saskia's. And meet them you will; with only 20 guests per evening, and all of them seated at the same communal table, you're guaranteed to rub shoulders with some of Amsterdam's most in-the-know hipsters. The setting is part of the draw, but it's the delicious 4-course dinners that makes this Amsterdam's most elusive reservation. Cross your fingers and call now. *Fri and Sat 7:30pm, by reservation only.* €€ (set menu) ▯▤ Albert Cuypstraat 203 (1e v.d. Helststr), 862-9839

Snel • Eastern Harbor • Dutch
It attracts a lot of visitors—it's housed in a migrant hotel-turned-prison-turned-hip hotel—but Snel pulls its share of stylish locals too. Simple yet appealing standards like club sandwiches and potato and leek soup please the palate, while the Dutch-design furnishings and soft white interior, designed by power-house architects MVRDV, subtly compete for attention. *Daily 7am-1am.* € ▤ Lloyd Hotel, Oostelijke Handelskade 34 (Lloydplein), 561-3636, lloydhotel.com

Wolvenstraat* • Jordaan • Fusion
Best Brunches It might take some basic map work to find this great cafe—it has no sign—but it's worth the hunt. The food is top-notch with Asian influences, and the owners have an eye for style that they share with the unpretentious, gorgeous patrons. Best of all: Everyone else in the cafe will be a native Amsterdammer. Ask them for some tips on the weekend's most promising events. Great at any hour, it's best on weekend mornings for chilled-out coffee and breakfast. *See Hip Nightlife, p.99. Mon-Fri 8:30am-1am, Sat 10am-2am, and Sun noon-1am.* € ▤ Wolvenstraat 23 (Keizersgracht), 320-0843

Zaza's • De Pijp • Fusion
This restaurant's long and narrow room is almost always full to capacity, and the tables are arranged so that things are often quite cozy. The décor features natural wood, cream walls, and purple and white upholstery, and the regulars—sexy 30-something locals—come for the casual but stylish atmosphere. The chef does his part by whipping up creations that are attractive and ambitious interpretations of standards like pan-fried cod, smoked duck breast, and roasted lamb. *Mon-Wed 6-10:30pm, Thu-Sat 6-11pm.* € ▤ Daniël Stalpertstraat 103 (1e v.d Helststr.), 673-6333

Hip Amsterdam:
The Nightlife

HIP

Arena:toDrink* • Plantage • Hotel Lounge
Locals come for after-work drinks, nightcaps, and warm-up drinks, enjoyed before heading to Arena:toNight, the hotel's nightclub (see below), and you should too. Grab your stool at the great-looking bar—it's made of red tiles seemingly inspired by public swimming pools—or head outside to either of the two large terraces and rub shoulders with Amsterdam's funky dance set. Exposed industrial beams, colorful lighting, and a dash of design features set a creative mood that's reflective of those who grace the space, and should you show up hungry you can order off a part-dinner-part tapas light menu that more than fits the bill. *Mon-Thu 7am-1am, Fri-Sat 7am-2am.* 's-Gravesandestraat 51 (Mauritskade), 850-2450, hotelarena.nl

Arena:toNight* • Plantage • Nightclub
Reach a higher level of hip and worship some sexy 20- and 30-somethings at this club located in a former church. The light show and architecture—a downstairs space and upper-level balcony—make a dramatic setting, but the real draw is the dance floor. Things here stay hot until late. Groups can add an exclusive touch to a night at Arena by reserving the "hidden" lounge space, complete with private bartender. *See Hip Restaurants, p.87. Fri-Sat 11pm-4am.* Arena Hotel, 's-Gravesandestraat 51 (Mauritskade), 850-2541, hotelarena.nl

De Badcuyp* • De Pijp • Jazz Club
Best Live Music The city's funkiest neighborhood is the perfect spot for this live music center located in a renovated public bath. A line-up of jazz, worldbeat, Latin, funk, and soul nights complements sets of DJ'd tunes. The very casual on-site cafe serving limited but hearty pre-concert dinners on a small patio draws a hipster clientele. *See Hip Restaurants, p.87. Most programs start between 9 and 10pm; call for specifics; cafe Tue-Sun 6-10pm.* Eerste Sweelinckstraat 10 (Albert Cuypstr.), 675-9669

Bar Ça* • De Pijp • Theme Bar
Best Restaurant-Lounges It's as sexy, arty, and Spanish as you'd imagine Dali's living room to be. Bar Ça has "cavas," a Spanish sparkling wine, and some very snackable tapas that provide the perfect kick-start to an evening. The rich, plush interior featuring red and black accents is divided into a formal dining area where warm dishes are served, and a casual drinking and noshing space—cold tapas only—complete with low couches and high stools. A small terrace rounds out the space. *See Hip Restaurants, p.87. Sun-Thu 3pm-1am; Fri-Sat 3pm-3am.* Marie Heinekenplein 30-31 (Ferdinand Bolstr.), 470-4144, bar-ca.com

Bitterzoet • Nieuwe Zijde • Nightclub
Best Live Music The name means "bittersweet," but it won't leave a bad taste in your mouth. Nights at this laid-back dance and music venue are mellow affairs and a friendly vibe rules the room. It isn't the city's most aesthetically noteworthy space, but good-looking locals in their 20s and 30s, as well as a program of documentary and art films, guarantee that something will catch your eye. *Sun-Thu 8pm-3am, Fri-Sat 8pm-4am.* Spuistraat 2 (Kattengat), 521-3001

Brix* • Jordaan • Jazz Club/Lounge

The location in the heart of the charming Negen Straatjes draws a youthful crowd to this bar and restaurant with an "all-appetizer" menu. Three times a week, jazz gets top billing. Funky jazz DJs make the Friday night scene, vocal jazz featuring local René van Beeck happens on Monday nights, and a rotating cast of musicians shows up on Sundays. If you think you'll pay a return visit, buy your drink by the bottle; the bartenders will store it until you come back. *Sun-Thu 5pm-1am, Fri-Sat 5pm-3am.* ≣ Wolvenstraat 16 (Keizersgracht), 639-0351, cafebrix.nl

Café Finch • West • Lounge

A great spot to start—or end—an evening, this bar has a retro '70s interior and a disdain for publicity that attracts a very in-the-know crowd. Head elsewhere for dinner, but stick around to nosh on finger foods, drink, and hang with the friendly regulars. Chilled-out background music and a small terrace that's packed in fair weather make this a worthy pit stop, particularly on Saturdays and Mondays, when the adjacent market attracts a crowd of its own. *Sun-Thu 9am-1am, Fri-Sat 9am-3am.* ≣ Noordermarkt 5 (Prinsengracht), 626-2461

Café Hoppe • Nieuwe Zijde • Bar

Best Dutch Drinking It's said that not much has changed since they first opened the doors in 1670, and it's easy to believe. Everything you'd expect from your local brown cafe—a sandy floor, lots of beer, and a dark interior weathered from use—is on hand here, as is one surprising element: a young and hip crowd. The scene builds after work and lasts until closing time, and the small tables crammed into the room don't come close to meeting the needs of the crowd; in good weather patrons spill into the street. *Sun-Thu 8am-1am, Fri-Sat 8am-2am.* ≣ Spui 18-20 (Kalverstr.), 420-4420

Café de Jaren* • Oude Zijde • Bar

Best Terraces Stop in for lunch or drinks and watch the boats float by while enjoying one of Amsterdam's hippest and most scenic terraces. In good weather, the terrace here is a favorite spot for scenesters to hang out and watch the afternoon fade away, but the vibe is friendly and without pretension. *See Hip Restaurants, p.87. Daily 10am-10:30pm; cafe Sun-Thu until 1am, Fri-Sat until 2am.* ≣ Nieuwe Doelenstraat 20-22 (Binnengasthuisstr.), 625-5771, cafe-de-jaren.nl

Café 't Schuim* • Nieuwe Zijde • Bar

Best After-Work Drinks An Amsterdam institution, this high-energy informal scene—keep your expectations low and you won't be disappointed—is a come-as-you-are and leave-slightly-hammered hip watering hole. A friendly staff, an array of beers, and rotating art on the walls make for a consistently chaotic and highly recommendable good time. Sooner or later all locals make their way to Het Schuim, so do it the way they do: Drop in for a pint, stay for three more, and make some friends along the way. *See Hip Restaurants, p.88. Sun-Wed 11am-1am, Thu-Sat 11am-3am.* ≣ Spuistraat 189 (Wijdestr.), 638-9357

Chocolate Bar • De Pijp • Lounge

The chocolate bar doesn't serve chocolate, but the white and brown '70s décor is sweet, and the locals who frequent it make for some fine eye candy, too. You're better off following their example: Eat elsewhere—the area is packed with outstanding restaurants—and come here for drinks and funky tunes, especially when the sun is out and the chilled-out terrace becomes the place to be in the neighborhood. Come for after-work drinks, or show up around 11pm to witness this bar at its happening best. *Sun-Thu 10am-1am, Fri-Sat 10am-3am.* ≡ 1e v.d. Helststraat 62a (Albert Cuypstr.), 675-7672

Club Magazijn • Oude Zijde • Nightclub

Best Dance Clubs Check your attitude at the door when you arrive at this industrial-retro space where reflective wallpaper and large orb-lamps set the mood. It's one of Amsterdam's least pretentious clubs, and soulful progressive music, weathered couches, and the complete absence of an elitist door policy make this a mellow-vibed, late-night dance destination of choice. Those looking for glamour are best to head elsewhere, but if you're looking for some atmosphere without the edge, you can't beat this deeply chilled, popular with the locals, spot. *Wed 9pm-3am, Thu 10pm-3am, Fri-Sat 10pm-4am, Sun 9pm-3am.* C≡ Warmoesstraat 170 (Sint Jansstr.), 669-4469

Diep • Nieuwe Zijde • Lounge

The kitschy interior featuring garish lighting and glass chandeliers suggests a nonchalant approach to décor, but details like an illuminated ticker-tape indicating the DJs' beats of choice attract a local and alternative-hip crowd. Deep on the cool-without-trying scale, Diep's legion of friendly regulars comes for the array of whiskeys as well as a decent beer selection, making it worth a stop mid-evening or later at night when it's at its crowded-cosy best. *Sun-Thu 5pm-1am, Fri-Sat 5pm-3am.* ≡ Nieuwezijds Voorburgwal 256 (Wijdesteeg), 420-2020

18 Twintig* • De Pijp • Bar

A popular dining spot that also draws a crowd for after-work drinks. *See Hip Restaurants, p.88, for details. Daily noon-11pm.* ≡ Ferdinand Bolstraat 18-20 (Marie Heinekenplein), 470-0651, 18twintig.nl

11* • Eastern Harbor • Nightclub

This dance club is elevated, both literally and culturally. It's located on the 11th floor of an industrial building. If you like a hip and groovy dancing crowd, show up after midnight to find your tribe. *See Hip Restaurants, p.88, for details. Daily 11am-4pm and 6-10pm. Dancing Thu-Sat until 4am.* C≡ Oosterdokskade 3-5 (De Ruyterkade), 625-5999

Escape • Rembrandtplein • Nightclub

You never know what sort of scene you'll find at this club that hosts a rotating repertoire of dance parties. Hip-hop, Latin, R&B, house, and dance classics are all in heavy rotation, but each night's musical offerings differ, attracting crowds—always 20- and younger 30-somethings—that dress to reflect the urban-hip tunes. Check the online agenda or get the word on the street for up-to-the-minute party listings, or simply show up ready to dance and go with the bass-heavy flow. *Thu 11pm-4am, Fri-Sat 11pm-7am, Sun 11pm-4am.* C≡ Rembrandtplein 11 (Halvemaansteeg), 622-1111, escape.nl

GeSpot • Jordaan • Bar
Views of the Jordaan's romantic canals, a modern interior that incorporates classic elements of a wooden Amsterdam "brown bar," and an extensive list of delicious cocktails have made this a popular destination for Amsterdam's casual-lounge set. That being said, a fast-growing reputation for poor service and food in the restaurant proper means you should eat before you arrive, and show up late to get the most out of this attractive waterside scene. *Sun-Thu 11am-1am, Fri-Sat 11am-3am.* ≡ Prinsengracht 422 (Raamstr.), 320-3733, restaurant-gespot.nl

Herengracht* • Canal Belt • Bar
A popular dining spot that also draws a crowd for after-work drinks. *See Hip Restaurants, p.89, for details. Daily 10am-10:30pm.* ≡ Herengracht 435 (Leidsestr.), 616-2482, deherengracht.nl

De Huyschkaemer • Canal Belt • Bar/Lounge
With its contemporary interior and cozy, welcoming vibe, this "living room" attracts a loyal following of gay and straight hipsters of all ages. Stay in the thick of the action on the main floor, or retreat to the upstairs balcony to survey the attractive and informal goings-on from above. In fine weather, regulars lounge on the fabulous street-front patio. *Sun-Thu 4pm-1am, Fri-Sat 4pm-3am.* ≡ Utrechtsestraat 137 (Utrechtsedwarsstr.), 627-0575

Kamer 401 • Jordaan • Bar
Wedged in between two equally worthy watering holes—Weber and Lux—and situated perfectly on the edge of both the Jordaan and the Leidseplein, Kamer 401 forms part of a hip trifecta of bars that are close enough to the action but removed enough to attract laid back, local, regulars. Notable cocktails, deejayed tunes, and a young and trendy crowd help set the mood, and although comfort and coziness trump up-to-the-minute style, the red walls and earth toned sofas and stools add to the visuals. *Wed-Thu 6pm-1am, Fri-Sat 6pm-3am.* ≡ Marnixstraat 401 (Leidsegracht), 620-0614

Lime • Oude Zijde • Lounge
From the color of the walls to the vodka Gimlets, Lime will leave you green with envy and wanting more. This pre-clubbing hangout is cosy—low chairs, soft couches, dim lights, and mellow beats set the mood—and for all its '60s den style, the scene remains friendly and unpretentious. You can always drop in for a nightcap or do like the locals and indulge in some yummy cocktails. Before heading out to dance, stop in at the Chinese Temple next door, light some incense, and pray that the rest of the night is just as good. *Mon-Thu 5pm-1am, Fri-Sat 5pm-3am, Sun 5pm-1am.* ≡ Zeedijk 104 (Molenstr.), 639-3020

Lux • Jordaan • Lounge
"Mix and match" comes to mind when describing Lux, but "mix and mix some more" might be more accurate. A kitschy anti-design ethos rules this space where faux-leopard curtains, black tables, golden walls, and red chairs play off of junky curios. So what's the draw? Mellow grooves, a friendly staff, a decent stock of alcohol, and a crowd of approachable, casually styled in-the-know locals. *Mon-Sat 8pm-3am.* ≡ Marnixstraat 403 (Rozengracht), 422-1412

Melkweg • Canal Belt • Nightclub/Performance

A venerable institution on the city's nightlife scene, and the historical ground zero for the legendary Cannabis Cup, Melkweg—the Milky Way—is a multidisciplinary art space where the only rule is "anything goes." Concerts featuring groups like the Beastie Boys and Supergrass, modern dance shows, parties with big-name DJs, and even art cinema happen here. Tickets are necessary for most events and the program changes nightly; check the online calendar for highlights before you arrive. *Times and prices vary according to events.* C≣ Lijnbaansgracht 234 (Lauriergracht), 531-8181, melkweg.nl

Odeon* • Canal Belt • Nightclub

With a name like Odeon, you expect a show and this place delivers. No longer the student venue it once was, it attracts 20- and 30- somethings with its renovated dance floor, earth tone décor, and vaulted ceilings that make for a classic-meets-right-now scene. Dancing to soulful and funky tunes, guests share the spotlight with capable DJs and there's always enough room for everyone's egos, although by 1am things can get intimate. *See Hip Restaurants, p.91. Thu 11pm-4am, Fri-Sat 11pm-5am.* ≣ Singel 460 (Koningsplein), 521-8555, odeontheater.nl

Odessa* • Eastern Harbor • Lounge

Drab port city? Nyet! Cargo ship turned bourgeois-hipster hot spot? Da! Drinking, dining, and dancing rule the evenings at this shipboard modern restaurant-lounge (skip dinner and come for fun). By 10pm, the small but vibe-y dance floor complete with house tunes is packed. *Sun-Thu 11:30am-1am, Fri-Sat 11:30am-3am.* ≣ Veemkade 295 (Lloydplein), 419-3010

Pilsvogel • De Pijp • Bar

This traditional cafe in the middle of Amsterdam's hippest residential neighborhood attracts a buzzing young crowd. The beer-in-hand patrons at the Pilsvogel spill out over the terrace and into the adjacent streets. You'll hear the place before you see it, so you can bet that this is not the spot for intimate conversations despite the number of romances that have doubtlessly been kindled over beers here. *Sun-Thu 11am-1am, Fri-Sat 11am-3am.* ≣ Gerard Douplein 14 (1e v.d. Helststr.), 664-6483

Proust* • Jordaan • Restaurant/Lounge

What Proust lacks in elbow room—late night it's standing room only—it makes up for with ample and trendy charm, and wall-to-wall good-looking locals. A small fair-weather terrace with views of the historic 17th-century Noorderkerk reminds you that you're abroad, while cheerful and funky servers will make you feel right at home. You can eat here, but the low-attitude, high-energy vibe and under-35 crowd make it ideally suited to scenesters in the mood for cocktails and flirting. *Mon noon-1am, Tue-Thu 5pm-1am, Fri noon-3am, Sat 10am-3am, Sun 10am-1am.* B≣ Noordermarkt 4 (Prinsengracht), 623-9145

Royal Café de Kroon* • Rembrandtplein • Lounge

An 1898 institution that has managed to grab a modern crowd with a laid-back lounge atmosphere and upscale cafe food. *See Hip Restaurants, p.91, for details. Sun-Thu noon-1am, Fri-Sat noon-3am.* ≣ Rembrandtplein 17 (Halvemaansteeg), 625-2011

Soho • Rembrandtplein • Bar

Best Gay Scenes It's tiny and has an English pub theme on the inside, but don't let that fool you. This is one of the hottest gay bars in Amsterdam, drawing an upscale, sophisticated crowd, especially on weekends. Come early, have a few drinks, and snag a comfortable seat before it gets really, really packed. *Sun-Thu 8pm-3am, Fri-Sat 8pm-4am.* ☰ Reguliersdwarsstraat 36 (Openhartsteeg), 422-3312

Sugar Factory • Canal Belt • Live Music

Best Live Music One of the city's newest interdisciplinary art spaces, Sugar Factory is arguably the most exciting venue to open in a long time. Each night's agenda has an early slot—poetry readings, musical performances, live theater, and even fashion shows—while the late-night slot is dedicated to dancing. Big-name DJs drop in to spin Thu-Sat. The funky-clubby jazz jams often feature accompanying DJs, last until 5am, and are a weekly must. If you're in town, check the online agenda or just drop in and be surprised. *Thu-Sun; times vary so check ahead.* ⓒ☰ Lijnbaansgracht 238 (Lauriergracht), 627-0008, sugarfactory.nl

Suite Rest-O-Bar • Nieuwe Zijde • Lounge

The buzzword at this split-level space, tucked in a small sidestreet, is *gezellig*, meaning cozy, and the friendly vibe, mellow beats, and idle housecat seal the deal. More shabby than shabby-chic—think Grandma's musty basement—the purple, red, and orange themed Suite is a perfect chill-out drinking spot anytime post-dinner, when a crowd of casual, regulars makes the scene. Sweet indeed. *Sun-Wed 7pm-midnight, Thu 7pm-1am, Fri-Sat 7pm-2am.* ☰ Sint Nicolaasstraat 43 (Nieuwezijds Voorburgwal), 489-6531

Suzy Wong • Canal Belt • Lounge

Plush red fabrics on walls and furniture play off black wooden accents, giving this narrow lounge space with two rooms the feel of an Asian boudoir. You'd expect that from Jimmy Woo's little sister; she has an eye for style too, and like her more famous sibling, manages to turn some heads—check out the rainforest-themed room, literally overrun with foliage. Order a delicious cocktail, enjoy the mellow music, and use the ceiling mirrors to scope out your fellow loungers; you can't dance here but you can plan ahead! *Tue-Thu 6pm-1am, Fri-Sat 6pm-3am.* ☰ Korte Leidsedwarsstraat 45 (Leidsegracht), 626-6769, tao-group.nl

De Trut • West • Nightclub

Best Gay Scenes A Sunday night spent dancing and flirting at De Trut is a time-honored tradition for hip, trendy, and slightly alternative gays and lesbians. The weekly dance event was started by squatters and an egalitarian-edgy vibe remains both in the price of drinks and the unpretentious atmosphere. Expect a handsome, high-energy crowd, a host of international guests—manning the turntables as well as hitting the dance floor—and one of Amsterdam's longest lineups at the door; show up after the doors open and run the risk of getting turned away. *Sun 11pm-4am.* ⓒ☰ Bilderdijkstraat 165 (Kinkerstr.), (no phone)

TWSTD • Canal Belt • Nightclub

Consider this: The best thing that can be said about this club's interior is that it's on the small side with an average-looking bar and awfully tired couches. And yet it makes the grade. Why? What this places lacks in interior design, it makes up for with music. Well-known DJs—some of them with international reputations—enjoy the low-key atmosphere enough to drop in and spin. The program varies nightly so check the online agenda or just drop in. Dutch techno, pop, progressive, drum and bass, house, and disco beats keep the dance floor busy. *Sun-Thu 6pm-1am, Fri-Sat 6pm-3am.* ≡ Weteringschans 157 (Vijzelgracht), 320-7030, twstd.nl

Weber • Jordaan • Lounge

Close to the Leidseplein—Amsterdam's touristy nightlife epicenter—yet attracting a local crowd, the instantly likable Weber strikes the perfect balance between obvious and insider. The subtle swaths of floral wallpaper and mix-and-match furniture are positively shabby chic, while fur accents on the walls give this split-level lounge the feel of an urban après ski spot. The regulars are as warm as the soft-glow cast from the large Art-Deco chandelier, and the doors open late, making this a popular spot for post-theatre nightcaps. *Sun-Thu 9pm-3am, Fri-Sat 9pm-4am.* ≡ Marnixstraat 397 (Leidsegracht), 622-9910

Westergasfabriek • West • Nightclub

To borrow a phrase from dance icons the Village People, "Go West"! But before you do, call ahead: This collection of renovated buildings that was once part of a gas refinery frequently—but not always—hosts popular dance parties that are among the best in the city. On event nights, you can count on a trendy alternative crowd grooving to beats in the post-industrial space that's billed as a "totally immersive culturally environment"—loosely translated, that means "Dance here, it's hip." *Hours and prices vary according to the event.* C≡ Pazzanistraat 41 (Haarlenmerweg), 586-0710, westergasfabriek.com

Wolvenstraat* • Jordaan • Bar

A locals-only spot that's great for breakfast, and not so bad for a drink any time of day. *See Hip Restaurants, p.92, for details. Mon-Fri 8:30am-1am, Sat 10am-2am, and Sun noon-1am.* ≡ Wolvenstraat 23 (Keizersgracht), 320-0843

Youll Lady's Dancing • Rembrandtplein • Nightclub

Best Late-Night Scenes What started as Amsterdam's hip lesbian dance space has evolved into the most popular early morning dance destination for the younger gay and lesbian set. Chart-topping dance hits added to a low-attitude vibe; a stylish-good-looking crowd; and a DJ that spins until sunup ensure that long after the city's other gay clubs have closed their doors for the night, Youll is still packing the dance floor. *Fri-Sat 10pm-5am.* C≡ Amstel 178 (Engelse Pel Steeg), 421-0900, youii.nl

Hip Amsterdam:
The Attractions

Albert Cuypmarkt • De Pijp • Market

Best Outdoor Markets For serious browsing, the Albert Cuypmarkt is a local favorite. Selling everything from fresh produce to clothing and CDs, the 300 stalls that line Albert Cuypstraat have made this century-old open-air market a centerpiece of trendy De Pijp. Owing to its location—smack in the middle of one of the city's insider-hip residential neighborhoods—the market draws a mixed but generally young crowd, in search of vintage finds as much as deals, giving the scene a slight student flea market feel. Be sure to come on an empty stomach because traditional food vendors also make the scene, and where browsing ends, the noshing begins. Treats like homemade chocolates and gelato are in abundance, as are traditional Dutch favorites like French fries served with mayonnaise, poffertjes (tiny pancakes under an avalanche of icing sugar), delicious cheeses, and the Dutch equivalent of sushi—raw herring with onion. Try it, if you dare, wherever you see the words "Hollandse Nieuwe." *Mon-Sat 9:30am-5pm, weather permitting.* Albert Cuypstraat (between Ferdinand Bolstr. and van Woustr.)

De Appel Centre for Contemporary Art • Canal Belt • Art Gallery

Best Contemporary Art Spaces This first-rate center showcases work by emerging talents, and art forms that might not otherwise find a home in Amsterdam's vast cultural landscape—so you know things can get provocative. Unconventional exhibitions with themes like "Policing," "Mobility," and "Idealism" get top billing in the unique, creative space, while the well-attended Tuesday Night Program adds an intellectual perspective to the creative works on display; video presentations, lectures by visiting artists and curators, and highbrow versions of "bring your own art" nights, organized around themes like "(In)security and Fear," make for Amsterdam's most stimulating Tuesday night out (reservations required). *Tue-Sun 11am-6pm.* € Nieuwe Spiegelstraat 10 (Herengracht), 625-5651, deappel.nl

De Balie • Canal Belt • Art Gallery

Best Contemporary Art Spaces Exhibitions at this epicenter for hip and savvy locals often reflect the edgier side of creativity, and although you never know what you'll encounter—installation art, new media, design exhibits, documentary films, decorative arts, and interdisciplinary efforts all make the cut—you can be sure that your visit will be thought-provoking. A program of public symposiums on themes like "How Globalized Are You?" and "Islam and Multiculturalism" keep people chatting when the art browsing stops, and for those who wish to continue heated artistic-intellectual debates into the wee hours, an on-site cafe serves up coffee, beer, and bites to the same crowd. *Opening times vary according to events and exhibitions. Cafe Sun-Thu 10am-1am, Fri-Sat 10am-2am.* € Kleine Gartmanplantsoen 10 (Leidseplein), 553-5100

Droog Design • Oude Zijde • Art Gallery/Store

Best Dutch Design Admired by the *Wallpaper* magazine set, Droog Design is known worldwide for presenting quirky-yet-functional takes on everyday household items. That's why Droog—equal parts design showroom, exhibition space, and artistic think tank—is a design fan's must-see. The permanent collection features such well-known pieces as Marcel Wanders' "Knotted Chair," and Tejo Remy's "Chest of Drawers" and "Milk Bottle Lamp," while exhibitions from the globe's coolest upcoming designers and artists mean that there is always something new to surprise. On a classical note, the building is one with a history: The façade dates from 1641 and Rembrandt had hoped that his masterpiece, "The Sampling Officials," would hang inside. *Tue-Sun noon-6pm.* Staalstraat 7b (Groenburgwal), 523-5059, droogdesign.nl

Erotic Museum • Oude Zijde • Cultural Museum

Best Sex-in-the-City Popular at all hours of the day, and particularly so at night, this five-story museum dedicated to all things erotic might sound titillating, but in reality the displays have an educational and straightforward quality that's far more studious than sensual. Nevertheless, the Erotic Museum is a fun and informative distraction featuring a full-scale mock-up of a Red Light window, some ribald John Lennon sketches done during the legendary bed-in at the Amsterdam Hilton, sexual art and artifacts, and mannequins showing prostitute fashions throughout history. *Sun-Thu 11am-1am, Fri-Sat 11am-2am.* € Oudezijds Achterburgwal 54 (Oude Kennissteeg), 624-7303

Female and Partners • Nieuwe Zijde • Store

Want a taste of the exotic without the seediness of the Red Light District? Female and Partners will have you scantily covered. This lingerie and sex shop has a friendly and knowledgeable all-female staff, and you'll find both men and women happily shopping here. *Tue-Sat 11am-6pm, Thu 11am-9pm, Sun-Mon 1-6pm.* Spuistraat 100 (Nieuwe Spaarpotsteeg), 620-9152, femaleandpartners.nl

Game Over? Retrogames Amsterdam • Nieuwe Zijde • Store

Pac-Man anyone? If you think the modern age was born when the Atari 2600 was released, then Game Over, just steps from the Centraal Station, is not to be missed. The shop stocks vintage game consoles and cartridges for every home platform ever built, and the owners have an exhaustive knowledge of gaming history that trumps that of even the most in-the-know Gen X-ers. If you played it growing up, chances are they have it in stock. *Tue-Sat noon-6pm.* Hasselaerssteeg 12 (Nieuwendijk), 624-7841, gameover.nl

The Hash Marihuana & Hemp Museum • Oude Zijde • Cultural Museum

If your opinions of Amsterdam were largely formed by watching Cheech & Chong movies, this permanent exhibition of all things cannabis is a small, but fun, diversion. It's the only museum in the world dedicated to the cannabis plant and its uses, and surprisingly refrains from promoting the plant, instead aiming to make visitors better informed about soft drug use. Artwork celebrating cannabis use, an exhibition of medical marijuana use, and displays extolling the benefits of industrial hemp have drawn visitors to this joint (I couldn't resist) for over 20 years. *Daily 11am-10pm.* € Oudezijds Achterburgwal 148 (Stoofsteeg), 623-5961, hashmuseum.com

Heineken Experience • De Pijp • Brewery

Best Beer-Lovers' Spots No longer a working brewery, this enormous red-brick building now operates as a museum-shrine dedicated to all things Heineken. Get some tips on brewing, check out beer-making equipment, trace the nearly 250-year history of the company, and go on the Bottle Ride, which follows the production route of

Holland's most famous brew. Have a pint or two along the way and finish with the obligatory gift shop stop. *Tue-Sun 10am-6pm.* € Note: last tickets are sold at 5pm. Stadhouderskade 78 (PC Hooftstr.), 523-9666, heinekenexperience.com

Huis Marseille: Foundation for Photography • Jordaan • Art Museum
Housed in a 17th-century historical monument canal house, this small but very worthwhile gallery space features rotating photo exhibitions that are varied, yet uniformly high in caliber. International photography forms the basis of the exhibitions. Photo fanatics should try to time a visit for a Friday or Saturday when the library containing 1,500 important books of photography is open. *Tue-Sun 11am-6pm.* € Keizersgracht 401 (Hartenstr.), 531-8989, huismarseille.nl

Kadinsky • Nieuwe Zijde • Coffeeshop
Best Coffeeshops Some coffeeshops consider grunge to be a design statement, but Kadinsky has clean, modern lines that make it a pleasant standout. That little bit of style helps to draw a hip, sophisticated crowd, as does the nearby nightlife scene. They've also got Amsterdam's infamous "spacecakes," but take it slow—they are very powerful treats. *Daily 10am-1am.* Rosmarijnsteeg 9 (Nieuwe Spaarpotsteeg)

Lambiek Comics Shop • Canal Belt • Store
Graphic novels like *Maus* and *Persepolis* have added some hipster cachet to reading comic books, so drop in to Lambiek to reconnect with your inner youth the trendy way. Founded in 1968, it was Europe's first antiquarian comic shop, and it remains the finest on the continent, both in terms of its on-hand collection and knowledgeable staff. Having published and edited two encyclopedias on "sequential art," they are widely recognized for their expertise. Browsers will appreciate the small but significant collection of original artwork and reproductions by masters such as Robert Crumb. *Mon-Fri 11am-6pm, Sat 11am-5pm, Sun 11am-5pm.* Kerkstraat 132 (Leidsegracht), 626-7543, lambiek.net

MacBike Bicycle Rentals • Various • Bicycle Rentals
There isn't a more bike-friendly city in the world, so if you want to feel like an insider, grab a bicycle and hit the streets. With three locations and a massive fleet of bikes, MacBike is the best bet for those wanting an independent ride; but for those looking for a bit of guidance, they also offer a variety of self-guided routes. Some tours take in the city centre and traditional venues like working windmills, while the hands-down hipster favorites are the three- and six-hour modern architecture rides. They'll give you bragging rights for having glimpsed the off-the-beaten-track contemporary buildings that the city has become famous for. A word to the wise: Get the optional insurance and always lock your bike—theft is common. *Daily 9am-5:45pm.* € Stationsplein 12 (Centraal Station), Oude Zijde, 620-0985; Weteringsschans 2 (Nieuwe Vijzelstr.), Canal Belt, 620-0985; Mr. Visserplein 2 (Jodenbreestr.), Oude Zijde, 620-0985, macbike.nl

Sexmuseum Amsterdam • Nieuwe Zijde • Cultural Museum
Amateur social anthropologists—particularly those with naughty imaginations—will enjoy the erotic paintings, curio objects, recordings, and of course photographs that are on display in the two 17th-century houses that form the self-anointed "Venus Temple." Focusing on sexuality through the ages, and sexual imagery from different cultures, this small and amusing collection of artifacts is both educational and

saucy, and much more tasteful than you might expect—with the exception of the room decorated almost entirely with pornography. *Daily 10am-11:30pm.* €
Damrak 18 (Karnemelksteeg), 622-8376, sexmuseumamsterdam.com

Splash Healthclub • Various • Health Club
Splash offers day visitors access to solariums, Turkish baths, massage services, and a beauty parlor with limited spa treatments. For those who don't want to miss a session of their latest workout regime, a full agenda of classes including a variety of yoga styles, spinning, and aerobics is also available to drop-in guests, and classes can be conducted in English—just let them know when you show up. Perhaps best of all, the two Splash locations feature modern décor that attracts a fun crowd; hit the "Juice and Shake" bar post-workout and get the lowdown on the weekend's happenings from the hottie in your step class. *Daily 7am-midnight.* €€
Looiersgracht 26-30 (Hazenstr.), Jordaan, 624-8404; Lijnbaansgracht 241 (Leidsegracht), Canal Belt, 422-0280, healthclubsplash.nl

Stedelijk Museum CS • Eastern Harbor • Art Museum
Best Art Museums Although the Stedelijk's permanent collection of "Classic Modern Highlights" won't be on display—this is a temporary venue and the main collection is warehoused until the museum proper reopens in 2008—the satellite venue hosts one of the city's most vibrant art agendas, and it's a must for contemporary art fans. The large site hosts well-organized, innovative exhibitions on a variety of themes, and in addition to installation art, graphic design, sculpture, and video, performances from the fields of poetry, dance, and film round out the agenda, as do topical symposiums and evening lectures. *Daily 10am-6pm; closed 1 Jan.* €
Oosterdokskade 5 (Piet Heinkade), 573-2911, stedelijk.nl

Waterlooplein Market • Oude Zijde • Market
Best Outdoor Markets Amsterdam locals are chock-full of character, so you just know that the city's largest open-air flea market will offer the chance to score some far-out hidden treasures. Collector's items, books, CDs, clothing, and curios make up the bulk of the wares, and the possibility of finding must-have accessories alongside rare albums has given the market a measure of cool cachet among students, clubbers, and "starters"—those at the beginning of their professional careers. *Mon-Sat 9am-5pm.* Waterlooplein (Mr. Visserplein)

World of Ajax - Ajax Museum • East • Sports Museum
This *voetbal* team has one of the richest histories in Europe and some of the top names in the game have proudly worn the red and white jersey of Amsterdam's beloved club. A visit to the World of Ajax includes a tour of the visually impressive Amsterdam Arena—it was Europe's first to feature a retractable roof—a behind-the-scenes look at the team's operations, and a visit to the Ajax Museum where guests trace the history of the legendary club. Multimedia presentations factor large in the exhibitions as do memorabilia, the club's trophy room, and biographies about on-field luminaries like former World Footballer of the Year Marco van Basten and the father of "total football" Johan Cruyff. *Apr-Sept Mon-Sat 10am-6pm, guided tours from 11am; Oct-Mar Mon-Sat 10am-5pm, guided tours from 11am.* € Arena Boulevard 3 (Haakbergweg), 311-1336, ajax.nl

HIP

Classic Amsterdam

This city's been hosting the world's who's who since the height of the Golden Age when it was Europe's epicenter of culture and sophistication. Today's Amsterdam offers activities that are rich in art and history, topped off by restaurants celebrating the finest culinary traditions. Things this good never go out of style. Perhaps that's why those that experience the classier side of this city think of Venice as the Amsterdam of the south.

Note: Venues in bold are described in detail in the listings that follow the itinerary. Venues followed by an * asterisk are those we recommend as both a restaurant and a destination bar.

Classic Amsterdam:
The Perfect Plan (3 Nights and Days)

Perfect Plan Highlights

Thursday

Morning	**Anne Frank House**
Lunch	**Het Tuynhuys, Le Pêcheur**
Afternoon	**Boat tour, ARTTRA**
Cocktails	**Het Proeflokaal Wynand**
Dinner	**La Rive, Christophe**
Nighttime	**Jazzcafé Alto, Café Gollem**
Late-night	**Café Cuba, Café Nol**

Friday

Morning	**Rembrandt House, Yellow Bike Tour**
Lunch	**Quartier Sud, Café Vertigo**
Afternoon	**Rijksmuseum, Dutch Flowers, Flower Mkt.**
Cocktails	**De Admiraal, De Drie Fles.**
Dinner	**De Kas, d'Vijff Vlieghen**
Nighttime	**Theater Casa Rosso, In 't Aepjen**
Late-night	**De Twee Zwaantjes, Bourbon St. Blues Club**

Saturday

Breakfast	**Roberto's**
Morning	**Van Gogh Museum**
Lunch	**La Terrasse, Hudson's Terrace**
Afternoon	**Ams. Historical Museum, Amstel Hotel Health Club**
Cocktails	**Café 't Smalle**
Dinner	**Bordewijk, Ciel Bleu***
Nighttime	**Reijnders**
Late-night	**Twee Prinsen, De Duvel*, 't Kalfje***

Morning After

Brunch	**La Sirene**

Hotel: **Hotel Seven One Seven**

Thursday

9am Head to the Jordaan, home to many of the city's most picturesque canals and boutiques, and a host of cultural attractions. First stop: the solemn but fascinating **Anne Frank House**. Don't miss its small museum, where exhibitions on tolerance and understanding are staged.

11am Lighten the mood by heading to the nearby Negen Straatjes (Nine Streets), lined with one-of-a-kind shops. Look out for Van Ravenstein selling woman's clothing, Galerie Zilver offering original art pieces, and Café Pompadour dishing out luscious cakes, pastries, and teas to a well-dressed crowd of locals.

12:30pm Lunch Get a helping of sophistication at **Het Tuynhuys**. The former carriage house has a tranquil garden terrace that's perfect for romance. Or, to sample some of the Netherlands' excellent seafood, stop at **Le Pêcheur**, where the courtyard garden has views of canal houses.

2pm **Holland International Boat Tours** provide a number of options to explore the labyrinth of Amsterdam's canals. Or, if art's more your thing, allow the

CLASSIC

expert art historians at **ARTTRA** Cultural Agency to share their insight into Amsterdam's greatest treasures.

5pm The bar at **Het Proeflokaal Wynand Fockink**, a 400-year-old tasting house, serves jenevers to a smartly dressed local crowd. Or go to **In de Waag***, the medieval weigh-house-cum-bar and restaurant with a patio.

7:30pm Dinner After a hotel stop, dine with the stars—the Michelin stars, that is—at these spots: **La Rive** in the Amstel Hotel, where Edwin Kats' French cuisine makes for a refined evening; the charming but grand **Vermeer**, with sophisticated fish and game; or **Christophe** for creations that marry French with North African flavors.

9:30pm Non-stop good times and live music can be found nightly at **Jazzcafé Alto**, a dark joint known equally for the friendly regulars and the possibility of catching local legend Hans Dulfer—he has a standing Wednesday night gig, but drops in unannounced. Pay a visit to **Café Gollem** if your idea of a great night out means a pub. This brown bar stocks over 200 beers, and the locals will always make room for a guest.

Midnight For people-watching and great mojitos, check out **Café Cuba**. Or for a more obviously Amsterdam experience head to **Café Nol**.

9:30am In Waterlooplein, the Jewish heart of the city until World War II, stop by the Monument to Jewish Resistance. Then cross over the Magere Brug (skinny) bridge, one of the city's most photographed landmarks en route to **Rembrandt House**. His former digs are still decorated in the style of the Golden Age; art pieces from his personal collection adorn the walls, and prints from the master's hand grace a new annex. Or stretch your legs on a guided **Yellow Bike Tour**, since cycling the city's endless paths is a local rite of passage.

Noon Lunch **Quartier Sud**, located in the city's Oude Zuid or "Old South" neighborhood, is a lovely spot, but nature lovers can dine al fresco at **Café Vertigo** overlooking the beloved Vondelpark or, better yet, in the park. The folks here will pack you a gourmet picnic basket, and you can join the locals lunching on the grass.

1:30pm Go to the **Rijksmuseum**, and immerse yourself in Amsterdam's legendary art scene. Designed by Pierre Cuypers and finished in 1885, the neo-Gothic building is home to one of the world's most significant art collections and should not be missed. Highlights include Rembrandt's *The Night Watch* and *The Jewish Bride*.

3pm Nearby Spiegel Kwartier is home to Amsterdam's largest concentration of classic art galleries and antique shops. Highlights among these include Gebroeders Douwes, selling fine art including Dutch master paintings; Kunsthandel Frans Leidelmeijer, which specializes in Art Deco wares; and the Delft Shop, selling—you guessed it—porcelain and ceramics from the Netherlands' top houses. For a wilder taste of the city, drop into either the **Coffeeshop de Dampkring** or **Dutch Flowers**, two of the city's venerable "coffeeshops," or if it's really Dutch flowers that you're interested in, stroll over to the city's floating **Flower Market**.

5pm Sample the collection of classic liquors at either **De Admiraal** or **De Drie Fleschjes**. Since 1650 they've been serving jenevers to weary travelers and locals alike.

7:30pm Dinner Gentlemen, it's time to bust out the dinner jacket. Dine in a greenhouse where ingredients are grown for your meal at **De Kas**. **d'Vijff Vlieghen** is located in a warren of period houses. It has delicious interpretations of Dutch classics in a romantic candlelight environment, with original Rembrandt sketches on the walls. For its fine wines and Burgundian cuisine, **Chez Georges** is lauded as one of the city's finest restaurants.

10pm Since you can't leave Amsterdam without having walked the legendary Red Light District, head over to the live show at **Theater Casa Rosso**, the—all things being relative—classiest option among sex shows. If it's not your cup of t-and-a, stop at **In 't Aepjen** for drinks, in a setting crowded with antique curios and an accordion player.

Midnight **De Twee Zwaantjes** is perfect if you're in the mood to listen to rollicking Dutch drinking songs, or, to mingle with people from across the globe, wander the bars of Rembrandtplein.

2am If you're homesick for the Delta—or if you're simply wanting to keep the party going—head to **Bourbon Street Blues Club**, a good-times spot where locals party until sunup.

Saturday

9am Breakfast Start your day with breakfast at **Roberto's** in the Hilton Hotel.

10am Lines are somewhat shorter at the opening time of the **Van Gogh Museum**. View the world's largest collection of the artist's work, including his most famous paintings—*Sunflowers*, *Self Portrait as an Artist*, and *The Potato Eaters*.

Noon Lunch Head to **La Terrasse** if the weather works in your favor, **Hudson's Terrace** if it doesn't, or **De Compagnon** under any circumstances. Combining gracious style and fundamental cooking, each is worth a stop.

CLASSIC

1pm The **Amsterdam Historical Museum** documents the city's growth in fascinating exhibits. Continue your history lesson outdoors at the nearby **Begijnhof**—the enclosed courtyard containing two churches dates back to the 14th century—and the **Royal Palace**, where the short tour will give you a glimpse into royal life.

3pm **Bierbrouwerij 't IJ** has just opened its tasting house in time to satisfy your need for one ot its microbrews. If you prefer to unwind, **Amstel Hotel Health Club** has a whirlpool, Turkish bath, steamroom, pool, and massage.

7pm Warm up for dinner with a pre-meal drink at **Café 't Smalle**; the brown café is a neighborhood classic and the waterside patio is a fair-weather hot spot. Or drop into **'t Arendsnest** if you're a fan of microbrews. Every one of the Netherlands' breweries is represented in the 180-plus selections that make up the menu, and visiting neophytes are just as welcome as regulars.

8:30pm Dinner Make a reservation at **Bordewijk** to experience elevated cuisine along with inspired wines. **Ciel Bleu*** is where Michelin-starred French dishes and attentive service benefit from the city's grandest vistas. If your tastes lean toward the exotic, reserve a table at **Tempo Doeloe**. Amsterdam is chock-full of Indonesian restaurants, but this is the best.

10:30pm The Leidseplein is Amsterdam's come-one-come-all area for bar hopping—plan on staying late. **Reijnders** is the most authentic joint among them—but all offer patio seats and people-watching. To keep it strictly Dutch, head to the canal-side **Twee Prinsen**, where friendly locals and a heated terrace make the perfect bar scene.

11:30pm Whiskey aficionados should make a stop at **De Still**, where 150 brands and a tasting menu help you broaden your horizons, while those looking for a more general watering hole can head to **De Duvel***.

2am Getting hungry? **'t Kalfje*** serves a full menu well into the morning and can satisfy all of your late-night needs. Pretty it's not, but the beer is cold and the crowd is warm.

The Morning After

Located at the confluence of five canals and dishing out seafood-heavy tasty brunches, **La Sirene** is a gracious, scenic, and sophisticated end to your Amsterdam adventure.

Classic Amsterdam:
The Key Neighborhoods

The **Canal Belt** encompasses the area south of the city center and is characterized by grand canal houses—although most are offices nowadays. It also includes diverse attractions such as the buzzing Leidseplein, where you'll find crowds dining and lounging at any hour of the day, and the antique-shopping area concentrated around Nieuwe Spiegelstraat.

The **Museumplein** is home to Amsterdam's world-class museums—the Van Gogh, the Rijksmuseum, and the Stedelijk. It's also where you'll find the Vondelpark, Amsterdam's equal to London's Hyde Park and New York's Central Park.

The **Nieuwe Zijde**, or "New Side," is only new in relation to the Old Side (its development started in the 16th century), and you'll find many of Amsterdam's main attractions here. In addition to the Dam Palace, Nieuwe Kerk, the Begijnhof, and the Amsterdam Historical Museum, you'll find the commercial heart of the city.

The **Oude Zijde**, literally "the Old Side," is the area where Amsterdam was first developed and includes the old harbor, the Stopera and Theater Carré—two of the city's leading performing arts venues—and the famous Red Light District.

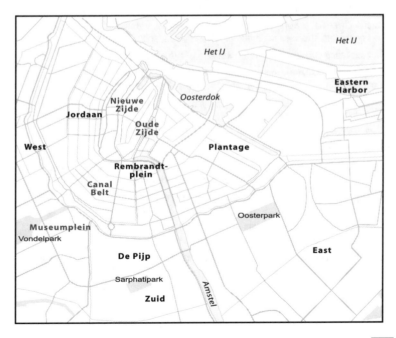

Classic Amsterdam:
The Shopping Blocks

Kalverstraat

Featuring reliable chain stores alongside standout boutiques, Kalverstraat is Amsterdam's buzzing come-one-come-all shopping stroll.

Bijenkorf Amsterdam's answer to Harrods. Dam 1 (Damrak), 900-0919

Hunkemöller A Euro Victoria's Secret. Kalverstraat 162 (Spui), 623-6032

Perrysport A huge sporting goods store. Kalverstraat 99 (Watersteeg), 624-7131

Rituals Boutique Skin care, beauty, and home products meant to add self-pampering to your daily routine. Kalverstraat 73 (Wijde Kapelsteeg), 344-9222

Negen Straatjes (Nine Streets)

Nestled between the romantic canals of the Jordaan, the Negen Straatjes are as rich with authentic character as they are with one-of-a-kind boutiques.

Antiquariaat St. Joris Maritiem Ephemera, engravings, and nautical antiques from Holland's storied past. Reestraat 3 (Keizersgracht), 623-5466

Art Deco-Djoeke Wessing Art Deco furnishings and accessories, upholstery, and salvaged items. Huidenstraat 20 (Keizersgracht), 627-4110

Galerie Zilver Gallery of local artist Eric Zilverberg; sculpture and paintings of Amsterdam streetscapes predominate. Prinsengracht 234 (Reestr.), 624-3395

De Kaaskamer Cheese emporium. Runstraat 7 (Keizersgracht), 623-3483

Pompadour Chocolaterie An Amsterdam institution. Tea room known for delicious cakes, pies, and chocolates. Huidenstraat 12 (Keizersgracht), 624-7919

The Spiegelkwartier

Concentrated around Nieuwe Spiegelgracht, the Spiegelkwartier is home to an astonishing number of high-end galleries and antique dealers.

Antique Wines Amsterdam Noteworthy antique wines as well as some recent, instant classics. Eerste Weteringdwarsstraat 2a (Spiegelgracht), 422-9315

Archea Ancient Art Etruscan, Greek, Roman, Egyptian, and Near Eastern treasures for discerning collectors. Nieuwe Spiegelstraat 37A (Kerkstr.), 625-0552

Aronson Antiquairs of Amsterdam Antique boutique. Delftware, and antique Chinese earthenware. Nieuwe Spiegelstraat 39 (Kerkstr.), 623-3103

E.H. Ariëns Kappers Print shop with Dutch art, as well as Old Masters (Rembrandt and Israel's etchings). Nieuwe Spiegelstraat 32 (Kerkstr.), 623-5356

Classic Amsterdam:
The Hotels

Amstel Hotel InterContinental • Plantage • Grand (79 rms)
Since opening its doors in 1867, the riverside Amstel has been synonymous with refinement and sophistication. It's hosted everyone from royalty to celebrities like George Clooney, Brad Pitt, and Matt Damon, who stayed during the filming of *Ocean's Twelve*. Palatial common areas feature Persian carpets, soaring ceilings, and Delft lamps, and that classic theme continues in guest rooms that are decorated in subdued style, part Laura Ashley and part classic Dutch. The hotel is located within walking distance of Amsterdam's major attractions, including Stopera (Opera House) and Theatre Carré, which hosts international musical and theatrical acts nightly. But should you choose to spend your evening at the hotel, the Amstel has it all. Wireless internet can be accessed throughout the hotel, a 24-hour business center complete with technical concierge is on hand to meet your communication needs, and there's a health and fitness club—massage, sauna, whirlpool, and indoor pool—to help you work off the jet lag. Dining options include La Rive (see p.120), the two-Michelin star restaurant that's one of the city's best dining destinations. The 55 executive rooms and 24 suites are divided almost evenly between those with street views and those like room 206, with views of the river and charming Magere Brug (skinny bridge), and as you might expect, rooms on the higher floors offer the most panoramic glimpses of the city. €€€€ Professor Tulpplein 1 (Sarphatistr.), 622-6060 / 800-327-0200, amsterdam.intercontinental.com

Amsterdam American Hotel • Canal Belt • Timeless (174 rms)
Classicists who still like to hit the town and cut loose will love the American. Renowned as an Art Nouveau monument as well as being the only hotel of note situated on the never-sleeping Leidseplein, the canal-side hotel is a sophisticated oasis in the heart of this city's action. A wealth of shopping, dining, drinking, and dancing options are just outside the hotel's front door, and most of Amsterdam's big draws, like the canals and the Rijksmuseum, can be reached in five minutes on foot. Back in the hotel, spacious guest rooms feature elegant—if standard—hotel furnishings that are upstaged by ornate architectural elements like original stained glass windows, elegant granite bathrooms, and Art Nouveau detailing. International visitors that tend toward moneyed 30-something-and-up couples can choose between Leidseplein or canal views, and should keep in mind that the preferred rooms—both with respect to size and views—are found on the fifth floor. An on-site restaurant and the attractive Bar Americain (p. 124) also feature that timeless Art Nouveau décor, and are classy dining and drinking options with views of the Leidseplein, so you'll never feel removed from the action—unless you choose to. Guest rooms offer a respite from the Amsterdam action, and a sauna and exercise room will help you to recharge and chill out. A private boat launch adds convenience for those wishing to travel by water taxi, and a nearby tram line to Centraal Station means that even distant attractions are well within range. €€€ Leidsekade 97 (Leidsestr.), 556-3000 / 800-327-0200, amsterdamamerican.com

The Grand Amsterdam Sofitel Demeure • Oude Zijde • Timeless (182 rms)
A convent in the 15th century, an inn hosting royalty in the 16th century, the headquarters for the Dutch admiralty in the 17th century, and host to Dutch royals from William of Orange—the father of the Netherlands—to the current regent, Queen Beatrix, the ornate Grand has certainly earned its name. Nowadays, well-heeled international guests, visiting A-listers, and the occasional royal figure come for custom-made inlaid furnishings, high ceilings, French doors, and large windows that enhance the chic but classical atmosphere in the hotel's public spaces and generous guest rooms where fabrics in bold stripes and floral prints—all in salmon and blue—suggest an English country manor. Few details are overlooked: Roger & Gallet products complement black-and-white Art Deco bathrooms, high-speed internet is on hand in every room, and every morning visitors receive international newspaper delivery to their rooms. Weather permitting, guests can dine in the leafy and tranquil garden courtyard, and the Art Deco Café Roux (see p.115), the hotel's only à la carte restaurant, is a worthy destination regardless of whether or not you choose to stay at the hotel; in addition to numerous culinary awards, it has received a Wine Spectator Restaurant Award for four consecutive years. Health-conscious visitors are delighted by the fitness center's pool, sauna, Turkish bath, and workout room, and art lovers shouldn't miss the mural by the co-founder of the Cobra movement, Karl Appel; it's located in the hallway across from the entrance to Café Roux. Request room 348; it has picture-perfect canal views, or ask for room 321 to enjoy views of the serene courtyard gardens. €€€€ Oudezijds Voorburgwal 197 (Sint Agnietenstr.), 555-3111 / 800-221-4542, thegrand.nl

Hotel de l'Europe • Oude Zijde • Grand (100 rms)
When the riverside Hotel de l'Europe opened its doors in 1896, it set a benchmark for class and luxury that continues to this day. The traditionally decorated, ornate common areas feature details that evoke old-world charm, and while the guest rooms are similarly appointed, all 100 feature modern conveniences like wireless access and roomy marble baths. Two destination restaurants, the waterside La Terrasse (see p.121) and the Michelin-star Excelsior (see p.117), guarantee that you won't have to look far for a great meal, but then again, many of Amsterdam's highlight restaurants and attractions are only steps from the hotel's front door: the city opera house, the flower market, and the famous canals can all be reached within five minutes on foot. As a member of the Leading Hotels of the World, it offers guests luxuries like a limousine service, a jetty for those who choose to arrive by boat, and one of the city's finer hotel fitness centers, complete with swimming pool, whirlpool, massage room, and sauna, all in splendid classical style. For some of the best views that Amsterdam has to offer, try to book rooms ending in -26, -32, -34, -36, or -38; on higher floors if you want a skyline vista, and on lower floors to view the river up close. €€€ Nieuwe Doelenstraat 2-8 (Oude Turfmarkt), 531-1777, leurope.nl

Hotel Pulitzer • Jordaan • Timeless (230 rms)
The Pulitzer, featured in the film *Ocean's Twelve*, consists of 25 restored 17th- and 18th century canal houses all linked together and framed by two of the city's main canals as well as the boutique shops on the trendy Negen Straatjes. It's the perfect Amsterdam location for the sophisticated and discerning international crowd that makes it their home away from home. The deluxe rooms are all uniquely decorated, but each features the modern amenities, furnishings,

and service consistent with a five-star home away from home. Details like a high tea—served in the tranquil garden in fair weather—and twice monthly art exhibitions in the hallways, add to the atmosphere of sophistication and culture that reaches its yearly climax during the Prinsengracht Concert. The daylong, canal-side classical concert is staged outside the Pulitzer's front door, turning canal-view rooms into symphony box-suites. Rooms with classic architectural elements like high ceilings, exposed beams, and larger baths, stand out, as do those with canal views: Rooms 418 and 272 offer both. Room 418 has grand views of the Prinsengracht, making it a hot commodity at any time of the year—particularly so on the evening of the annual concert—while room 272 has an equally enviable view of the Keizersgracht. €€€€ Prinsengracht 315-331 (Westerchurch), 523-5235 / 800-326-3535, starwood.com

Hotel Seven One Seven • Canal Belt • Grand (8 rms)

With only eight elegantly appointed suites, the Hotel Seven One Seven—a canal house decorated with antiques and rich fabrics—promises top-notch personal service. There are ample lounge areas with fireplaces overlooking the Prinsengracht (one of the city's main canals), a secluded garden patio, and a small but well-rounded library. The romantic, sophisticated theme continues in the rooms, with brass beds dressed in the finest of linens, full-length baths appointed with Hermès products, ISDN wiring, Bang & Olufsen TV/DVD sets, and stereos with radio and CD. Guest rooms range in size from a large 450 square feet to an astonishing 750 square feet, and included in the price of a stay are luxuries like ironing, shoe shines, house wines, afternoon tea and pastries, in-room refreshment cabinets, and sumptuous made-to-order breakfasts. The well-connected staff can arrange anything from transportation to hard-to-get tickets for big events. If stairs present an obstacle—the hotel has no elevator—ask for the Franz Liszt room; it has a separate street-level entrance as well as access to the dining area. Otherwise splash for the Schubert or Picasso suites; in addition to being the largest of the guest residences, they both feature sweeping canal views, and each has a wall of windows, making the rooms beautiful, bright, and airy. €€€€ Prinsengracht 717 (Leidsestr.), 427-0717, 717hotel.nl

NH Barbizon Palace • Nieuwe Zijde • Timeless (275 rms)

This five-star luxury hotel opposite Centraal Station is a convenient home base for visitors planning on making day trips by rail. Much of the hotel is situated behind the restored façades of 19 Golden Age homes, and many of the guest rooms—all decorated in a style that's best described as updated English country; think modernized and reissued period furnishings, and fabrics featuring floral patterns and bold stripes—show a respect for tradition, incorporating original architectural features like split levels and exposed oak beams that date back to the 17th century. Destination restaurants like Hudson's Terrace (see p.118) and the Michelin-starred Vermeer (see p.122) mean that guests can experience Amsterdam's finest dining without even leaving the hotel, but neighborhood options are far from limited, as many of Amsterdam's top dining and sightseeing options are just a short walk away. A business center, a small health and fitness club, private boat moorage, secure on-site parking, and the proximity of Amsterdam's extensive tram lines, make this one of the more practical options in the city and a very popular option for business travelers. €€ Prins Hendrikkade 72 (Zeedijk), 556-4564, nh-hotels.com

NH Grand Krasnapolsky • Nieuwe Zijde • Timeless (468 rms)

Location, location, location—the adage of realtors the world over holds true at this large chain hotel. Located right on the Dam Square—the spiritual and geographic heart of the city—and opposite the Dam Palace (the Queen's offices), it affords its guests views of the palace, the Nieuwe Kerk, (see p.132) and the bustling square. Like the common areas and lobby, the guest rooms are spacious yet warm and cozy. Expect ample baths, but furnishings that are strictly standard-issue hotel, albeit of the five-star variety: smart wooden bedframes, richly colored curtains, burnished TV cabinets, and dark wall-to-wall carpeting. Of course, they contain all of the amenities that you'd expect from a big-name property: wireless internet, roomy baths, airport shuttle service, and a well-appointed communications and business center. The picturesque Winter Garden, built in 1879, with a ceiling composed of cast iron and glass, is the preferred dining option from among the Krasnapolsky's four restaurants, and it hosts what is surely the most comprehensive breakfast buffet in the city. If size matters more than dramatic views, opt for any room in the Royal Wing—they have extra-spacious sitting areas and baths—otherwise do like most of the business guests, honeymooners, and sophisticated sightseers: Request a Dam Square-view room when making your reservation ... the higher the better to take in the sights. €€ Dam 9 (Warmoesstr.), 554-9111, nh-hotels.com

Classic Amsterdam:
The Restaurants

De Belhamel • Jordaan • French
Best Tables with a View Located at the junction of two canals, and boasting a fair-weather waterside terrace, de Belhamel is virtually synonymous with "that place with the good views." They serve decent classical French-Italian and Dutch dishes to a wide variety of guests, and if you can pry your eyes away from the canal, the Art Nouveau interior has many original design elements to admire. It's a no-brainer, but be sure to ask for a window table if the terrace is closed. *Daily noon-4pm and 6-10pm.* €€ ▭ Brouwersgracht 60 (Herengracht), 622-1095, belhamel.nl

Bordewijk • Jordaan • French-Mediterranean (G)
Outstanding food, professional service, a casual-chic crowd, and an intelligent wine list that includes some surprising choices make this one of the best restaurants in Amsterdam. White walls and black tables in metal and wood give the space a cool-ly minimal feel, and large windows make it light and airy. The ambience is casual yet refined, and of course the summer-only terrace is popular, but the main event remains chef Wil de Mandt's Mediterranean-influenced French country fare. *Tue-Sun 6:30-10:30pm.* €€ ▭ Noordermarkt 7 (Prinsengracht), 624-3899

Café Luxembourg* • Nieuwe Zijde • Tavern
Brown bars aren't known for their food, but Luxembourg breaks the mold with a decent menu that helps you lounge away a pleasant afternoon. *See Classic Nightlife, p.125, for details. Sun-Thu 9am-1am, Fri-Sat 9am-2am.* € Ⓑ▭ Spui 24 (Kalverstr.), 620-6264, cafeluxembourg.nl

Café Roux • Oude Zijde • French
Since the 1920s, people have come to bask in the Art-Deco glory of Café Roux, and the period lighting, glazed glass sconces, and ebony-accented chairs still look timeless and elegant. Lately guests come to enjoy the delicious, traditional French fare and selections from the 15,000-bottle wine cellar, among the best in the country. The wine list consistently garners the Wine Spectator Award of Excellence, and 2005 saw genius-sommelier Noël Vanwittenbergh earn a personal Wine Spectator Diamond Award of his own, making Café Roux a classic must. *Daily 6:30-10:30am, 12:30-3pm, and 6:30-10:30pm.* €€ ▭ Grand Amsterdam Sofitel, Oudezijds Voorburgwal 197 (Sint Agnietenstr.), 555-3560, thegrand.nl

Café Vertigo • Museumplein • Cafe
The large patio offering gorgeous views of the city's beloved Vondelpark is only one of the attractions at Vertigo. By virtue of its location in the Netherlands' Film Museum, the cafe is a gathering place for the local hipster-media savvy set. Drop in for tapas on the terrace or a full meal in the dining room, a modern, stylish space with oversized photos of classic film icons like John Wayne and James Dean—either way you'll find your tribe relaxing and gossiping contentedly. *Daily 10am-1am.* € Ⓑ▭ Vondelpark 3 (R. Visscherstr.), 612-3021, vertigo.nl

Café Wildschut* • Museumplein • Tavern

A grand cafe that draws a mostly drinking crowd, Wildschut also makes for a pleasant meal. *See Classic Nightlife, p.126, for details. Mon-Thu 9am-1am, Fri 9am-3am, Sat 10am-2am, Sun 10am-1am.* € B≡ Roelof Hartplein 1-3 (Cornelis Anthoniszstr.), 676-8220

Chez Georges • Jordaan • French (G)

Belgian owner-chef Georges Roorda is a gracious host, his foie gras is the stuff of local legend, and the loyalty of his regular customers is unwavering. Consistently excellent cooking and superior wine pairings showcase his love for Burgundian fare, motivating smartly dressed fans of classic cuisine to fill the tables every night. The room is decorated with classic wall moldings, mirrors, and antique-looking wallpaper, and it's perfect for wooing business and romantic partners alike. Order the five- or seven-course "gastronomic" menu and you'll have plenty of time to get the job done! *Mon-Tues and Thu-Sat 6-10pm.* €€ ≡ Herenstraat 3 (Herengracht), 626-3332

Christophe • Jordaan • French-North African (G)

Owner-chef Christophe Royer's cuisine combines French classic cooking with traditional Mediterranean ingredients like chorizo, saffron, and couscous, and he's earned a Michelin star for his efforts. His Algerian-French roots are evident in dishes like brochette of lamb with dates, mint, and eggplant puree, and his reputation for unpretentious cooking, combined with a subtly elegant décor (pale walls, light wooden tables, and white linen), has made Christophe a favorite among deep-pocketed 30-plus diners. Complex cuisines demand fine wine pairings and Royer's range of familiar classics and selective surprises aptly fit the bill, providing the perfect companion to consistently delicious meals. *Daily from 6pm.* €€€ ⊒ Leliegracht 46 (Keizersgracht), 625-0807, christophe.nl

Ciel Bleu* • De Pijp • French (G)

Best Tables with a View Onno Kokmeijer's delicious, Michelin-star French cuisine and the dining room's location on the 23rd floor of the Okura Hotel make this a culinary highpoint in more ways than one. The classic interior complete with crisp white linens is quietly sophisticated, as are the business diners who share the space with locals and tourists. From the discerning service to the fine wines and the sweeping city views, nothing disappoints. *See Classic Nightlife, p.126, for details. Daily 6:30-10pm.* €€€ ⊒ The Okura Hotel, Ferdinand Bolstraat 333 (Jozef Israelskade), 678-7111, okura.nl

De Compagnon • Nieuwe Zijde • French

Visitors and locals rave about de Compagnon and you can't blame them. The service is unfailingly attentive yet never stuffy, the interior is romantic—imagine a candlelit space that's part wine cellar and part period home—and the meals are consistently memorable. Head chef Bert van Buschbach uses wild and organic ingredients whenever possible, and his French-Burgundy dishes, which include a mouth-watering suckling pig and whole fried guinea fowl with a creamy truffle sauce and sliced fresh truffle, show off both his skill and respect for tradition. Request a table on the small balcony, or try to reserve a table with canal views to round out the perfect experience. *Mon-Fri noon-2pm and 6-10pm, Sat 6-10pm.* €€ ⊒ Guldehandsteeg 17 (Warmoesstr.), 620-4225, decompagnon.nl

Côte Ouest • Nieuwe Zijde • French

Paris is only a five-hour drive away, but step into this smart French bistro—or sit down at a sidewalk table—and you'll be whisked to the City of Lights faster than you can say "Garçon!" Galettes, quiches, steak frites, and five varieties of mussels—all served with fries of course—make up the bulk of the simple menu, and like the cuisine, the décor stays true to its roots. The acres of rich dark wood, tables covered with paper cloths, and scene-stealing standing-room-only bar all enhance the experience. *Tue-Sun 5-10pm.* € ⊟ Gravenstraat 20 (Blaeustr.), 320-8998, coteouest.nl

De Duvel* • De Pijp • Continental

The name means "the devil," but the scene is heavenly for a bite to eat or a night out. *See Classic Nightlife, p.126, for details. Sun-Fri 11am-1am, Sat 11am-3am.* € ⊟ 1e v.d. Helststraat 59-61 (Daniël Stalpertstr.), 675-7517, deduvel.nl

Dynasty • Rembrandtplein • Asian

The predominantly non-Dutch clientele and clichéd parasols and rattan chairs can make it hard to understand Dynasty's big draw. See for yourself: Save this spot for a sunny summer evening and head through the restaurant into the beautiful garden. It's a serene oasis in the heart of downtown, and whether you're wooing a lover or a business contact, it sets the perfect mood. And the menu? It covers Malay, Filipino, Cantonese, Thai, and Vietnamese dishes—but despite its lack of focus, it works. *Wed-Mon 5:30-11pm.* €€ ⊟ Reguliersdwarsstraat 30 (Sint Jorisstr.), 626-8400

l'Entrecôte et les Dames • Museumplein • French

This attractive steak house pays a fitting homage to the famous l'Entrecôte in Paris by replicating the Parisian concept identically. All diners start with a signature walnut salad and move onto pre-cut steak (or sole) and fries, finishing with an optional dessert. The setting is equal parts antique pharmacy and modern French bistro, and the combination of a simple menu and well-dressed crowd makes it perfectly suited to pre-concert dinners for those headed to the nearby Concertgebouw. *Mon-Sat 5:30-11pm.* € ⊟ Van Baerlestraat 47-49 (Moreelsestr.), 679-8888, entrecote-et-les-dames.nl

Excelsior • Oude Zijde • French (G)

With Amstel River views, soft piano music, exceptional formal service, an old-money crowd that includes the occasional royal, and the rarest of Amsterdam rarities—a "jacket required" dress code—this is one of the city's grandest dining experiences. In a fittingly elaborate classic style, ornate crown moldings, fresh bouquets, and brilliant antique chandeliers set the mood for chef Jean-Jacques Menanteau's Michelin-star cuisine, which includes a gourmet vegetarian menu and an abbreviated "theater menu" in case dinner is only the beginning of the evening's entertainment. *Mon-Fri 12:30-2:30pm and 7-10:30pm, Sat-Sun 7-10:30pm; theater menu daily 6-11pm.* €€€ ⊟ Hotel de l'Europe, Nieuwe Doelenstraat 2-8 (Oude Turfmarkt), 531-1777, leurope.nl

Hostaria • Jordaan • Italian

Best Italian Eateries "La Vita Bella" could be the motto of this tiny and informal Italian eatery. With one of the city's best reputations for warm hospitality and authentic, homestyle cooking, it's garnered a strong local following in a neighborhood filled

CLASSIC

with worthwhile dining options. Book ahead and enjoy exquisite dishes like the shrimp risotto and lobster spaghetti. Depending on your love of kitschy-campy "mama mia" antics, request a table nearer to, or farther away from, the legendarily dramatic chef. *Tue-Sun 6:30-10pm.* € ▤ 2e Egelantiersdwarsstraat 9 (Egelantiersstr.), 626-0028

Hudson's Terrace and Restaurant • Nieuwe Zijde • French

The restaurant is named after Henry Hudson, who discovered New York, and in his honor, the room is decorated with dark wooden furniture and nautical brass accents throughout. Huge barometers and ship's clocks telling the times in international cities provide the only flourishes in the room aside from that on the plates. Consistently recommendable—if unadventurous—dishes, the enjoyable terrace, and the close proximity to Centraal Station make this a popular spot for the above-30 local crowd to book for special lunches and dinners. *Mon-Fri 6:30am-11pm; Sat-Sun 7am-11pm.* €€ ▤ NH Barbizon Palace, Prins Hendrikkade 72 (Zeedijk), 556-4875

In de Waag* • Oude Zijde • French-Dutch

What looks like a small canal-side castle was once the weighing house for goods entering the city. Nowadays it's a restaurant that serves cafe fare by day and decent French food by night, but the main draw is the setting. Outdoors, a buzzing terrace proves ideal for summertime people-watching, while indoors, the high ceiling, exposed beams, and dark wood set a classic mood that's best seen at night when it's candlelight only. Access the internet for free at the well-stocked reading table. *See Classic Nightlife, p.127. Daily 10am-10:30pm.* €€ ▤ Nieuwmarkt 4 (Geldersekade), 422-7772, indewaag.nl

't Kalfje* • Jordaan • Cafe

Best Late-Night Scenes Finding a decent neighborhood bar at 2am on a Monday night can be a challenge in Amsterdam, and rarer still is finding a place with an open kitchen. Enter 't Kalfje. Show up mid-evening and the place looks dead. Show up after midnight and things are just heating up. Sure, you'll find prettier bars, but spare-ribs and rib-eye steaks are hard to come by in the wee hours of morning, and as many locals can tell you, 't Kalfje can be a loyal friend in times of need. *See Classic Nightlife, p.128. Mon-Thu 4pm-3am, Fri-Sun 4pm-4am.* € Ⓑ▤ Prinsenstraat 5 (Keizersgracht), 626-3370

De Kas • East • New Dutch (G)

Best Dutch Dining A sexy clientele, a garden setting, and a beautiful décor that incorporates subtle touches from Holland's hottest designers all help make this one of this city's most coveted reservations, but the top draw is on the plates. Fans of the slow food movement take notice: The ingredients used at De Kas couldn't be fresher or more locally sourced. De Kas is situated in a stylish greenhouse, and while some of the provisions, like meats and fish, come from their dedicated farm, most of your meal is grown just yards away from where you dine. Five-course menus celebrate the best of this country's culinary traditions while also pointing toward the future of European cuisine. Opt for the rarefied chef's table for a glimpse of the workings of one of Holland's most prestigious restaurants. *Mon-Fri noon-2pm and 6:30-10pm, Sat 6:30-10pm.* €€ (set menu) ▤ Kamerlingh Onneslaan 3 (Middenweg), 462-4562, restaurantdekas.nl

Klein Paardenburg • Ouderkerk aan de Amstel • French (G)

From the dishes—think baked fresh-caught pike with cabbage, potato muslin, smoked eel, and Riesling sauce—to the smart-fashionable 30-plus crowd and the restaurant's riverside locale, old-world charm and sophistication abound. Alfresco dining on the waterfront terrace provides opportunities to spot waterfowl—as well as the Amsterdam elite who come for lunch and dinner—while indoors, the updated classical interior offers comfort and warmth that's as perfect for intimate business as it is for romance. Should you need more privacy post dinner, wander Ouderkerk aan de Amstel's charming laneways for an up-close glimpse of small-town Holland. *Sun-Fri noon-2:30pm and 6-10pm, Sat 6-10pm.* €€€ ▭ Amstelzijde 59 (Oranjebaan), 496-1335

Marius • West • French-Mediterranean (G)

You can divide the locals into two camps: Already-ardent fans of Marius, and those who are dying to go. It's that good. The intimate space feels like a country cottage (rustic cupboards and checkered tablecloths abound), suggesting the romantic good life that most people only dream about. That quality comes through in the four-course set menus (there's no à la carte option). The owner-chef earned his stripes at Chez Panisse in California, and his menu reflects his love of his craft. Servers do their part in creating the perfect leisurely ambience; they'll enthusiastically offer up insightful perspectives on dishes and appropriate wine selections, and will go the extra mile to ensure that every experience is a memorable one. Just remember to book well in advance. *Tue-Sat from 6pm.* €€ (set menu) ▭ Barentszstraat 243 (van Linschotenstr.), 422-7880

The Pancake Bakery • Jordaan • Cafe

Unlike North Americans, the Dutch regard pancakes as a cheap, uncomplicated, and hearty lunch—or more often, dinner—option. Located in a 17th-century canal warehouse, and catering to a mixed-bag come-as-you-are crowd, the noisy Bakery has a large menu of sweet pancakes featuring stroop (Dutch syrup), icing sugar, and fruit, as well as savory options like ham and cheese. It's the perfect introduction to this lowbrow staple of Dutch cuisine. *Daily noon-9:30pm.* € ▤ Prinsengracht 191 (Prinsenstr.), 625-1333, pancake.nl

Le Pêcheur • Rembrandtplein • Seafood

Best Romantic Dining With a wide range of dishes on offer and understated but fine touches in the décor—flower arrangements, wall moldings, and a ceiling mural—Le Pêcheur is the ideal place to sample some of Holland's choicest seafood. Fresh Zeeland oysters are seasonal must-eats, as are mussels, plaice, turbot, and sole. The largely 30-plus crowd is comprised of locals and tourists who come for the consistently high-quality food and wines, as well as the charming courtyard garden that's surrounded by patrician canal homes. *Mon-Fri noon-3pm and 5:30-11pm, Sat 5:30-11pm.* €€ ▭ Reguliersdwarsstraat 32 (SintJorisstr.), 624-3121, lepecheur.nl

Pulitzer's • Jordaan • French

The movie *Ocean's Twelve* made the Pulitzer Hotel famous, but for locals and tourists with an eye for style—particularly mature visitors—this handsome restaurant was already on the radar. Traditional bistro fare that's prepared with a flourish is served in a warren of rooms with off-white walls and black accents and furnishings. Original artwork adorns the walls—be sure to check out the whimsical take on

Rembrandt's *The Night Watch*—and in warmer weather, lunch and dinner are served in the courtyard gardens, along with a worthwhile high tea. *Daily 7am-11pm.* €€€ ▤ Hotel Pulitzer, Keizersgracht 234 (Reestr.), 523-5282, pulitzer.nl

Quartier Sud • Zuid • French

Best Lunch Spots Plush rich red chairs stand out against the dark floor and ceiling, creating a stylishly updated backdrop for traditional, older, moneyed locals. The small terrace is always popular with business diners who come for the attentive servers and the unique menu—with no distinction between lunch and dinner selections, you eat what you want when you want it—and some of the city's best house wines. Meats and fish from the grill are perennial pleasers as is steak tartare served with salad and pommes frites. *Mon-Fri 10:30am-10:30pm.* €€ ▤ Olympiaplein 176 (Parnassusweg), 675-3990

Restaurant Greetje • Oude Zijde • Dutch

The Delft blue-meets-antique-wooden décor gives this restaurant old-world charm, and the menu does nothing to ruin the mood. Classic dishes like braised game with gingerbread, red cabbage, and mashed potatoes, or roasted pheasant with "hotch potch" of the day and creamy gravy have earned the respect of culinary critics and the general public alike, making this comfortable and welcoming spot an instant classic. Try to reserve one of the few tables offering views of the historic Montelbaanstoren. Built in 1512, the waterside tower is one of the few remaining pieces of the city's medieval walls, and was a popular subject for Rembrandt. *Sun and Wed-Fri 5-10pm, bar until 1am, Sat 5-11pm, bar until 3am.* € Ⓑ▤ Peperstraat 23-25 (Rapenburg), 779-7450, restaurantgreetje.nl

La Rive • Canal Belt • French (G)

Best Fine Dining Politicians, royalty, old money, and the global who's who have all dined on chef Edwin Kats' two-Michelin-star cuisine, enjoying what is unquestionably Amsterdam's finest classic culinary experience. Wood paneling and books create a conservative ambience similar to a gentleman's club as do the formal, yet friendly, servers. An impressive wine list, a seasonal terrace, and private booths offering Amstel River views create an air of refined distinction that rivals that found in any of Europe's finest grand-dining rooms. *Mon-Fri noon-2pm and 6:30-10:30pm, Sat 6:30-10:30pm.* €€€ ▢ Amstel Hotel, Professor Tulpplein 1 (Sarphatistr.), 520-3264, restaurantlarive.nl

Roberto's • Zuid • Continental

Ask many Amsterdammers about the Hilton Hotel and they'll assume you're curious about John and Yoko's famous "bed-in." Ask a foodie and you'll get a knowing nod to Roberto's, a prime destination for elegant seafood dinners and sophisticated breakfasts. Plenty of your fellow diners will be visiting guests of the hotel, but enough of a crowd is drawn from the exclusive community around the hotel to avoid the tourist clichés. *Daily 7am-10:30pm.* €€ ▤ The Hilton Hotel, Apollolaan 138 (Breitnerstr.), 710-6025, amsterdam.hilton.com

Rosario • Oude Zijde • Italian

Simple wooden tables—try to reserve the one that has a canal view—and equally simple white walls provide the ideal backdrop for Rosario to work his magic. You can order à la carte, but regulars opt for the inclusive menu; antipasto, pasta or risotto, secondo, and dolce. Dishes are authentic and pure, showing a respect for the finest Sicilian cuisine, and a legion of loyal locals packs the restaurant nightly. Attentive servers and Rosario's proximity to the Stopera, this city's opera house, have bolstered its strength as a pre-concert dining destination. *Tue-Sat 6-10:30pm.* €€ ▤ Peperstraat 10 (Rapenburg), 627-0280

Sama Sebo • Museumplein • Indonesian
This contender for top Indonesian honors is popular with locals as well as visitors looking to try the blended exotic-spice flavors of Holland's favorite imported cuisine. Order à la carte or opt for a delicious 20-plus dish tasting menu called rijsttafel; you can't go wrong either way. Batik fabrics and reed mats make for simple, arguably tired décor, but that doesn't deter the mixed crowds, including the well-heeled shopping set and the occasional celebrity, from filling this place. Heaping lunch specials are worthy, too. *Mon-Sat noon-2pm and 6-10pm.* € ▤ PC Hooftstraat 27 (Stadhouderskade), 662-8146, samasebo.nl

Segugio • Rembrandtplein • Italian
Best Italian Eateries Best Italian? Don't take our word for it: While standing outside the restaurant contemplating the menu, two locals weighed in on Segugio. "Excellent place," said a passerby on foot. "Yes, you must!" yelled a passenger from a passing car. The somber gray interior, pale wooden floors, and crisp white linens are sophisticated and subtle, lest they distract from the high quality of the food. Refined cooking—especially the risottos and original pastas—thoughtful wine pairings, and service to match make this an excellent choice for romance or a special night out. Try to reserve the table in the window. *Mon-Sat 6-11pm.* €€ ▢ Utrechtsestraat 96a (Prinsengracht), 330-1503, segugio.nl

La Sirene • Zuid • Seafood
Best Brunches Every Sunday, chef Rob Blaauboer sets out a buffet of fine meats, seafood, and of course champagne that lures well-to-do tourists and locals looking for a splurge. Waterside dining with views of five canals, a fair-weather terrace, impeccable service, and a classic décor in dark woods attract a sophisticated crowd that arrives by car and by boat, tying up at the hotel's private dock. During the week, locals come here to dine on some of Amsterdam's best prepared seafood. *Mon-Sat noon-2:30pm and 6-10pm, Sun noon-2:30pm.* €€€ ▢ Le Méridien Apollo, Apollolaan 2 (Bernhard Zweerskade), 570-5724, lasirene.nl

Tempo Doeloe • Canal Belt • Indonesian
Best Tastes of the Exotic Chef Ghebrial draws upon an arsenal of flavors like coriander, anise, and curry to create delights. Exotic dishes—some mild, some hot—make this place an Amsterdam institution. Order a rijstafel (rice table), the Indonesian equivalent of a tasting menu. If you're looking for a quiet dinner, that's exactly what you'll get here, but should you take the bait from the friendly staff, the often hilarious servers will unleash one-liners and quips with abandon. *Mon-Sat 6-11pm.* €€ ▢ Utrechtsestraat 75 (Herengracht), 625-6718, tempodoeloerestaurant.nl

La Terrasse • Oude Zijde • French (G)
Best Terraces With a vista that takes in the Muntplein and the Amstel River, this highbrow patio offers a feast for the eyes as much as for the palate. While the menu is unique to La Terrasse, the excellent dishes are prepared indoors at the Michelin-star restaurant Excelsior (see p.117), posing one dilemma. Can you pry your eyes from your plate long enough to take in the views? *Easter–mid-Oct noon-10pm weather permitting.* €€ ▤ Hotel de l'Europe, Nieuwe Doelenstraat 2-8 (Oude Turfmarkt), 531-1705, leurope.nl

Toscanini Ristorante • Jordaan • Italian

This stalwart of the dining scene has been around for long enough to be considered an Amsterdam institution, but luckily for devoted local fans and visiting guests, the quality never wanes. Toeing the line between classic and contemporary, the renovated coach house has a glass roof that lets in a generous amount of natural light—and which almost gives the space a trendy ambience—and the updated-classic theme runs deep into the cuisine. Organic ingredients are used whenever possible, all breads and pastas are made in-house, and the wine selections are exclusively Italian, giving the whole scene the air of mouth-watering authenticity. *Mon-Sat 6-10:30pm.* € ⊟ Lindengracht 75 (Noorderkerkstr.), 623-2813, toscanini.nl

Het Tuynhuys • Rembrandtplein • Continental

Sure, it's the gorgeous garden terrace that lures people to "the Townhouse," but without the unwavering commitment to service and pleasing dinner options, the mid-30s-plus crowd would have moved on long ago. Instead locals and tourists alike still crowd the former carriage house, dining on fish and meat dishes and sipping stellar wines. And the garden? It's beautiful and charming, with tables (thankfully) placed far enough apart to allow the romantic conversations a European garden restaurant demands. *Mon-Fri noon-2:30pm and 6-10:30pm, Sat-Sun 6-10:30pm.* €€ ⊟ Reguliersdwarsstraat 28 (Sintjorisstr.), 627-6603, tuynhuys.nl

Utrechtsedwarstafel • Canal Belt • French

You never know what you're going to get at this popular restaurant, but you can be sure that you're in for a meal to remember. Owners Hans and Igor decided to do something different: Eschewing menus, they insist that guests choose only between three to five courses, and wines that are further classified into simple, medium, and complex combinations. The details of your meal remain a secret until the dishes arrive, and somehow it works. The space is minimally decorated with light wooden floors and furniture; all the better to focus on your meal of French classics that come married with carefully selected wines. Critics—both professionals and the armchair variety—have been raving since the doors opened. *Tue-Sat from 7pm.* €€ (set menu) ⊟ Utrechtsedwarsstraat 107-109 (Utrechtsestr.), 625-4189, utrechtsedwarstafel.com

Van Vlaanderen • Canal Belt • French-Mediterranean (G)

Best Fine Dining Although this city standout was already one of the most popular tables in town, the Michelin star has raised Chef Philippart's French-Belgian cuisine to the status of local legend. Sophisticated dishes paired with special wines, all selected by resident genius-sommelier Bas, ensure that each dinner lives on in memory despite the bland décor. Oh well, enjoy the service and focus your eyes on the cuisine; the mature and sophisticated local dine-about crowd has heralded it as "edible art" and in a town filled with Rembrandts and Van Goghs, they know their stuff. *Tue-Thu from 6:30pm, Fri-Sat from 7pm.* €€€ ⊟ Weteringschans 175 (Nieuwe Vijzelstr.), 622-8292

Vermeer (NH Barbizon Palace) • Nieuwe Zijde • French (G)

Retreat into a bygone era with an evening at Vermeer. Housed in three adjoining 17th-century buildings and with a menu made up of equal parts fish and game—all of it up to Michelin-star snuff—Vermeer offers bygone grandeur with panache. Fireside aperitifs, cigar menus, acres of fine linens, marble, art, and black and white tiled floors, set a mood of old-world charm, while the wine list, compiled by two very competent in-house sommeliers, includes many of the globe's finer choices. Whether you're celebrating a special occasion or simply dining with your special someone, Vermeer guarantees that it's done with uncommon sophistication. *Mon-Fri noon-2:30pm and 6-10pm, Sat 6-10pm.* €€€ ⊒ Prins Hendrikkade 72 (Zeedijk), 556-4885, restaurantvermeer.nl

d'Vijff Vlieghen • Nieuwe Zijde • Dutch

Best Dutch Dining Although this Amsterdam institution is vastly more popular with well-to-do visitors than locals, it shouldn't be hastily dismissed. The staff rightfully pride themselves on excellent service, a comprehensive wine cellar, tasty interpretations of traditional Dutch cooking, and seasonal menus that add a gourmet touch by featuring items like European game. Located in a warren of 17th-century rooms, the many nooks and crannies offer diners the opportunity for romantic intimacy, while those interested in classic art will appreciate the four original Rembrandt prints hanging on the walls. *Daily from 5:30pm.* €€ ⊒ Spuistraat 294-302 (Mosterdpotsteeg), 530-4060, thefiveflies.com

Visaandeschelde • Zuid • Seafood (G)

Outstanding food and perfectly attentive service distinguish this fine seafood restaurant from the competition, and the contemporary classic décor—mirrors, wood panels, and black-cushioned bench seats—does its part to draw the style-conscious but classically minded crowds. Deep-pocketed locals and tourists compete for tables with those who have saved for the big night out, and everyone dresses up, creating a festive special occasion. Magical dishes reflect the chef's intimate understanding of a variety of cuisines and feature Asian, French, and international flourishes that invite being paired with adventurous but reliably high-quality wines. *Mon-Fri noon-2:30pm; and Mon-Sun 5:30-11pm.* €€ ⊒ Scheldeplein 4 (Scheldestr.), 675-1583, visaandeschelde.nl

Yamazato • De Pijp • Japanese (G)

Best Fine Dining For some of the best dining this side of Tokyo, head to this Michelin-star spot that's popular with local gourmands, tourists, visiting Japanese businessmen, and those celebrating a big occasion. Chef Akira Oshima's lovingly prepared and extravagant ten-course menu is perfect for those with time to spare, but you won't go wrong ordering à la carte either. Focus on the sushi—it's by far the best in town—or explore some less-common elements of Japanese cuisine. Whatever you choose, count on fresh ingredients, subtle flavors that delight the palate, and attentive and warm service to make the meal a memorable one. *Daily 7:30-9:30am by appointment only, noon-2pm and 6-9:30pm.* €€€ ⊒ The Okura Hotel, Ferdinand Bolstraat 333 (Jozef Israelskade), 678-7111

Zuid Zeeland • Jordaan • Italian

In part it's the delicious food—well-executed game and fish with obvious Mediterranean accents—and in part it's the warm interior with its cheery yellow terra cotta walls, and bright flower arrangements, that make this restaurant a local favorite with a reputation for value. Ruinart Champagnes, Gabriel & Andreu Cognacs, and a selection of fine wines round out the appealing dining experience. Sidewalk tables are available in warm weather, but you can't go wrong with the seats near the front window: they have views of the Herengracht. *Mon-Fri noon-2:30pm and 6-11pm, Sat-Sun 6-11pm.* € ⊟ Herengracht 413 (Beulingstr.), 624-3154, zuidzeeland.nl

Classic Amsterdam:
The Nightlife

De Admiraal • Jordaan • Bar
Best Dutch Drinking Friendly servers, 30-plus locals who are quick to extend a warm hand, pub fare that will do in a pinch, and a large selection of liquors, beers, and wines make this a local favorite—particularly for after-work drinks. And speaking of locals, do like a regular and stick to the gins; this is the only place to feature concoctions from van Wees, Amsterdam's last remaining independent distiller. There's a small outdoor terrace, and sofas for when you get tired or tipsy. *Mon-Sat 4:30-10:30pm.* ▤ Herengracht 319 (Treeftsteeg), 625-4334

't Arendsnest • Jordaan • Bar
Best Beer-Lovers' Spots Every one of the Netherlands' 50-plus breweries is represented at "the Eagle's Nest" and with 180 varieties of bottled beer on hand and 18 more on tap, the place is a beer-lover's paradise. Friendly locals and tourists are bound together by their love of the drink, and although the focus is on having a good time, a visit can take on an educational quality too: The barman-owner is passionate, knowledgeable, and quick to share his expertise, and for true aficionados, tasting tutorials can be organized. *Sun-Thu 4pm-midnight, Fri-Sat 4pm-2am.* ▤ Herengracht 90 (Korsjespoortsteeg), 421-2057, arendsnest.nl

Bar Americain • Canal Belt • Hotel Bar
Best Hotel Bars Buzzing at all hours, the Leidseplein is perfect for people-watching, and the Bar Americain offers an ideal vantage point. The barmen are skilled in drink mixing as well as conversation, and on a clear, warm evening, there's no better place than the large terrace. Indoors, light wooden floors and pale walls give the Art Deco room a bright and airy appeal, and international guests mingle with 30-plus locals who have a taste for classic styling. Even if you don't score a coveted window seat, you'll still have a great-looking beginning—or end—to your evening on the town. *Daily 5pm-1am.* ▤ Amsterdam American Hotel, Leidsekade 97 (Leidesplein), 556-3000, amsterdamamerican.com

Bierbrouwerij 't IJ • Plantage • Brewery
Best Only-in-Amsterdam Even if it wasn't located beside a windmill, this brew pub, attracting diverse locals after work and on weekend afternoons, would still be a classic; their beers are considered among the country's best, and with standard, seasonal, and occasional brews to sample, ardent ale and lager fans would need multiple visits to try them all. The springtime-only "Paasij" should definitely be sampled as should the autumn-only "bockbiers," but it's the always available and complex- tasting "Struis" that's the perennial crowd-pleaser. *Wed-Sun 3-8pm.* ▤ Funenkade 7 (Alexanderkade), 622-8325, brouwerijhetij.nl

Boom Chicago • Canal Belt • Comedy Club
With an excellent all-American troupe, this dinner-comedy spot featuring English-language improv, scripted comedy, and short sketches, is an Amsterdam institution. The reliably funny shows touch on current events—read: American politics—as well as the humorous side of life in Holland, providing visitors with

a rare late-night live-entertainment option. The only caution: Eat before you arrive—you'll dine far better elsewhere. *Showtimes vary. See website for details.* C≡ Leidseplein 12 (Leidsestr.), 423-0101, boomchicago.nl

Bourbon Street Blues Club • Canal Belt • Live Music

Best Late-Night Scenes If you love live music, and late nights, do like Sting, Jeff Healey, and the Rolling Stones have done before you and head down to Bourbon Street for a long night of blues, rock, soul, and funk. A mixed crowd comprised mostly of 30-plus locals drinks and dances the night away—literally, since the place is open until 5am on weekends—with the only common thread between them being a passion for good times. *Fri-Sat 10pm-5am with live music 11pm-4am, Sun-Thu 10pm-4am with live music 10:30pm-3am.* C≡ Leidsekruisstraat 6-8 (Prinsengracht), 623-3440, bourbonstreet.nl

Café Cuba • Oude Zijde • Theme Bar

Even in the coldest and wettest weather, locals know they can find a taste of sunshine at Café Cuba. Come early for after-work drinks or be prepared to fight the crowd for a seat: Amsterdam's best caparinhas and mojitos mean that people from all walks of life pack the place. The Nieuwmarkt-facing patio offers fine people-watching and the chance to watch occasional buskers perform. *Sun-Thu 1pm-1am, Fri-Sat 1pm-3am.* ≡ Nieuwmarkt 3 (Koningsstr.), 627-4919

Café Gollem • Nieuwe Zijde • Bar

Best Beer-Lovers' Spots Amsterdam has its share of "brown bars," watering holes with classic wooden interiors and pervasive old-world authenticity. Two things help to distinguish this city center bar from its competitors: the selection of over 200 artisan brews from Belgium and beyond, and the decidedly hip crowd. Drop in any day of the week and you'll find a warm and friendly crowd—all of them armchair connoisseurs—celebrating its love for the drink. *Sun-Thu 4pm-1am, Fri-Sat 2pm-2am.* ≡ Raamsteeg 4 (Spuistr.), 626-6645, cafegollem.nl

Café Luxembourg* • Nieuwe Zijde • Pub/Tavern

Best After-Work Drinks Thankfully the rave reviews haven't driven away the loyal locals that give this excellent brown cafe its appealing neighborhood vibe. The traditional hallmarks are present—acres of dark wood, small weathered tables, and an often smoky atmosphere—but Luxembourg distinguishes itself with a well-stocked reading table, a Wi-Fi zone, and a decent menu that means you don't have to leave when you get hungry. There's also a short-list of only-in-Holland liquors, and a small selection of cigars. Try to secure one of the storefront seats. *See Classic Restaurants, p.115. Sun-Thu 9am-1am, Fri-Sat 9am-2am.* ≡ Spui 24 (Kalverstr.), 620-6264, cafeluxembourg.nl

Café Nol • Jordaan • Bar

Best Only-in-Amsterdam At times surreal, but always entertaining, this outrageously decorated, campy cafe manages to attract locals—young and old, hip and not—as well as curious tourists looking for a slice of authentic, albeit bizarre, Amsterdam-icana. Whether you come for the beer or to gawk at the décor, you'll soon find yourself singing along to the corny oompah-pah tunes that are part of this neighborhood's history. And who cares if you don't know the words? Plenty of the locals don't either! *Sun-Thu 8pm-1am, Fri-Sat 8pm-3am.* ≡ Westerstraat 109 (Tichelstr.), 624-5380

Cafe 't Smalle • Jordaan • Bar

This canal-side brown cafe has all the characteristics of an Amsterdam neighborhood classic. The black and white tiled floor, cramped wooden tables, and decent selection of draft beers draws a crowd of young to middle-aged professionals with classic tastes, and never is that more the case than when the sun is shining; suspended over the leafy canal is a small patio offering a perfect view. *Sun-Thu 9pm-3am, Fri-Sat 9pm-4am.* ⊟ Egelantiersgracht 12 (1e Egelantiersdwarsstr.), 623-9617

Café Wildschut* • Museumplein • Pub/Tavern

Best After-Work Drinks The terrace and the Jugendstil-Art Nouveau interior continue to make this long-standing grand cafe a perennial hotspot for thirsty locals who like to drink with a splash of classic style. From local businessmen to students, international visitors, and the pre-concert crowd—the Concertgebouw, home of the Royal Dutch Symphony is a short stroll away—everyone drops by, and during the extra-crowded "happy hours," they might all show up at once. Come for after-work drinks, and on weekend afternoons and evenings to see Wildschut at its best, and try to score a window-side table. *See Classic Restaurants, p.116. Mon-Thu 9am-1am, Fri 9am-3am, Sat 10am-2am, Sun 10am-1am.* ⊟ Roelof Hartplein 1-3 (Cornelis Anthoniszstr.), 676-8220

Ciel Bleu Bar* • De Pijp • Hotel Bar

Best Hotel Bars Some of Amsterdam's best drinks come with an added bonus: a panoramic view that's arguably the best in town. The Amstel River, the residential southern neighborhoods, and even the harbor can be spotted from this bar on the 23rd floor of the Okura Hotel that's popular with the city's business crowd, mature and deep-pocketed tourists, and those dining at the Ciel Bleu* restaurant (see p.116) next door. Save your visit for a fair-weather day or, better yet, for dusk when sunsets give the vista an added touch of color. *Daily 6pm-1am.* ⊟ The Okura Hotel, Ferdinand Bolstraat 333 (Jozef Israelskade), 678-7111, okura.nl

Cristofori Salon • Jordaan • Live Music

Best Jazz Scenes Known for hosting classical recitals, Cristofori's also hosts a lesser known, but equally popular Sunday Jazz series. Sunday concerts are mellow affairs characterized in part by great music, and in part by the charming setting: What's now an intimate and plush canalside performance space was once a 17th-century tobacco warehouse. *Sun 8:30pm.* ⊆⊟ Prinsengracht 581-583 (Runstr.), reservations 624-4969, cristofori.nl

De Drie Fleschjes • Nieuwe Zijde • Bar

The "Three Little Bottles" has been open since 1650 and judging by the looks of things, little has changed. Those interested in authenticity will appreciate the wall of wooden casks opposite the bar—it used to be a distillery—and the numbers of casual locals who frequent the space at happy hour, adding character by the truckload. *Jenever*, Dutch liquors, and spirits are the drinks of choice, but a small but passable selection of wines will satisfy the less adventurous. *Mon-Sat noon-8:30pm, Sun 3-8pm.* ⊟ Gravenstraat 18 (Blaeustr.), 624-8443

De Duvel* • De Pijp • Pub/Tavern

The name is a variation on "the devil" but the nightlife at this local eatery is positively angelic: Good-looking, friendly locals spill off of the patio and into the street. Show up mid-late evening and don't dress up too much: The 25-45 year old crowd's idea of a good time is a beer or glass of wine, some good conversation, and a cozy and welcoming vibe. Check your attitude at the door, order yourself a Heineken, settle in for the night, and make a few friends. *See Classic Restaurants, p.117. Sun-Fri 11am-1am, Sat 11am-3am.* ≣ 1e v.d. Helststraat 59-61 (Daniël Stalpertstr.), 675-7517, deduvel.nl

Het Proeflokaal Wynand Fockink • Nieuwe Zijde • Bar

Best Dutch Drinking The name of this "tasting bar" suggests an evening of wild debauchery although in truth, the atmosphere in this 400-year-old room is quite civilized. The mostly well-dressed and professional 30-plus crowd packs the room—literally—at happy hour, as much to sip spirits, liquors, and the ubiquitous *jenevers* (Dutch gins), as they do for conversation. The crowd knows its history and its booze, so if you don't know your *advocaat* from your *hemeltje* ask the bartender to guide you through the menu or hit a friendly regular up for a tip. *Mon-Sun 4-9pm.* ≣ Pijlsteeg 31 (Oudezijds Voorburgwal), 639-2695

Holland Casino • Canal Belt • Casino

700 slot machines, a VIP area, 55 gaming tables—including roulette, blackjack, poker, and punto banco—and a late-night restaurant, all make this casino an entertaining destination. Ladies get free drinks on Wednesdays, and on weekends guests listen to live bands in the Lido Club. Cars, diamonds, and other luxury prizes are given away weekly, and of course there's always the chance to strike it rich. Note: Visitors entering a casino must present a passport as identification. *Daily 1:30pm-3am, restaurant until 2am nightly, live music Fri-Sat 8pm-2am.* ℂ꤭ Max Euweplein 62 (Weteringschans), 521-1111, hollandcasino.com

In 't Aepjen • Oude Zijde • Bar

Located in one of the two remaining wooden houses in the city, this watering hole has over 450 years of history, and charm to match. The name means "In Little Monkeys" and legend has it that when it was a sailor's inn, primates from the Dutch East Indies were accepted as payment. That nautical past is trotted out every Saturday night when an accordionist plays ye olde sea shanties. *Sun-Thu 3pm-1am, Fri-Sat 3pm-3am.* ≣ Zeedijk 1 (Warmoesstr.), 626-8401

In de Waag* • Oude Zijde • Lounge

A beautiful terrace and a building that looks like a small castle make this a charming spot to eat, and also to enjoy a cocktail at any time of day or evening. *See Classic Restaurants, p.118, for details. Daily 10am-10:30pm.* ≣ Nieuwmarkt 4 (Geldersekade), 422-7772, indewaag.nl

Jazzcafé Alto • Canal Belt • Jazz Club

Best Jazz Scenes For an unpretentious, sometimes raucous jazz joint, Alto tops the list. A broad audience turns out nightly to hear famous—and less famous—artists, but aficionados shouldn't expect anything alternative as the music is as mainstream as the crowd. Nevertheless, it's hard to beat this small dark room where friendliness makes up for the lackluster décor. Local jazz legend Hans Dulfer plays a regular gig on Wednesdays. *Sun-Thu 9pm-3am, Fri-Sat 9pm-4am.* ≣ Korte Leidsedwarsstraat 115 (Leidsestr.), 626-3249, jazz-cafe-alto.nl

't Kalfje* • Jordaan • Bar

Best Late-Night Scenes This spot heats up after midnight with one of the area's only late-night kitchens, and a lively bar crowd as well. If you're eating, stick to the basics. *See Classic Restaurants, p.118, for details. Mon-Thu 4pm-3am, Fri-Sun 4pm-4am.* ☰ Prinsenstraat 5 (Keizersgracht), 626-3370

Reijnders • Canal Belt • Pub/Tavern

Though it's located in the middle of Amsterdam's tourist ground zero, Reijnders stands out from the crowd by retaining an aura of charm and authenticity, while rarely conforming to tourist-trap clichés. Eat elsewhere, but come for a drink as waiters dressed in traditional black and white garb, high ceilings, and a glassed front that allows access to a street-front terrace in good weather, make this a perfect spot for people-watching. *Sun-Thu 9am-1am, Fri-Sat 9am-3am.* ☰ Leidseplein 6 (Leidsestr), 623-4419, hoopman.nl

De Still • Nieuwe Zijde • Bar

Even the most determined whiskey fan could never work their way through the 150-plus brands on hand at De Still. The 30-something-and-up regulars store their bottles-in-progress behind the bar while neophytes order from tasting menus. Aficionados can order a la carte or allow Bas, the resident whiskey guru, to surprise them with obscure drinks. Usually crowded, often smoky, and always friendly, it's a must. *Sun-Thu 3pm-1am, Fri 5pm-3am, Sat 3pm-3am.* ☰ Spuistraat 326 (Mosterdpotsteeg), 427-6809

Theater Casa Rosso • Oude Zijde • Sex Show

Best Sex-in-the-City A handful of live sex shows contribute to Amsterdam's reputation as an "anything-goes" destination, so if it's vicarious hedonism you're after, a visit to Casa Rosso is sure to satisfy your deepest curiosities. It offers a slightly elevated experience, and while many of these theaters are the domain of stag parties and conventioneers, Casa Rosso hosts the lion's share of curious couples. Witness a one-hour show—featuring performers alone and in any number of combinations—and you'll return home with some travel stories that are sure to get the attention of your friends. *Sun-Thu 8pm-2am, Fri-Sat 8pm-3am.* Ⓒ☰ Oudezijds Achterburgwal 106-108 (Stoofsteeg), 627-8954, janot.nl

Twee Prinsen • Jordaan • Bar

The popular-with-the-locals "Two Princes" cafe has a lively atmosphere and staff that are among the friendliest in the city, making it the ideal destination for your first foray into the local pub scene. Large windows, an attractive mosaic floor, and the omnipresent wooden interior lend an authentic vibe to the room, while outside you'll find an all too rare Amsterdam treasure—a heated terrace that's perfect when the autumn chills set in. *Sun-Thu 10am-1am, Fri-Sat 10am-3am.* ☰ Prinsenstraat 27 (Keizersgracht), 624-9722

De Twee Zwaantjes • Jordaan • Bar

With a canal-side terrace, traditional décor, and a crowd made up of locals that spans as many generations as it does styles, this intimate bar offers visitors a great opportunity to experience a charming and authentic view of Amsterdam. Characters pack the room beyond capacity and beer flows freely, but the big draw is the impromptu weekend sing-alongs that feature traditional Dutch songs. *Sun-Tue and Thu 3pm-1am, Fri-Sat 3pm-3am.* ☰ Prinsengracht 114 (Egelantiersgracht), 625-2729

Classic Amsterdam:
The Attractions

Amstel Hotel Health Club • Plantage • Spa
It's dedicated to serving the needs of the Amstel Hotel guests—read; the visiting elite—and it more than fits the bill. A 15-meter pool, sauna, Turkish bath, Jacuzzi, cold plunge pool, solarium, health bar, and a handful of massage rooms make the Amstel Hotel's fitness space one of the city's best. Factor in the river-view workout room, fitness instructors, and spa treatments, and hitting the hotel gym has never looked so good. *Mon-Fri 7am-11pm, Sat-Sun 8am-10pm.* € The Amstel Hotel, Professor Tulpplein 1 (Sarphatistr.), 622-6060, amsterdam.intercontinental.com

Amsterdam Historical Museum • Nieuwe Zijde • History Museum
Best Historic Sites This large collection of documents, paintings, archaeological objects, and prints illustrates Amsterdam's growth from medieval fishing village to the world-class city it is today. Temporary exhibitions, on themes like the German occupation of the city or Amsterdam's struggle against flooding, complement the permanent exhibits—highlights include the reconstructed 't Mandje, the world's first gay bar, and period fashion—but even those who elect to pass on the museum proper can still get a small dose of history at no cost. In the museum courtyard, tiny lockers are the last obvious signs of the building's former use as an orphanage, and the adjacent Civic Guard Gallery is one of the city's most unique alleyways: Golden Age paintings line the walls. *Mon-Fri 10am-5pm, Sat-Sun 11am-5pm.* € Nieuwezijds Voorburgwal 357 (Wijde Kapelsteeg), 523-1822, ahm.nl

Anne Frank House • Jordaan • Historic Site
Best Historic Sites Touring the secret hiding place of Amsterdam's most famous citizen, Anne Frank, is an inspiring yet solemn affair: Anne's original diary (on display here) shows the strength of the human spirit, while the pencil marking growth chart—still visible on one wall of the secret annex—reminds us that the diminutive Anne, and her sister, Margot, died so young. Most visitors come to see the legendary place where eight people hid for more than two years, but the adjacent museum has documents and temporary exhibitions on themes like "Freedom & Democracy" that address the more theoretical questions raised by the visit to the annex. *Apr-Aug 9am-9pm; Sept-Mar 9am-7pm; closed Yom Kippur.* € Prinsengracht 267 (Westermarkt), 556-7105, annefrank.nl

ARTTRA Cultural Agency • Jordaan • Guided Tour
Best Guided Tours For those wanting to immerse themselves deeply in Amsterdam's rich artistic scene, the folks at ARTTRA can open doors to private collections and historical locations that are otherwise closed to the visiting public. All of ARTTRA professional guides are academically trained art historians, and while you can select a pre-planned tour, you can also have one tailor-made to your preferences and interests. *By appointment.* €€€€+ Tweede Boomdwarsstraat 4 (Boomstr.), 625-9303, arttra.nl

Begijnhof • Nieuwe Zijde • Historic Site

Best Historic Sites This enclosed courtyard was built in the 14th century to house religious women and remains one of Amsterdam's most picturesque settings. Beautiful houses, including the city's oldest surviving residence, Het Houten Huis (The Wooden House), overlook a well-kept garden. Two historic churches are also located here: The 15th-century Protestant "English Church" and the "clandestine" Catholic chapel that dates back to the 17th-century when Catholicism was driven underground. Today the Begijnhof (as it's called in Dutch) houses are still occupied by single women and visitors are asked to respect their privacy and to be mindful when taking photos. *Daily 9am-5pm.* Entry off Gedempte Begijnensloot (Spui), 622-1918, begijnhofamsterdam.nl

City Picnic (Café Vertigo) • Museumplein • Park

Forget dining al fresco. Try barefoot in the park for your perfect respite from the city streets. Stop in at Café Vertigo, pick up a gourmet picnic basket, and head to the scenic Vondelpark, Amsterdam's largest and most adored greenspace. The "City Lovers" basket features delicacies like fine cheeses, fresh strawberries, paté, champagne, croissants, and chorizo, and the classic wicker baskets include cutlery, glasses, a tartan blanket, and candles for those wanting to add an element of romance to the occasion. *Available Apr-Oct by reservation only.* €€€ Vondelpark 3 (R. Visscherstr.), 616-8727, citypicknick.nl

Coffeeshop de Dampkring • Nieuwe Zijde • Coffeeshop

Best Coffeeshops This is an old-school spot that knows both its clientele and its cannabis. Don't expect a chic setting, but if you've come for that menu behind the counter, you won't be disappointed. When the cast of *Ocean's Twelve* was in town, they were known to make an appearance or two here, but most days, you'll just find the very mellow locals. As an added plus, they serve booze. *Daily 10am-1am.* Handboogstraat 29 (Heiligeweg), 638-0705

Dutch Flowers • Jordaan • Coffeeshop

Best Coffeeshops They've got cigars, but that's not what most patrons are smoking. This is a great place to check out exotic varieties of Amsterdam's favorite herb, all while lounging on a pretty outdoor patio and enjoying a drink—yes, this is also one of the city's few coffeeshops that serves liquor. *Sun-Thu 10am-1am, Fri-Sat 10am-2am.* Singel 387 (Heisteeg), 624-7624

Dutch Resistance Museum • Plantage • History Museum

The occupation of the Netherlands by Germany during World War II is undoubtedly the low point in Dutch history, and this museum documents that era in exhibitions that are a must for armchair historians and anyone interested in remembering important past events. Primary documents, film and audio clips, propaganda posters, photographs, and personal accounts retell the story of Holland's darkest days, while an accurate re-creation of a city alleyway attempts to capture the atmosphere in the streets. From the German invasion to the Dutch capitulation and resistance, the story is laid out in fascinating detail—even including the post-war dilemma of dealing with wartime collaborators. *Tue-Fri 10am-5pm, Sat-Mon and public holidays noon-5pm.* € Plantage Kerklaan 61 (Plantage Muidergracht), 620-2535, verzetsmuseum.org

Flower Market (Bloemenmarkt) • Rembrandtplein • Market
Best Outdoor Markets Look closely and you'll see that this fragrant and colorful market is not on solid ground; situated on a row of houseboats, it's the only floating flower market in the world. Open year round, the market sells cut flowers and bulbs to locals and tourists alike, and not surprisingly, tulips hold pride of place. Many bulbs are pre-approved for export to North America, but if you want to take some home with you, ask before you buy. *Daily 9am-8pm.* The Singel canal between the Koningsplein and the Muntplein

Hermitage Amsterdam • Plantage • Art Museum
Dedicated to exhibitions on loan from Russia, Amsterdam's newest permanent museum is a satellite branch of St. Petersburg's famous Hermitage Museum. Although it's a relatively recent addition to Amsterdam, well-received exhibitions of Venetian art, the personal collections of Nicholas and Alexandria, and art from Byzantium and Jerusalem suggest that this small museum will have a powerful impact on Amsterdam's cultural landscape. *Daily 10am-5pm.* € Nieuwe Herengracht 14 (Amstel), 530-8755, hermitage.nl

Holland International Boat Tours • Various • Guided Tours
Best On-the-Water You'll want to experience Amsterdam's gorgeous canals from the water, and Holland International's comfortable canal boats offer the perfect vantage point. Most of the narrated tours last one hour, sticking to the canal belt and taking in the major sights, but specialty tours offering wine and cheese by candlelight, or focusing on contemporary architecture, are longer in duration and stray farther from the city centre. No matter which tour you opt for, you'll want to score one of the outdoor seats at the rear of the boat, especially if you're looking to take some memorable photographs of your voyage. *Daily, Apr-Oct 10am-10pm; Nov-Mar 10am-6pm; sailings every 30 min; architecture tours Sat at 11am only.* €€ Prins Hendrikkade 33a (Damrak), 622-7788; Plantage Kerklaan 61 (Plantage Muidergracht), Plantage, 620-2535, hir.nl

Hortus Botanicus • Plantage • Botanical Gardens
For visitors with an interest in plants that reaches beyond "coffeeshops" and their wares, the city's botanic garden is not only an interesting attraction, but an oasis of tranquility as well. Founded in 1638 to supply the city with medicinal herbs, the collection grew with Dutch trade networks. Today, over 4,000 varieties of plants are on display. Flora from former colonies like Indonesia, Suriname, and the Western Cape of South Africa lend an exotic touch to what is one of the oldest public gardens in the world. *Mon-Fri 9am-5pm, Sat-Sun 10am-5pm, July and Aug until 9pm.* € Plantage Middenlaan 2 (Plantage Parklaan), 625-9021, dehortus.nl

Jewish Historical Museum • Oude Zijde • History Museum
The Jewish history of Amsterdam is a rich one, and this museum documents its highs and lows. Photographs, ephemera, objects, and works of art on display illustrate the religious and cultural identity of Jews in the Netherlands. Of particular interest are the celebrated works of artist and Auschwitz victim Charlotte Salomon, as well as Master paintings relating to Judaic themes, and fascinating large-scale exhibits like 2006's "The 'Jewish' Rembrandt." *Daily 11am-5pm.* € Nieuwe Amstelstraat 1 (Turfsteeg), 531-0310, jhm.nl

CLASSIC

Looier Art and Antique Centre • Jordaan • Market
This daily indoor antique market, the largest in the Netherlands, has large shops and 72 smaller stands that ensure that there's an incredible array of items on display: Porcelain and ceramics, prints, jewelry, furnishings, and toys are only a few of the diverse offerings on hand, and an on-site cafe offers weary shoppers a place to rest their feet. If you're looking for an original Rembrandt print, though, save your time and head to the rarified shops of the Spiegelkwatier. *Sat-Thu 11am-5pm.* Elandsgracht 109 (1e Looiersdwarsstr.), 624-9038, looier.nl

Museum Van Loon • Jordaan • Historic Site
Had "Lifestyles of the Rich and Famous" broadcast in the 17th century, surely this double-wide canal house with 14 elegantly appointed rooms would have made the cut. The period home now houses a gorgeous collection of personal items compiled from the estate of one of Holland's wealthiest patrician families. Highlights include family portraits, ornate signed furniture, porcelain, silverware, and a beautiful garden. *July-Aug daily 11am-5pm, Sept-June Fri-Mon 11am-5pm.* € Keizersgracht 672 (Leidsegracht), 624-5255, museumvanloon.nl

Museum Willet-Holthuysen • Canal Belt • Historic Site
When Louisa Holthuysen died in 1895, she left her gorgeous canal house, its contents, and her husband's significant art collection to the city of Amsterdam on the condition that her home would become a museum. Today, that home is the only fully furnished 19th-century house on Amsterdam's canals that's open daily to the public. In addition to providing a glimpse into aristocratic life during the 18th and 19th centuries, it offers an annual agenda of exhibitions focused on 19th-century life. Fashion, illustration, jewelry, crafts, and art all appear on the museum's program. *Mon-Fri 10am-5pm, Sat-Sun 11am-5pm.* € Herengracht 605 (Utrechtsestr.), 523-1822, willetholthuysen.nl

Nieuwe Kerk • Nieuwe Zijde • Art Museum
Along with the Royal Palace, this picturesque church dominates the Dam Square, and when it's not hosting royal functions like coronations or weddings, the "New Church" is home to large-scale temporary exhibitions. Most are fascinating, showcasing treasures from foreign cultures and countries, and lately the agenda has broadened to include exhibitions that focus on "world religions," making it one of Amsterdam's most well-attended museums. *Daily 10am-6pm during exhibitions.* € Dam Square (Mozes en Aaronstr.), 638-6909, nieuwekerk.nl

Oude Kerk • Oude Zijde • Historic Site
Since the early 13th century when it was built, the "Old Church" has grown from a single-aisled chapel into a massive basilica, and its role in the city has changed from house of worship to burial site to cultural center. Today the oldest church in Amsterdam hosts organ concerts and art exhibitions in a medieval setting, complete with gravestones (some belonging to famous residents like Rembrandt's wife, Saskia), and soaring stained-glass windows that evoke the building's rich history. *Mon-Sat 11am-5pm, Sun 1-5pm.* € Note: Concerts and exhibitions may have an extra charge. Oudekerksplein 23 (Oudezijds Voorburgwal), 625-8284, oudekerk.nl

Rembrandt House • Oude Zijde • Art Museum
Rembrandt's life is the focus of this museum located in his former house. The 17th-century home contains furnishings that are typical of that era, as well as paintings from Rembrandt's own collection—he was such an avid collector that

it brought about his bankruptcy—and static displays are supplemented with live demonstrations. In Rembrandt's former graphic workshop, visitors can watch demonstrations on etching and printmaking, while upstairs in the artist's reconstructed studio, paint-making demonstrations illuminate Rembrandt's craft. A modern annex contains a broad collection of prints and etchings from the artist's own hand. *Mon-Sat 10am-5pm, Sun 11am-5pm.* € Jodenbreestraat 4-6 (Houtkopersdwarsstr.), 520-0400, rembrandthuis.nl

Rijksmuseum • Museumplein • Art Museum
Best Art Museums Anyone with even the slightest interest in classic art should bump the Netherlands' national museum to the top of their Amsterdam agenda. Its collection is considered among the best in the world, and although the museum is being renovated until Dec 2008, the ongoing "Masterpieces" exhibit keeps the most well-known paintings on display. Vermeer's *The Kitchen Maid*, and *The Jewish Bride* and *The Night Watch*, both by Rembrandt, are the top draws, but even the lesser-known works from the Netherlands' Golden Age are standouts, and works by Frans Hals, Jan Steen, and van Ruisdael shouldn't be missed. *Daily 9am-6pm, Fri until 10pm.* €€ Jan Luijkenstraat 1 (Hobbemastr.), 674-7000, rijksmuseum.nl

Royal Palace • Nieuwe Zijde • Historic Site
Situated on the Dam Square in the center of Amsterdam, the Royal Palace was built to serve as Amsterdam's city hall, and once was home to Louis Napoleon—his famous collection of Empire furniture is still on display—before becoming one of three palaces available to the reigning Dutch monarch. Nowadays, it's used for official state functions like the Queen's New Year reception and the awarding of royal prizes. Painters like Rembrandt and Ferdinand Bol added their touches to the inside of the palace, and fine sculpture and stonework can be found throughout. *July-Aug daily 11am-5pm, Sept-June Tue-Thu and Sat-Sun 12:30-5pm. Free guided tours in English at 2pm on Wed and Sun, in July-Aug only. Note: The palace is still in use and is subject to closure for special events; call ahead.* € Dam Square (Paleisstr.), 620-4060, koninklijkhuis.nl

Scheepvaart Museum (Netherlands Maritime) • Oude Zijde • Museum
The Netherlands' maritime tradition is documented in paintings, models, antique instruments, and full-scale ships at this museum located in the 300-year-old former arsenal of the Dutch Navy. Visitors of all ages will enjoy learning about Holland's history of overseas trade, the role that shipping played in the Golden Age, the importance of the VOC (Dutch East India Company), and the Netherlands' colonial past. Plan to spend an hour. *Mid-June–mid-Sept daily 10am-5pm, mid-Sept–mid-June Tue-Sun 10am-5pm.* € Kattenburgerplein 1 (Prins Hendrikkade), 523-2222, scheepvaartmuseum.nl

Tropenmuseum • Plantage • Cultural Museum
Holland's colonial past sparked a Dutch fascination with other cultures, and this museum explores that interest. Permanent collections like "Art, Culture, and Colonialism" and "Music and Theatre" are augmented with temporary ones like "20th-Century Surinamese Painting." Of course, the cultures of former Dutch colonies like Indonesia, the Dutch Antilles, Suriname, and the Western Cape of South Africa feature heavily, but exhibitions like "The Golden Age of Islam" ensure that the museum isn't too Dutch-centric in its scope. *Daily 10am-5pm.* € Linnaeusstraat 2 (Mauritskade), 568-8215, kit.nl

Van Gogh Museum • Museumplein • Art Museum

Best Art Museums The world's largest collection of Van Gogh's work is on display at this modern museum, housed in two noteworthy buildings, and it's a classic art lover's dream. Paintings and sketches are arranged chronologically, and also according to periods in the artist's life, so those looking to understand the collection's context will find it. *Sunflowers*, *The Potato Eaters*, and *Self-Portrait as an Artist* are the most famous works on display among many others, and the large museum is bound to surprise as lesser-known works like the artist's attempts at Japanese-style painting are also on display, showing the depth, and virtuosity of—arguably—history's finest painter. *Sat-Thu 10am-6pm, Fri 10am-10pm.* €€ Paulus Potterstraat 7 (Van de Veldestr.), 570-5200, vangoghmuseum.nl

Westerkerk • Jordaan • Church

The largest Protestant church in the Netherlands has a long and storied past, earning it a special place in the heart of locals. Rembrandt is buried inside (his grave is anonymous so don't bother looking for it) and the bells of the church tower are mentioned in Anne Frank's diary. In addition to its reputation as a lookout spot—those who climb the church tower are rewarded with some of Amsterdam's best canal views—the church is known for an agenda of music events. *Apr-Sept 11am-5pm.* Note: Some events have an admission charge. Prinsengracht 281 (Westerstr.), 624-7766, westerkerk.nl

Yellow Bike Tours • Nieuwe Zijde • Guided Tour

Best Guided Tours Amsterdam is a cyclist's paradise, and riding a bike through the city's streets and along its scenic canals is the first step towards calling yourself an insider. Yellow Bike's three-hour guided city tour takes up to 12 people to many of the city's highlights, offering a basic orientation to the city, and it's the perfect way to start your visit. They also offer a 6.5-hour country village tour, if you find yourself wanting a taste of rural Holland complete with dikes and polders (land reclaimed from the sea). When you muster up the courage to bike the streets without a guide, check out MacBikes (see p.102); Yellow Bike doesn't have rentals. *Daily 8:30am-5:30pm.* €€ Nieuwezijds Kolk 29 (Nieuwezijds Voorburgwal), 620-6940, yellowbike.nl

PRIME TIME
AMSTERDAM

Everything in life is timing (with a dash of serendipity thrown in). Would you want to arrive in Pamplona, Spain, the day *after* the Running of the Bulls? Not if you have a choice and you relish being a part of life's peak experiences. With our month-by-month calendar of events, there's no excuse to miss out on any of Amsterdam's greatest moments. From the classic to the quirky, you'll find all you need to know about the city's best events right here.

Prime Time Basics

Eating and Drinking

Locals rarely sit down for breakfast, but lunch is about noon-1pm, dinner as early as 7pm, and Sunday brunch at noon. Cocktails are enjoyed before dinner (around 6pm), but some bars, notably those with an after-work crowd, can get busy as early as 5:30pm. While bars fill up around 10pm, nightclubs won't heat up until 1am. Many places serve finger food late into the night, and while there are a few restaurants serving full menus late, most will have wrapped things up by 10 or 11pm.

Weather and Tourism

Holland is on the North Sea and it's a very flat country with no natural features to break up winds: Things can get breezy but the weather is rarely extreme—think consistently mild. It's not often freezing cold in Amsterdam, and it's only occasionally hot and humid. Rain is spread fairly evenly throughout the year, and as a result there's not much point in trying to avoid it. It can get chilly in the summer, and those who do visit then contend with Amsterdam's largest crowds and peak hotel rates.

Dec-Feb: Winter can be quite cool (37°F, 3°C on average in January), windy, and wet, but the museums are invitingly quiet, hotel rates are at their lowest, and the crowds are at their smallest: You won't battle long line-ups, and you won't jockey for position to view the Van Goghs. If you're lucky and the canals freeze over during your visit, you'll witness the Dutch passion for skating.

Seasonal Changes

Month	Celsius		Fahrenheit		Hotel
	Low	High	Low	High	Rates
Jan.	1	5	33	42	L
Feb.	0	6	32	43	L
Mar.	2	9	36	49	S
Apr.	4	12	39	54	S
May	8	17	46	63	S
June	10	19	51	67	H
July	13	21	55	71	H
Aug.	12	22	54	71	H
Sept.	10	18	50	65	S
Oct.	7	14	45	57	S
Nov.	4	14	39	49	S
Dec.	2	6	35	44	L

H-High Season, S-Shoulder, L-Low

Mar-May: Spring tends to be slightly colder and wetter than the autumn, and visitors benefit from shoulder-season hotel rates. With the exception of Queen's Day, crowds are virtually non-existent, and for those hoping to see flowers, this is the season of choice: April for daffodils, May for tulips.

June-Aug: Most tourists visit Amsterdam in summer and it's difficult to argue with that logic. When the sun is out, the city comes alive, buzzing with energy, and it's undeniably the best time of the year to hang out on a terrace overlooking the canals.

Sept-Nov: In addition to enjoying shoulder-season hotel rates and low crowds, visitors can enjoy mild weather well into October. By the end of October, local residents expect the weather to take a turn for the colder and wetter, but clear and sunny stretches are still possible.

National Holidays • Nationale Feestdagen

New Year's Day • Nieuwjaarsdag	January 1
Good Friday • Goede Vrijdag	The Friday before Easter Sunday
Easter Sunday • Eerste Paasdag	The first Sunday after the first full moon in spring
Easter Monday • Tweede Paasdag	The day after Easter Sunday
Queen's Birthday • Koninginnedag	April 30
Liberation Day • Bevrijdingsdag	May 5
Ascension Day • Hemelvaartsdag	Forty days after Easter Sunday
Whit Sunday • Eerste Pinksterdag	Seven weeks after Easter
Whit Monday • Tweede Pinksterdag	The day after Whit Sunday
Christmas Day • Eerste Kerstdag	December 25
Boxing Day • Tweede Kerstdag	December 26

Listings in blue are major celebrations but not official holidays.

The Best Events Calendar

January	February	March
• Jumping Amsterdam	• Maastricht Carnaval	• TEFAF European Fine Art Fair

April	May	June
• Koninginnedag - Queen's Day	• Dodenherdenking · Remembrance Day & Bevrijdingsdag · Liberation Day • KunstRAI	• Amsterdam Roots Festival • Dutch TT Assen • Holland Festival • Open Garden Days • Parkpop

July	August	September
• Amsterdam Tournament • Julidans - July Dance • North Sea Jazz Festival • Summer (Zomer) Carnival • White Sensation and Black Sensation	• Amsterdam Pride • Dance Valley • FFWD Heineken Parade • Grachtenfestival • Preuvenemint • Uitmarkt • Utrecht Festival	• Aalsmeer Bloemencorso • Jordaan Festival

October	November	December
	• The Cannabis Cup • Int'l. Documentary Film Festival • Museumnacht - Museum Night • Pictura Antiquairs Nationaal (PAN)	• New Year's Eve

The Night+Day's Top Five Events are in blue.
High Season is from June-Aug. represented by blue background.

The Best Events

January

Jumping Amsterdam

RAI Convention Center and other venues, 465-5446, jumping-amsterdam.nl

The Lowdown: When the Dutch horsey-set plays host to international equestrians, €300,000 is up for grabs. This World Cup event is the highlight of the Netherlands' horse calendars. In addition to the equine competitions that are centered on the RAI, off-site fashion shows and concerts offer entertaining evenings. *The last weekend in January, usually beginning on the last Thursday.* Tickets €10, event pass €100, World Cup €35.

February

Maastricht Carnaval

Various locations in Maastricht, 465-5446, jumping-amsterdam.nl

The Lowdown: Rio has Carnival, New Orleans has Mardi Gras, and Maastricht has Carnaval. Sure, other Dutch cities share in the celebrations, but Maastricht, the Netherlands' most Catholic city, puts on the best show. From the kick off parade on Sunday, to the slightly more family-oriented parade on Monday, beer flows like water and being silly is the name of the game. Floats, costumes, and sing-alongs are hallmarks of events Still need convincing? The three days of non-stop partying are so fun that locals ditch work, and over 100,000 people flood the streets. *The Sunday before Ash Wednesday until Shrove Tuesday, three days later.* Free.

March

TEFAF European Fine Art Fair

Maastricht Exhibition and Congress Centre, 041-164-5090, tefaf.com

The Lowdown: Wanna buy a Vermeer? With 200 leading art dealers in 290,000 square feet of exhibition space, the Fine Art Fair is the world's most prestigious art and antiques swap meet. As you'd expect, if you're in the market for a Flemish or Dutch master, TEFAF is the place to find it as well as African and Egyptian pieces, manuscripts, textiles, ephemera, musical instruments, jewelry, porcelain, furniture from every era; the list is endless and it's all for sale. The Thursday invitation-only advance viewing is the best time to be there, but the opening night is a good runner-up. *The second week in March, usually beginning on Thursday.* €40 (including catalog) or €60 for two.

April

Koninginnedag • Queen's Day
Museumplein, Dam Square, Jordaan, Vondelpark, everywhere else

The Lowdown: Ribald, a little drunken, and wholly good natured, Queen's Day is the can't-miss street party of the highest order and worth planning your Amsterdam visit around. The Dutch are notoriously indifferent toward their royal family, but every April 30 the streets of Amsterdam become a sea of orange colors as locals go crazy, dress in ridiculous costumes, and celebrate the ascension of Queen Beatrix to the throne. Concerts, street parties, fireworks, and what is surely the planet's largest spontaneous flea market all add up to the premier event on Amsterdam's fun calendar. Although the official date is April 30, the best night to join the fun is the evening before. *April 30.* Free.

May

Dodenherdenking • Remembrance Day & Bevrijdingsdag • Liberation Day
Museumplein, Dam Square, Westerpark, and various locations throughout the country

The Lowdown: World War II marked the low point in Dutch history and every year two consecutive days, the first solemn and the second joyous, are dedicated to remembrance. On May 4th, the Queen heads to the Dam Square where she lays a wreath on the National Monument, and at 8pm, two minutes of silence are observed nationwide—the entire country grinds to a halt, trains included. On May 5th, attention turns to celebrating the liberation of the country in May of 1945. Large concerts are held in most cities and impromptu street markets ensure that good-spirited fun rounds out the schedule, but Amsterdam's Dam Square is the focus of ceremonies. *May 4-5.* Free.

KunstRAI
RAI Convention Centre, 549-1212, kunstrai.nl

The Lowdown: The Netherlands is a hotbed of modern arts, and the 22-year-old KunstRAI, Amsterdam's annual contemporary arts fair, has established a strong reputation for showcasing new international talent alongside dealers selling post-1945 works. Lectures and interactive exhibits lend appeal to the event, and if you're unfamiliar with the world of contemporary art but are curious to learn about building a collection of your own, take advantage of the "Beginning Collectors" program. But don't miss opening night whatever you do. *The first or second Wednesday in May, until the following Sunday.* €15.

June

Amsterdam Roots Festival

Oosterpark and various locations, 531-8181, amsterdamroots.nl

The Lowdown: Bust a move global-style! The top musical artists from Africa, South America, Asia, and the Caribbean supply the worldbeat grooves in Amsterdam's best music venues. In the Oosterpark, up-and-comers give free concerts to the more adventurous. Listening to such diverse styles as the Afro-Cuban, Rai, and African percussion groups on hand, you're bound to expand your musical horizons, but in case the music doesn't get you thinking, a small but thought-provoking line-up of seminars on topics like globalization will. *Third week in June, beginning on Saturday.* Free–€35.

Dutch TT Assen

Circuit Assen, tt-assen.com

The Lowdown: Sure it's a day trip from Amsterdam, but if you've got the need for speed, head out to Assen and watch grand prix motorbikes scream past at more than 140 miles per hour. Each year over 100,000 international race fans gather to watch the Touring Trophy (TT), the Dutch leg of the world championship. With no Formula 1 race in Holland, this race is the highpoint of the country's motor racing calendar. *Third weekend in June.* €85.

Holland Festival

Various locations including the main concert and theatre halls, 788-2100, hollandfestival.nl

The Lowdown: As if to emphasize Amsterdam's reputation as a cultural mecca, the month-long Holland Festival, the largest arts festival in the low countries, offers it all. Following opening night gala performances, the festival celebrates theatre, music, dance, opera, film, and art (both Western and non-Western), and for more than 55 years, Europe's cultural cognoscenti have joined in the party. Performances tend to draw arts fans with adventurous but classical leanings. *Month long.* Individual tickets free–€85.

Open Garden Days

Various locations on city canals, 320-3660, canalmuseums.nl/en

The Lowdown: If you are smitten with canal houses and you'd like to have a closer look, Open Garden Days gives you that rare chance. Over 30 private canal houses, many dating back to the 17th century, open their beautiful gardens to the public for a once-a-year look. Boat tours stop at key houses, and such civilized activities as wine tasting and classical recitals make for a sophisticated weekend with rare behind-the-scenes access. *Third weekend in June.* €12.

Parkpop

Zuiderpark, The Hague, parkpop.nl

The Lowdown: Like music and crowds? Head over to Parkpop. It's Europe's largest free-of-charge, day-long, open-air music festival, and each year over 375,000 fans—most of them under 30—show up to groove to the sounds of big-name, quality talent. Past performers include Hugh Masekela, INXS, The The, Shaggy, and Dave Matthews, and the recent addition of a side stage means that the music, and the fun, is non-stop. *The last Sunday in June.* Free.

July

Amsterdam Tournament

Amsterdam Arena, Southeast Amsterdam, amsterdamtournament.nl

The Lowdown: Ajax, Amsterdam's professional *voetbal* team is one of the most storied in Europe, and scoring a ticket for a regular season game can prove virtually impossible. Thanks to the weekend-long Amsterdam Tournament, fans are afforded a rare opportunity to see the home side taking on top clubs from South America, England, and continental Europe. With plenty of beer-fueled singing and chanting, it's soccer at its best. *The last weekend in July.* €27-55 per day (2 games).

Julidans • July Dance

The Leidseplein and main theater venues, 523-7716, julidans.com

The Lowdown: Holland's only summer dance festival showcases performances featuring the world's elite dancers and choreographers. With a mandate to include performances of "non-Western origin," Julidans has a reputation for surprising diversity; African and Asian dance troupes are well represented as is urban dance, while the presence of film and other visual media give the program an interdisciplinary touch. *The first two weeks of July.* €-€€€

North Sea Jazz Festival

Rotterdam (moved from The Hague after 2005), northseajazz.nl

The Lowdown: If your idea of musical genius is summed up in the names of Oscar Peterson, Dave Brubeck, and Wynton Marsalis, get your funk on and make the pilgrimage to the North Sea Jazz Festival, one of the largest and best-attended jazz events in the world. While all styles of jazz are represented in the lineup of international acts, you'll find blues, gospel, funk, soul, hip-hop, R&B, worldbeat, and Latin sounds on the menu too. *The last week in July.* Day tickets €65; 3-day tickets €155; all-event VIP tickets €320.

Summer (Zomer) Carnival

Various locations, Rotterdam, zomercarnaval.nl

The Lowdown: This Caribbean festival is a dance party extravaganza that draws more than one million people from all over Europe. It includes a "battle of the drums," lots of colorful and scanty costumes, and an anything-goes attitude.

Thursday kicks off with a pre-party, and Saturday offers a street parade. *The last weekend in July, beginning on Thursday.* €€

White Sensation and Black Sensation

Amsterdam Arena, Arena Boulevard 1, East, id-t.com

The Lowdown: The annual White Sensation and Black Sensation—actually two separate events—are billed as the world's leading dance parties, and who's to argue? Staged a week apart, each draws upward of 40,000 revelers to the Amsterdam Arena, where they dance until sunup to beats supplied by the globe's hottest DJs. Plan ahead. Way ahead. Tickets to both parties completely sell out in February within one week of going on sale. VIP tickets offer access to exclusive lounges and cool-down spots, and those sell out within the hour. Oh, and since you're planning ahead, select your outfit now: Dancers dress head-to-toe in the color of the night—black for Black and white for White—and those who don't, get turned away at the door. *White Sensation is the first Saturday in July, and Black Sensation occurs one week later.* €60 each, VIP €110 each.

August

Amsterdam Pride

Various locations, amsterdampride.nl

The Lowdown: Combine the loudest and proudest of Holland's gay community, 80 boats, 250,000 spectators, and a decade of tradition and you've got the world's only floating Pride parade. The Canal Parade, Amsterdam's third-largest event by attendance, is simply the highpoint in a week full of diverse, gay-themed events. Street parties, an open air-film festival, fashion and art gallery shows, sports tournaments, a youth fair, and an amazing number of club events ensure that the fun never ends at Amsterdam Pride. Note—the Prinsengracht, the Amstel, and the area around the Stopera provide the best vantage points for watching the parade. Go early if you want to stake some prime real estate. *The first weekend in August.* Free.

Dance Valley

Spaarnwoude Recreation Area, Velsen, dancevalley.nl

The Lowdown: Grab your dancin' shoes and your tent! Dance Valley is the week-end-long dance party where world-class techno, drum & bass, and ambient DJs spin for crowds of 45,000. There are camping facilities for 15,000 but should you prefer to burn the midnight oil, a cinema, cafe, game area, and "silent disco"—DJ'd tunes are broadcast through headphones only and people appear to be dancing in silence—promise round-the-clock entertainment. *The first weekend in August, usually beginning on Friday.* €88.

FFWD Heineken Dance Parade

Various locations in Rotterdam, ffwdheinekendanceparade.nl

The Lowdown: Rotterdam's answer to Berlin's Love Parade is now the largest of its kind in Europe, attracting 350,000 spectators who move to the beat of international DJs on parade floats. When the parade ends, the party continues at the south end of the Erasmus Bridge, where eight soundstages showcase top-name talent. After-parties guarantee that the vibe continues until sunrise. *The second weekend in August.* Free or grandstand seating for €17.50.

Grachtenfestival • Canal Festival

Various locations, 421-4542, grachtenfestival.nl

The Lowdown: For five days every August, Amsterdam's most scenic locations—private houses and gardens, museums, public squares, concert halls, and historic buildings—play host to 90 classical concerts. But as good as the other 89 concerts may be, let's be honest, the one everyone wants to attend is the Prinsengrachtconcert. Held on Saturday evening, it's staged in a gorgeous location at the conflux of two scenic canals and it features top talent. For the best seat, book a room at the Pulitzer Hotel that overlooks the concert. *Third week in August, usually beginning on Saturday.* Free for Prinsengrachtconcert. Other concerts free-€20.

Preuvenemint

Vrijthof Square, Maastricht, preuvenemint.nl

The Lowdown: The name literally translates to "tasting event," and food lovers won't be disappointed. Held on the Vrijthof, the city square, more than 30 restaurants and bars turn out for a block party with live music. *The last full weekend in August, and the three days preceding it.* Free.

Uitmarkt

Leidseplein, Museumplein, and various other locations

The Lowdown: Uitmarkt, second only to Queen's Day in attendance, marks the official kickoff to Amsterdam's arts season. Virtually every cultural organization in the city gets in on the party, offering free performances in theatre, music, dance, and film, while book fairs and cultural symposiums round out the agenda. Sure, some of the events, particularly theatre, will be in Dutch, but the vibe is excellent and the majority of international acts perform in English. *The last weekend in August.* Free.

Utrecht Festival of Early Music

Utrecht (see p.182), oudemuziek.nl

The Lowdown: The most prestigious artists and ensembles offer a packed agenda of concerts when scenic Utrecht hosts its annual early music jam. Workshops and seminars lend a scholarly air to the gathering while the side attraction "Fair," where instruments, crafts, scores, books and records are traded, adds a classy swapmeet touch. *Ten days beginning on the last Friday in August.* Free-€50, *depending on event.*

September

Aalsmeer Bloemencorso
Variable routes, bloemencorso.com/aalsmeer

The Lowdown: The Dutch love parades almost as much as they love flowers, so it shouldn't surprise that they've combined the two passions in creating the annual Bloemencorso. The five-kilometer-long, moving floral pageant incorporates over one million blossoms and is a showcase for the legendary Dutch horticulture industry. Note: The parade starts in suburban Aalsmeer and usually ends at the Dam Square, but the route can change from one year to the next. Check the website for specifics. *The first weekend in September.* Free.

Jordaan Festival
On the Westermarkt and throughout the Jordaan,

The Lowdown: If ever there was a battle cry demanding that Amsterdammers remember their bohemian history, the Jordaan Festival is it. Street performances, pub crawls, dancing and singing along to Dutch oldies music (much of it in the grandest oom-pah-pah style) all factor prominently in the annual celebration of all that is Jordaanse. Don't know the words? It doesn't matter … neither do many of the locals. Think you're too hip to join in? Witness the scores of stylishly clad, local scenesters in conga lines with their elders. Silly fun reigns supreme—especially late-night. *The second weekend in September.* Free.

November

The Cannabis Cup
The Melkweg and various locations, cannabiscup.com

The Lowdown: Spare the jokes about a "buzzing scene" during this "high"-light event: Nearly 20 years old, this chilled-out good time grows larger every year. Opening ceremonies, awards shows, and nightly entertainment add to the agenda, but let's face it, there's one reason you're gonna attend. Splash out for a "Judges Pass," which includes some valuable, uh … information and the right to vote on the year's best crop. *The third week in November, usually beginning on Sunday.* Advance tickets sold in US dollars: Judges pass $175 early-bird online rate, $200 regular online rate; €200 at door.

International Documentary Film Festival
Various cultural venues, 627-3329, idfa.nl

The Lowdown: When Amsterdam hosts the planet's largest documentary film festival, everyone's invited and seemingly everyone shows up. Each year IDFA screens enough docs—200 works from 40-plus countries—to please even the most ardent fan, but the films are only part of the festival's draw. Competitions, debates, workshops, and daily "talk show" panel discussions add to the film-going experience. Off-site parallel industry events like Docs for Sale, which screens films for TV purchasers and festival organizers, and the Forum,

Europe's largest annual gathering of commissioning editors and producers, are staged concurrently. *The last week of November through the first weekend of December.* Tickets €7.50, festival pass €125.

Museumnacht • Museum Night

Various locations, primarily cultural venues

The Lowdown: As if the Amsterdam cultural agenda were not full enough, Museumnacht ups the ante. Drawing huge crowds, the city's leading cultural institutions stay open until 2am and play host to a vast array of one-off events, enriching tours, symposiums, performances in music and dance, and even fashion shows. The big 3 (the Van Gogh, Rijksmuseum, and the Stedelijk CS) draw the biggest crowds. *The first Saturday in November.* Tickets €17.50.

Pictura Antiquairs Nationaal (PAN)

The Parkhal at Amsterdam RAI, 549-1012, pan-amsterdam.nl

The Lowdown: Quality and elegance are the buzzwords at PAN Amsterdam, the city's annual fine art and antique fair. Over 110 galleries strut their stuff, and although the emphasis is on Dutch and Flemish art, classic works, glassware, ethnographic art, jewelry, contemporary art, and furnishings can all be found at PAN. *The third week in November.* Day pass €12.50, event pass €35.

December

New Year's Eve

Dam Square and other locations

The Lowdown: Although the Dutch party hard on New Year's Eve, there are no typical Amsterdam traditions associated with the night. Instead, locals tend to follow the Western model of celebrating; dancing until dawn with friends, recklessly shooting off fireworks, and drinking themselves silly—literally. If you don't end up with an invite to a private party, plan early enough to score tickets to an event at a local restaurant, hotel, or club. If you'd rather experience the Dutch equivalent of Times Square, grab a can or six of Heineken, head to the Dam Square, and join in the party. *December 31.* Free.

HIT the GROUND RUNNING

Enjoying an Amsterdam insider experience is easy—just keep this chapter's key tips in mind when you plan your trip. From the lowdown on local transportation to finding English-language newspapers, from what to wear to how to call home, we give you the resources to help plan a flawless visit. You'll also get advice on mixing business with pleasure, as well as some surprising, in-the-know facts to impress the locals.

City Essentials

Getting to Amsterdam: By Air

Amsterdam Airport Schiphol (AMS)
900-7244-7465 (inside Netherlands), 20-794-0800 (international), schiphol.nl

As the Netherlands' only significant airport, Amsterdam Airport Schiphol is Europe's fourth busiest. 97 airlines service 217 destinations; more than 1.6 million kg of freight—chiefly flowers—move through each year; and it's chronically expanding. However, year after year, Schiphol ranks as one of the best airports in the world for user-friendliness, and its reputation for convenience, accessibility, dining, artwork, shopping, signage, and business services is well deserved. Arrivals in Amsterdam are typically swift and smooth, and hotel transfers are efficient.

Schiphol's layout is very simple. There is only one terminal with three departure halls that are quickly traversed using the extensive system of moving walkways. Departures with curbside check-in are located on the second level, while the baggage claim—complete with free luggage carts—is on the ground level. Steps away in Schiphol Plaza, you'll find hotel shuttle services, the entrance to the subterranean train station, and the taxi stand.

If you find yourself killing time at AMS, explore some of the airport's many pieces of art. A free copy of "Art at Schiphol," available at any info desk, will help you to locate outstanding installation pieces, such as Dale Chihuly's *The Niijima Floats* and Atelier van Lieshout's *Schiphol Skulls*. If your tastes lean towards the classics, simply head to the airport's wing of the Rijksmuseum, which shows small collections of Dutch master paintings according to themes, and admission is free.

If you'd rather get some work done, head to the Business

Flying Times to Amsterdam

Nonstop From	Airport Code	Time (hr.)
Atlanta	ATC	9½
Barcelona	BCN	2
Chicago	CHI	8½
Frankfurt	FRA	1
London	LHR	1
Los Angeles	LAX	11
New York/ Newark	JFK/ EWR	8
Paris	CDG	1
Rome	FCO	2½
San Francisco	SFO	10½
Toronto	YYZ	8
Washington, D.C.	IAD	8½

Major Airlines Serving Amsterdam Airport Schiphol (AMS)

Airlines	Website	Local Phone (area 020)	Departure Hall
Aer Lingus	aerlingus.com	623-8620	2
Air Canada	aircanada.com	346-9539	3
Air France	airfrance.com	654-5720	2
Alitalia	alitalia.com	470-0118	1
British Airways	britishairways.com	346-9559	1
Cathay Pacific	cathaypacific.com	653-2010	3
China Airlines	china-airlines.com	646-1001	3
Continental Airlines	continental.com	346-9381	3
Delta Airlines	delta.com	201-3536	3
El Al	elal.co.il	644-0101	3
Japan Airlines	jal.co.jp/en	305-0075	3
KLM	klm.com	474-7747	2
Korean Air	koreanair.com	655-6333	3
Lufthansa	lufthansa.com	0900-123-4777	1
Malaysia Airlines	malaysiaairlines.com	521-6262	3
Martinair	martinair.com	601-1767	3
Northwest Airlines	nwa.com	474-7747	2
Singapore Airlines	singaporeair.com	548-8888	3
United Airlines	united.com	201-3708	3
US Airways	usairways.com	201-3550	3

HIT THE GROUND

Center on the top floor between piers E and F, where you can rent a PC, fax, phone, and even a conference room with secretarial support. In concourses C and D, and also in the corridor between E and F you will find Communication Centers where you can take advantage of wireless LAN at the "laptop bars" and get technical support should you need it.

Schiphol has a variety of recommendable dining and lounging options. In Lounge 1, discerning travelers will enjoy Bubbles, a contemporary bar with an extensive seafood menu and a long list of wine and champagne (7am-9pm daily), as well as Grand Café het Paleis, a cozy Dutch cafe with high ceilings, wooden floors, and all-day breakfasts (6am-9pm). In Lounge 2, try Shirasagi Sushi Bar (9:30am-8:30pm) or head to the smart-looking Brasserie (7am-9pm) to order European fare à la carte.

Finally, in Lounge 3, head to Café Amsterdam (daily, 7:30am-8pm) for classic pub fare and drinks.

Schiphol Airport is about 20 minutes from downtown Amsterdam by car, although the crowded state of Dutch highways can add up to 40 minutes to the trip, especially during rush hours—7-9:30am and 4-7pm on weekdays, no matter which direction you are traveling.

Into Town By Taxi: Taxis can be found outside Schiphol Plaza at the *staandplaats*—"taxi stand." They offer a fixed rate of €39 to the city center, and anyone approaching you in the terminal and offering you a deal won't be doing you any favors.

Into Town By Shuttle Service: Tickets for the Connexxion Schiphol Hotel Shuttle (038-339-4741) can be bought at the company's desk at Schiphol Plaza, just outside the arrivals hall. The buses depart frequently between 6am and 9pm and cost €11 one way and €17.50 for a return trip.

Into Town By Public Transit: Trains depart for the city from underneath Schiphol Plaza every 15 minutes and arrive at Amsterdam Centraal Station 25 minutes later. A one-way ticket costs €3.40 and can be bought at the ticket counter in Schiphol Plaza.

Rental Cars: Car rental agencies, located in Schiphol Plaza, are open from 7am until 11:30pm daily, with the exceptions of Avis and Hertz, which open at 6:30am. Each requires a credit deposit for rentals and each agency has its own garage on-site. Reservations are strongly recommended.

Agency	Website	U.S. 800 Number	Local Number
Avis	avis.com	800-238-4898	655-6050
Budget	budget.com	800-472-3325	604-1349
Europcar	europcar.com	n/a	316-4190
Hertz	hertz.com	800-654-3001	502-0240
National	nationalcar.com	800-227-7368	316-4081
Sixt	e-sixt.com	n/a	405-9090

Luxury Self-Driven Cars: All of the airport-based car rental agencies have luxury car options, including 4x4s, sport convertibles, and luxury sedans.

Limos:
- Carey Chauffeur Drive — 631-4721
- Doelen Limousine Service — 653-0931

Getting to Amsterdam: By Land

By Car: The A10 Ring Road is the highway that completely encircles the city. Any and every highway that approaches Amsterdam links up with the A10 and it's from the A10 that you will exit the highway and enter the city proper. If your approach is from the eastern part of the Netherlands or from the region around Münster in Western Germany, you'll use the A1. If you approach Amsterdam from the south eastern cities—Maastricht, Eindhoven, 's Hertogenbosch (Den Bosch), or Utrecht—or if you're driving up from France or Belgium, you'll end up on the A2. Driving up from the southwestern cities of Rotterdam or Den Haag (The Hague) means that you'll approach Amsterdam on the A4.

Driving Times

From	Distance (km.)	(mi.)	Approx. Time (hr.)
Berlin	650	404	6½
Brussels	210	130	2
Frankfurt	720	447	7
The Hague	57	35	¾
London	540	336	6½
(+ waiting time at the Chunnel)			
Maastricht	215	133	2
Milan	1,070	665	10
Munich	820	510	8
Paris	500	311	5
Rotterdam	73	45	1
Utrecht	38	24	½
Zurich	820	510	8

By Train: By North American standards, Europe has an astonishingly comprehensive railway system. Trains are an excellent and convenient way to get to Amsterdam from elsewhere in Europe. Netherlands Railways (ns.nl) operates an astonishing number of trains that arrive in Amsterdam from within Holland itself, and they also operate overnight trains from other European destinations, including Zurich and Munich. You can travel from London, via Lille or Paris on Eurostar (eurostar.com), and you can travel from Brussels and France on the high speed Thalys (thalys.com). ICE International (iceinternational.com) operates trains to Amsterdam from Basel, Switzerland, and most major cities in Western Germany.

Amsterdam Centraal is the city's main train station. In addition to the usual amenities—newsstands, fast food, and ticket sales—a tourism info booth can be found on track 2b. Outside, you'll find taxis, trams, and the entrance to the subway.

HIT THE GROUND

Amsterdam: Lay of the Land

Located on the IJ river, bisected by the Amstel River, and crisscrossed with a veritable web of canals, Amsterdam is a compact city, and its 730,000 residents are never far from the water. All of the city's most visited neighborhoods, such as the Canal Belt, the Jordaan, and the Museumplein, are easily reached on foot or by bicycle, and even the farthest reaches of Amsterdam can be reached quickly by public transit—including boats, should you prefer to travel by water.

Getting Around Amsterdam

By Car: As a general rule: Don't bother! Amsterdam is a very compact city, and you don't need a car to get around. When it comes to leaving the city, keep in mind that Holland is a tiny country, about the size of Maryland and Connecticut combined. Most excursions can easily be accomplished by train. If you insist on hitting the highways, be prepared for incredibly high speeds ... until you find yourself stuck in one of the daily, multi-mile traffic jams; a rule of thumb dictates that if it's light out, it's rush hour. The clearly marked Lijnbus lanes are reserved for regional buses and you will face a whopping fine if you get caught driving in one. Similarly, it's illegal to have a cell phone or PDA in your hand while driving in Holland, so pull over if you have to make a call. The minimum fine is €140 and you can have your phone seized. Call 0800-0888 if you have car trouble while driving in the Netherlands. You'll reach the ANWB (Royal Dutch Touring Club), the Dutch equivalent of the AAA, whose yellow cars patrol major roads offering round-the-clock roadside assistance. The four 24-hour gas stations in Amsterdam are located at Marnixstraat 250, Gooiseweg 10, Sarphiastraat 225, and Spaarndammerdijk 218.

Park It: Street parking is very hard to come by, and if you do find a spot, be prepared to pay dearly; consider booking a hotel that has on-site parking if you anticipate needing it. In the city center, paid metered parking is in effect Monday through Saturday from 9am to 11pm and on Sundays from noon to 11pm. Bring lots of coins, expect to pay around €3.50 per hour, and don't even think about cheating the meter. Parking patrols are diligent, and if you overstay your time you risk having your wheel clamped. It costs €75 to get the clamp removed, and if you don't pay within 24 hours, the car is towed, spiking the cost of recovery to a minimum of €180. Public lots are expensive, but they offer added security. Two larger, centrally located facilities where you can pay a flat fee of approximately €44 per day or an hourly rate similar to meters are:

- Amsterdam Central, Prins Hendrikkade 20A
- Waterlooplein, Valkenburgerstr. 238

Note: No matter where you park your car in Amsterdam, remember to lock it at all times and never leave any belongings behind.

By Taxi: Taxis have strict limitations on where they can stop, making it hard to hail one in the street. Call the central

Sample Taxi Rates	
Route	Cost
Centraal Station-Museumplein	€13
Leidseplein-Dam Square	€11
RAI-Dam Square	€12
City Center-Schiphol Airport	€39

dispatch number (677-7777) or head for the nearest large hotel, main square, or designated taxi stand—Centraal Station, Leidseplein, and the Muziektheatre—where you'll always find one waiting. Drivers know the city well and more often than not, your ride will be a spotless, newer Mercedes.

By City Bus, Tram, and Subway: GVB (gvb.nl): Amsterdam has 37 bus lines, 18 tram lines, and 3 subway lines that start at 6am and run until 12:30am. There are overnight routes to serve your after-hours needs but they're limited so check the GVB website or with your concierge. Tickets for the night routes are bought from the drivers. Otherwise, to ride a bus, tram, or subway, you use Strippenkaarten (Strip Cards).

Strippenkaarten and Day Tickets: Amsterdam has been divided into transportation zones with set tariffs. Although you can pay cash each time you use public transport, purchasing a Strippenkaart (Strip Card) in advance will save you money if you're using the subway or trams often. Essentially a transit debit card, they're purchased at various locations—railway stations, post offices, department stores, variety stores, and large hotels—and they come in two formats; 15 strips (€6.70) or 45 strips (€19.80). Note: Prices change every January. To travel within one zone you pay a base rate of two "strips" and add one "strip" for each subsequent zone traversed. Before entering the subway, you stamp your card; on trams, enter the back door to find a transit worker who will do the job for you.

Tram and bus drivers can also sell you special Strip Cards (€6.70) that allow unlimited use of trams, buses and subways for 24 hours.

By Bike: It's no coincidence that most locals prefer to cycle. Amsterdam's 17th-century streets weren't designed with cars in mind. On the downside, cycling in Amsterdam takes a bit of getting used to and at times you'll think that utter anarchy has broken out. And yes, motor scooters are allowed on the bike lanes too. Keep your eyes wide open and look three times before crossing a street and you'll be fine. Bikes can be rented

HIT THE GROUND

anywhere that you see the sign "Fietsen Verhuur" and be sure to take out any offered insurance and use the locks—yes, plural—at all times. Bicycle theft is so rampant that the police have been known to stage sting operations to nab both the thieves as well as would-be buyers.

By Boat: Traveling Amsterdam by boat combines relatively efficient transportation with the chance to enjoy the city's romantic canals. All-day hop-on-hop-off service on the Canal Bus (canal.nl/uk) costs €15 and your pass is valid until noon the next day. It runs on three routes, making fourteen stops at museums, shopping areas, and other main attractions. A much pricier option is to call a water taxi (535-6363): For groups of up to eight people, the base rate is €85 for the first half hour, falling to €70 for each half hour thereafter.

On Foot: Be sure to bring along a detailed map when you head out to explore Amsterdam. Many of the small streets are obscure even to locals, and the maze-like layout of the canals can make things confusing. Amsterdam is shaped like a half-circle, with the Dam Square forming the hub of the "half-wheel" and the streets forming "spokes" that stretch outward to the concentric rings of the canals. Now for the tricky part: When walking on many canals you can walk south, then east, then north again, all while continuing in the same direction along the same street. If you paid attention during geometry class, you'll remember that the shortest distance is not around the edge of a circle, but rather straight through the center. That principle is at work here too, so even if you are headed to an address on the same canal, it's often quicker to cut through the city center than it is to walk the canal itself (though the canal route may be more scenic if you're not pressed for time).

Amsterdam Addresses: When it comes to addresses, they're straightforward but you'll find that the Dutch write the street name first and the address second: Leidsestraat 34, for example. Occasionally an address will start with 1e, 2e, 3e, or 4e, meaning first, second, third, or fourth. In those cases, there will be several streets that share the same name and are only distinguishable by their number; 1e v.d. Helststraat vs 2e v.d. Helststraat, for example. If you don't know whether you're searching for an address on a canal or a street, keep in mind the suffixes—*straat* (street), sometimes abbreviated to str., and -*gracht* (canal). Tacked onto the ends of names, they generally give you a clue as to what to look for, and you can call yourself an honorary local when you can name the exceptions to the rule. Finally, if you have any doubts about where you're headed, ask a concierge at your hotel or simply stop someone in the street and get directions. You'll be hard-pressed to find a local who doesn't speak excellent English and who's not happy to lend a hand.

Other Practical Information

Money Matters (Currency, tipping, taxes—and getting them back when you leave): As is the case in much of Europe, in the Netherlands it's Euros (€) and cents (100 to the Euro). For currency rates go to xe.com. Major credit cards are widely accepted, but always check before sitting down to dinner. There are plenty of 24-hour ATMs throughout the city, and most of those are located at major banks; the most common banks—ABN-Amro, Rabobank, ING, and Postbank—all have bank machines. Look for signs that say "Geldautomaat." If you need help in person, you'll find that business hours differ among banks, but most are open from Tuesday to Friday between 9am and 4pm. On Mondays most banks open at 1pm, and on weekends banks are closed. Currency can be exchanged at any GWK branch. And when it comes to tipping, it's customary to give taxi drivers and waiters a tip of about 10 percent unless you've dropped in for a coffee or snack, in which case rounding up the bill to the nearest Euro will suffice.

Metric Conversion

From	To	Multiply by
Inches	Centimeters	2.54
Yards	Meters	0.91
Miles	Kilometers	1.60
Gallons	Liters	4.54
Ounces	Grams	28.35
Pounds	Kilograms	0.45

Taxes: A Value Added Tax of 19% is included in your hotel rate, and in shops, taxis, and restaurants. Non-European Union residents are entitled to a refund on the taxes paid on some purchases—the key word being "some." Whenever you see a sign that says "Global Refund Tax Free Shopping," you can ask for a refund check provided that you spend more than €137 in that store on the same day. Those checks are redeemed at the Global Refund Cash Refund Office located in departure hall 3 or customs on level 2 at Schiphol airport. You'll need to present your purchases as well as the receipts and refund cheques so be sure to collect your refund before checking your bags for travel. For more information, go to globalrefund.com.

Netherlands Area Codes

City	Area Code
Amsterdam	020
The Hague	070
Maastricht	043
Rotterdam	010
Utrecht	030

Calling: Two kinds of pay phones are common in the Netherlands. Green KPN telephones accept major credit cards as well as dedicated phone cards available for purchase at train stations, tobacco stores, and the GWK currency exchange locations. Blue and orange Telfort phones,

HIT THE GROUND

located in train stations, accept coins or phone cards sold at the station's ticket window, as well as at GWK locations. From the Netherlands to North America, dial 00 (for an international call) followed by 1 (the country code for Canada and the United States), the area code, and finally the local number. Within the Netherlands, with the exception of 0900 numbers (ones with a service charge) or 0800 numbers (toll free), all phone numbers in Holland have ten digits. Dial the area code of the city (three digits starting with a zero) and the local phone number. For Amsterdam listings, we've provided you with the local number. For all other listings in Holland, we've included the area code. To call Holland from North America, dial 1 followed by 31 (the country code for Holland), the last two digits of the city's area code (Amsterdam's becomes 20 for example), and finally the local number.

Time Zones: The Netherlands is located in the Central European Time zone. Amsterdam is 6 hours ahead of New York (EST) and 9 hours ahead of Los Angeles (PST). Clocks in the Netherlands are turned forward one hour during daylight savings. Daylight savings starts on the last Sunday in March and ends on the final Sunday in October.

Safety: You are very unlikely to become a victim of violent crime during a visit to Amsterdam, but as is the case in any big city, Amsterdam has its share of petty crime. Most of it occurs in areas where unwitting tourists tend to gather, and most of it can be avoided with a street-smart approach. Keep your eyes on your valuables at Centraal Station, the Damrak, Leidseplein, and the Dam Square, where pickpockets operate. Keep an especially close watch on bags if you've stopped to eat on a terrace or if you're watching a street performer; pickpockets love distractions. On trains, never leave a purse or wallet lying in plain view. When walking in the Red Light District, avoid small unlit alleys and keep to yourself. If you are approached by anyone asking for spare change, selling something, or telling you a hard-luck story, do not engage the person whatsoever: Just keep walking. Scams abound. Since bicycle theft is rampant, make sure you lock yours at all times.

Gay and Lesbian Travel: Amsterdam is a progressive, laid-back city that has a deserved reputation for welcoming gay travelers. Naturally there are plenty of gay-specific lodgings, restaurants, and nightclubs but the high level of acceptance in Dutch society means that gays will feel at home on virtually any happening dance floor or crowded terrace. The Netherlands Tourism Board (holland.com) is a good starting place for information on gay Amsterdam, but if you want to know more, check out PinkPoint (pinkpoint.org). They offer up-to-the-minute info on events and nightlife. If you like your information first-hand, PinkPoint can also be visited on the Amsterdam Westermarkt daily from 11am until 6pm.

Numbers to Know (Hotlines)

Emergency, Police, Fire Department, Ambulance, Paramedics   112

Non-emergency police   0900-8844

Along the highways you'll find call boxes for emergency use or you can always call 0800-0888 to reach Holland's equivalent of the AAA.

On-Call Doctors   592-3307

You'll hear a taped message in Dutch but you can press # 1 in case of an emergency, or stay on the line for a non-emergency referral.

24-Hour Emergency Rooms

- Our Lady Hospital   599-9111
  Onze Lieve Vrouwe Gasthuis, Oosterpark 9,

- Centrum Free University Medical Center   444-3636
  Vrije Universiteit Medisch De Boelelaan 1118

Pharmacy

If you need a pharmacy (apotheek), you'll find many open Monday to Friday from 8 or 9am until 5:30 or 6pm. On nights and weekends, pharmacies open on a rotating schedule. Ask your concierge to call 694-8709 to locate the one nearest to you as the information is in Dutch.

On-Call Dentists   0900-821-2230

Traveling with Disabilities: In theory, all public buildings including hotels and restaurants are to be wheelchair-accessible. In practice, many of Amsterdam's older buildings simply cannot be retrofitted in order to conform to current standards. Call ahead or check with a concierge before making dinner plans.

If you're planning to travel on trains within the country, you are advised to call the Disability Assistance Office of Netherlands Railways (030-235-7822) three hours in advance of your departure. They're open daily from 7am until 11pm, and they ensure that a specific train is wheelchair-accessible. Unfortunately city trams are of little use to those in wheelchairs, so call Connexxion Taxi (606-2200) in advance of a local trip.

Restrooms: Many public restrooms, even those in McDonald's, are guarded by grim-faced sentinels who will demand €0.50 or so before letting you use the facilities. It's wise to keep a small supply of pocket change at the ready.

HIT THE GROUND

English Language Media: *The Amsterdam Times* and *Amsterdam Weekly*, both free and widely available at shops, cafes, restaurants, hotels, and cultural venues, contain local news as well as entertainment listings. The *International Herald Tribune* and *USA Today* are both available at many hotels and newsstands. Both CNN and the BBC can be found on television in the Netherlands, and you'll find many imported, un-dubbed English language shows wedged in between regular Dutch programming.

Radio Stations (a selection)

FM Stations

88.9	RTV Noord-Holland	Classic Hits
90.7	Arrow	Smooth Jazz
94.3	Radio 4	Classical
95.7	Fresh FM	Dance
96.1	FunX	Urban
96.5	3FM	Pop
98.0	CityFM	Classic Rock
99.6	Slam FM	Dance
101.2	SkyRadio	Pop & Classics, no DJs
102.1	Radio 538	Pop
103.6	CAZ FM	Pop

AM Stations

1008	Radio 10	Golden Oldies

Shopping: Most Amsterdam shops are open from Tuesday to Friday between 9am and 6pm, with the exception of Thursdays when they stay open until 9pm. On Saturday, shopping hours are from 9am to 5pm and on Sundays, many shops are open from noon until 5pm, while some stay closed; call ahead or ask a concierge if you're going out of your way. On Mondays, shops typically open between 11am and 1pm, and close at 6pm.

Most other large Dutch cities have shopping hours similar to Amsterdam's with three exceptions: Rotterdam has late-night shopping on Fridays instead of Thursdays, and Maastricht's and Utrecht's shopping areas are closed on all except the first Sunday of every month.

Travelex outlet (located at Leidseplein 1-3) keeps the longest hours: Daily from 8:30am to 10pm.

Attire: Summers can be hot and humid, but along with your beachwear, pack a raincoat and a light sweater. The odd shower can't be ruled out and things can turn cool quickly. Winter winds can be cold and you should certainly wrap up well in January and February, when the average temperature hovers just above 2 degrees Celsius. The Dutch are relaxed about clothing, and most people dress quite casually. (Even showing up to the opera in trendy-stylish jeans and T-shirts is perfectly acceptable.) That said, there is a difference between casual and sloppy—avoid the latter or you'll stand out. Except for trips to the beach or to play a sport, surprisingly few people—men or women—wear shorts in the Netherlands. When

Size Conversion

Dress Sizes

Europe	34	36	38	40	42	44
US	6	8	10	12	14	16
UK	8	10	12	14	16	18
France	36	38	40	42	44	46
Italy	38	40	42	44	46	48

Women's Shoes

Europe	38	38	39	39	40	41
US	6	6½	7	7½	8	8½
UK	4½	5	5½	6	6½	7

Men's Suits

Europe	46	48	50	52	54	56
US	36	38	40	42	44	46
UK	36	38	40	42	44	46

Men's Shirts

Europe	38	39	40	41	42	43
US	14½	15	15½	16	16½	17
UK	14½	15	15½	16	16½	17

Men's Shoes

Europe	41	42	43	44	45	46
US	8	8½	9½	10½	11½	12
UK	7	7½	8½	9½	10½	11

it comes to dining out and clubs, casual and smart-casual dress prevails. Men, leave the tie at home—locals rarely wear them, preferring to wear collared shirts with a sport blazer. Also, both men and woman should bring a couple of colorful pieces of their wardrobe on a trip to Amsterdam; you can't go wrong with black, but the Dutch adore vibrant colors. And finally, for hitting the dance floor: For men, designer jeans with collared shirts or even T-shirts, a sport jacket, and designer sneakers will make a great impression on the locals. For women, go with designer jeans, T-shirts, and blouses and you'll fit right in.

Drinking: The legal drinking age for beer in the Netherlands is 16, and for hard liquor that age rises to 18. It's legal to consume alcohol in public, so long as you don't cause a disturbance or appear intoxicated.

Smoking: Virtually no restaurants in Amsterdam completely forbid smoking, and even restaurants with dedicated non-smoking sections are scarce. Smoking tobacco is universally accepted in Amsterdam's nightclubs, bars, and pubs, and that's not likely to change soon—the debate simply isn't on city council's radar.

HIT THE GROUND

Drugs: It can't be said often enough: Do not attempt to buy drugs, soft or hard, on the street. Holland is the one place where you can buy marijuana in the safety of a friendly pub; take advantage of it. But don't assume that soft drugs' being legal in pubs extends to their being relaxed about hard drugs: they're not. Despite what your buddies in college told you, drug use remains technically illegal; however, there's a loophole: The Dutch policy on drugs distinguishes between cannabis (decriminalized for those over 18 years of age) and hard drugs like heroin, cocaine, and synthetic drugs, which remain illegal.

Although the sale of soft drugs remains an offense, the police ignore "coffeeshops" where they may be purchased and consumed. So what does that mean to you? First, if you want to sample a coffeeshop's wares, you'll have to ask for a menu; they're not allowed to advertise the availability of drugs. Secondly, don't stockpile! Even though it's unusual, police are allowed to search you and you probably don't want to be found with what looks like more than a personal stash. Third, remember that the liberal Dutch attitude towards soft drugs is not extended to hard drugs; don't push your luck. Fourth, if you want to light up somewhere other than a coffeeshop, like in a cafe or on a terrace, be courteous and ask permission first. Finally, don't buy on the street. In addition to being illegal, street transactions are risky and downright dangerous.

If it's the legendary "space cakes"—marijuana-infused snacks—you're after, beware! They're much more potent than smoked marijuana, but it takes a while to get a buzz going. Go slowly and be patient. Amsterdam is rife with tales of tourists who have spent a day or two in a stupor after pigging out. "Smart Shops" legally sell magic mushrooms, herbal ecstasy, and the like, although—as is the case with most drugs—the smartness of sampling remains open to debate. More detailed information about the Dutch policy on drugs can be found at minbuza.nl. Click "English" and search "drugs."

Sex: Since prostitution became legal in the Netherlands, the sex trade has been closely monitored, and workers receive frequent health check-ups. Nevertheless, visitors to Amsterdam are strongly encouraged to take all health precautions, including making use of condoms, when participating in sex—be it of the paid variety or not.

Additional Resources for Visitors

Amsterdam Tourism Offices—the VVV The Amsterdam tourism office, known as the VVV, can be a great resource during your stay. The knowledgeable staff can make recommendations, answer questions about the city, and arrange hotels, excursions or entertainment tickets. They can also sell "I Amsterdam Cards." Available for 24 hours (€33), 48 hours (€43), or 72 hours (€53), the cards offer convenience and excellent value if you plan to museum hop during your visit. In addition to free admission to most of the city's top attractions, the card includes a small user handbook, a canal cruise, and a ticket for unlimited public transportation while your card is valid. The card is also available at select hotels and at all participating museums.

Stationsplein 10 *Daily 9am-4:30pm* Across from Centraal Station.
Centraal Station *Mon-Sat 8am-10pm; Sun 9am-5pm* Beside Track 2b.
Leidseplein *Sept-May daily 9am-5pm; Apr-Aug daily 9am-7pm.* At the corner of Leidsestraat.
Schiphol Airport *Daily 7am-10pm* Schiphol Plaza, Arrival Hall 2.

Amsterdam Chamber of Commerce
De Ruyterkade 5, 020-531-40-00, kvk.nl

Foreign Visitors

Entry: A valid passport is all that Americans and Canadians need to enter the Netherlands.
US Consulate in Amsterdam: Consulate Museumplein, 19, 575-5309
US Embassy in The Hague: Embassy Lange Voorhout 102, 070-310-9209
Passport Requirements: travel.state.gov/travel/tips/brochures /brochures_1229.html
Cell Phones: The cellular phone network in the Netherlands is GSM 900/1800.
Useful Numbers: For the Netherlands' directory service call 0900-8008. To reach an operator dial 0800-0410, and to place a collect call, ring 0800-010.
Electrical: The voltage in Holland is 220 volts. Hotels may have a 110-volt outlet for electric razors, but unless your appliance has a built-in power converter, you'll need to bring one along. Also be sure to pack an adapter—the plugs in the Netherlands have two round pins set parallel to one another.

The Latest-Info Websites

Event Tickets: Visitors can purchase tickets to most events and concerts at the AUB Ticket Office. (Fri-Wed 10am-6pm; Thu 10am-9pm) Corner of Leidseplein and Marnixstraat
Last Minute Ticket Shop: Purchase tickets to performances on the day of the event for half-price. In person only. (Daily from noon-7:30pm) Leidseplein 26 (Marnixstr.), lastminuteticketshop.nl

And of course, **pulseguides.com.**

Useful Vocabulary

Yes	**Ja**	Jah
No	**Nee**	Nay
Hello (formal)	**Goedendag**	Ghood-uh-dagh
Hi (informal)	**Hoi**	Hoy
Good Morning	**Goedemorgen**	Ghood-uh-morg-uh
Good Afternoon	**Goedemiddag**	Ghood-uh-mid-dagh
Good Night	**Goedenavond**	Ghood-uh-nahv-font
Goodbye	**Tot ziens**	Tot seens
Please / You're welcome (formal)	**Alstublieft**	All-stew-bleeft
Please / You're welcome (informal)	**Alsjeblieft**	All-syuh-bleeft
Thank you	**Bedankt**	Buh-dahnkt
What's your name? (informal)	**Hoe heet je?**	Who hate yuh?
What is your name? (formal)	**Hoe heet u?**	Who hate ew?
My name is ...	**Ik heet ...**	Ick hate ...
Do you speak English?	**Spreekt u Engels?**	Sprake-t u Eng-uls?
I don't understand	**Ik begrijp het niet**	Ick buh-ghripe het neat
Excuse me	**Pardon**	Pahr-donn
To your health / Cheers	**Proost**	Proest
Where is the restrooom?	**Waar is het toilet?**	Wahr is het twa-let?
How much does it cost?	**Hoeveel kost het?**	Who-vail cost het?
Open	**Open**	Opuhn
Closed	**Gesloten**	Ghe-slow-ten
How much?	**Hoeveel?**	Who-vail?
Where?	**Waar?**	Wahr?
When?	**Wanneer?**	Wahn-ear?
The bill, please	**De rekening alstublieft**	
	De ray-kuh-ning all-stew-bleeft	

Do you want something to drink?
Or, if you really want to pretend to be Dutch, ask "Beer?"

Wil je iets drinken? Biertje?
Will yuh eats drink-en? Beer-tcha?

I would like to have a biscuit with you
(very common phrase in Dutch, it means you want to spend the night with someone, referring to breakfast)

Met jou zou ik wel een beschuitje willen eten
Met yow zow ick well un buh-schrout-juh wil-len a-ten

Do you have a light? *Literally ... Do you have some fire?*

Heb je een vuurtje voor me?
Hep yuh un vuur-tyuh voor muh?

Ooh, that gives me goose bumps!

**Oh, ik krijg er mierentietjes van!
(mierentietjes = ants boobs!)**
Oh, ick krige air mee-ruh-teet-yus van!

Where is the Red Light District?

Waar zijn de wallen / de rosse buurt?
Wahr sine de wal-len / de ross-uh buurt?

Can I use the internet here?

Kan ik hier internetten?
Kahn ick hear in-ter-net-en?

I am lost	**Ik ben verdwaald**	Ick ben vehr-dwald
I am hungry	**Ik heb honger**	Ick hep hong-ur
He / she is hot	**Hij / zij is lekker**	Hi / zi is lek-ker
Nice weather!	**Lekker weertje!**	Lek-ker weer-tcha!
Your place or mine?	**Bij jou of bij mij?**	By yow off by my?

Food

breakfast	**ontbijt**	ont-bite
lunch	**lunch**	loon-ch
dinner	**diner**	di-nay
coffee	**koffie**	cof-fee
tea	**thee**	tay
milk	**melk**	melk
ice	**ijs**	ice

Party Conversation—A Few Surprising Facts

- Amsterdam's 165 canals mean that it's a city of bridges as well—1281 to be exact. If you stand on the bridge where Reguliersgracht meets Herengracht and face away from Thorbeckplein (the open square), you can see 15 bridges at once. Go at night when the illuminated bridges are at their best.

- Parking a car in Amsterdam is difficult for locals too: People who move into the city center face waits of up to six years before being eligible for a parking permit.

- The Dam Square, a focal point of raucous Queen's Day celebrations, has a dark side: On May 7, 1945, Amsterdam residents flooded the square believing that the liberation of the Netherlands was complete. Remaining German officers opened fire, killing 19 and injuring 117 others.

- Amsterdam was home to the first openly gay bar in the world. Opened in 1927, 't Mandje, or "the Basket," only closed its doors in 1985. Regarded as a landmark, part of the bar has been rebuilt in the Amsterdam Historical Museum.

- The 730,000 residents own an estimated 600,000 bikes; 400 km of bike lanes wind through Amsterdam, and 40 % of all "movement" in the city takes place on two wheels.

- More than 6,300 international companies have their headquarters in the Netherlands, and the country hosts the distribution centers for 50 percent of all American and Japanese companies doing business in the European Union.

- Despite their symbolic association with Holland, tulips were only introduced in the 16th century. Shortly afterwards, the Dutch passion for the Turkish flowers was so great that speculators traded single bulbs for as much as the equivalent of $35,000 today. The collapse of the tulip trade in 1636 decimated the Amsterdam stock exchange as well as the Dutch economy.

- Modern, yes, but Amsterdam respects its roots—it is home to 6,800 buildings and 6 working windmills from the 16th-18th centuries.

- With almost 150 art galleries and more than 50 museums—which include, 22 paintings by Rembrandt and 206 by Van Gogh—Amsterdam is one of the world's leading centers of art.

- Some of Amsterdam's most coveted addresses are houseboat moorings, and over 2,500 can be found within city limits.

The Cheat Sheet
(The Very Least You Ought to Know
About Amsterdam)

Here's a countdown of the essential facts you need to keep from looking like a *buitenlander*.

10   Neighborhoods

The Canal Belt is located just south of the city-center Dam Square. It's home to the city's most stately canal houses and offices as well as the Leidseplein—a buzzing nightlife hub—and the high-end antique shopping of the Spiegelkwartier.

The Jordaan is the area west of the center where you'll find the city's iconic, leafy canals and one-of-a-kind shops. Some locals argue that the name is a variation on *jardin*—French for garden—while others suggest that it draws inspiration from the Jordan River. Once the bohemian heart of the city, the Jordaan is now an upscale and trendy residential, business, and dining hotspot.

The Museumkwartier (Museum Quarter) is Amsterdam's high-culture ground zero although it wasn't always so; until late in the 20th century, the area was home to the city's big breweries. Now the Rijksmuseum, the Van Gogh Museum, and the permanent home of the Stedelijk Museum CS are located here on the southern edge of the city.

Nieuwe Zijde (New Side), bordered on the west by the Singel and the east by Oudezijde Voorburgwal, is the western portion of medieval Amsterdam. Today, you'll find Centraal Station, the Dam Square, and the shopping mecca Kalverstraat there.

Oostelijk Havengebied (the Eastern Harbor), the newest of Amsterdam's neighborhoods, is located northeast of the city center. Home to an eclectic mix of residential, retail, and services, it's known worldwide for its outstanding contemporary architecture and burgeoning shopping and gallery scenes.

Oude Zijde (Old Side), east of Oudezijds Voorburgwal, was the center of medieval Amsterdam, and of the city's Jewish community until World War II. Today the area is known for its Jewish roots as well as for being home to the University of Amsterdam, Stopera (the city hall/opera house), and the infamous Red Light District.

The Oude-Zuid (The Old South), located south and west of the city, is a perfect place for a stroll. Leafy streets and stately period residences make this area a desirable address for locals.

De Pijp is quickly emerging as the vibrant destination for in-the-know dining. Terraces, lounges, and chic brasseries abound in the new, south-of-the-city-center hot spot that also doubles as a residential area for many of Amsterdam's hippest 30-something professionals.

Plantage is the area around Artis, Amsterdam's historical zoo, and Hortus Botanicus, the city's botanical gardens. Known for elegant villas, the area at the eastern edge of the city is also home to the Dutch Resistance Museum.

Red Light District is called the Walletjes (Little Walls). The area is seedy, garish, and tacky—but it's also world-famous. You know you're going to want to have a look, so go at night, stick to the main streets, and see it in all its neon-lit glory.

Performing Arts Venues

De Balie Exhibitions and performances compete with video installations and lectures at this hip anything-goes venue. It's also the heart of the International Documentary Film Festival. Kleine Gartmanplantsoen 10, 553-5100

Het Concertgebouw Built in 1888 and hosting over 650 concerts a year, the home to the acclaimed Royal Concertgebouw Orchestra also hosts jazz performances. Concertgebouwplein 2-7, 020-671-8345, concertgebouw.nl

Cristofori Salon These former tobacco warehouses host a wide agenda of piano recitals, chamber music, and jazz. Prinsengracht 581-583, 624-4969

Heineken Music Hall In addition to the best of pop music, old and new, medium-sized touring productions like Riverdance grace the Heineken stage. Arena Boulevard 590, 0900-68-742-4255, heineken-music-hall.nl

Koninklijk Theater Carré Along with musical acts, dance, and plays, this ornate historical venue hosts touring Broadway productions and circuses. Amstel 115-125, 524-9452, theatercarre.nl

Melkweg Dance Photography, film, and performances by big-name musical acts round out the agenda at this hip interdisciplinary space. Lijnbaansgracht 234, 531-8181, melkweg.nl

Muziekgebouw Aan 't IJ Amsterdam's newest classical music venue, an architectural showpiece, is the stage for medium-sized concerts and festivals. Piet Heinkade 1, 788-2000, muziekgebouw.nl

Het Muziektheater "Stopera," as it's known to locals, is Amsterdam's modern city hall that moonlights as the premier opera, ballet, and modern dance venue. Waterlooplein 22, 551-8117, muziektheater.nl

Stadsschouwburg Amsterdam From theater and music to poetry slams, anything goes on this stage that is the focal point of the "Julidans" dance festival. Leidseplein 26, 523-7700

Shopping Strolls

Albert Cuypmarkt This open-air market is a treasure trove of Dutch food stalls, clothing, art, books, and antiques. Located in De Pijp, the market is open 9:30am-5pm Monday through Saturday.

Bloemenmarkt The floating flower market—all of the shops are on houseboats—is the perfect place to buy cut flowers if you're invited for dinner or to buy bulbs as a souvenir. Check to make sure your purchase is OK for import.

Kalverstraat Lined with a wide range of shops carrying everything from tailored suits and books to haberdashery and sporting goods, this is Amsterdam's most popular one-stop shopping stroll. It's open, and equally packed, on Sundays. kalverstraat.nl

Looier Kunst en Antiekcentrum (Looier Art and Antique Centre) Over 72 market stalls, shops, and a cafe make this the largest permanent indoor antique market in the Netherlands and a great place to while away a rainy afternoon. Closed Fridays. Elandsgracht 109, 624-9038, looier.nl

Magna Plaza Located just steps from the Dam Square, Holland's most ornate shopping mall is a 19th-century neo-Gothic behemoth. It's also a great place to find top international brands in fashion, beauty, and giftware. magnaplaza.nl

Negen Straatjes (Nine Little Streets) Along the city's grandest canals you'll find one-of-a-kind galleries, boutiques, and studios as well as a range of excellent restaurants. It's the Jordaan's shopping hub and arguably Amsterdam's most charming area.

Pieter Corneliszoon (P.C.) Hooftstraat Shortened to "Pahy-Sahy" by the locals, P.C. is the see-and-be-seen shopping street. You won't know the names of the Dutch celebrities shopping here, but you will recognize the brands they're after: Cartier, Bulgari, Zegna, and D&G all hold court. pchooftstraat.nl

Spiegelstraat If a photo by David LaChapelle, a sketch by Picasso, or some antique Delftware is your idea of an Amsterdam keepsake, head on over to Spiegelstraat, where discreet galleries cater to the most discerning tastes in art and antiquities.

HIT THE GROUND

Monuments to Tolerance

Anne Frank Statue When you see the full-scale statue of Anne erected in her memory, you have to wonder how a body so small ever contained a spirit so large. Visitors headed for the Anne Frank House often pass by the monument without batting an eye. It's that unassuming. Westermarkt

Dock Worker Statue A statue of a dockworker might seem like an unlikely reminder to stand up for human rights and freedoms, but the dockworkers' strike of February 1941 was Holland's first large-scale protest against the anti-Semitism of their Nazi occupiers. Jonas Daniël Meijerplein

Homomonument Specifically intended to memorialize gays and lesbians persecuted during World War II, the Homomonument also acknowledges the suffering of gays and lesbians in general. Consisting of three pink granite canal-side triangles representing the past, present, and future, the monument invites pause and contemplation. Keizersgracht, behind the Westerkerk

Monument to Jewish Resistance This black, two-meter-high monument, erected in recognition of Amsterdam Jews who resisted the Nazi regime, is inscribed with the mournful text of a lamentation by the prophet Jeremiah: "Were my eyes fountains of tears then would I weep day and night for the fallen fighters of my beloved people." South end of Waterlooplein where the Amstel meets the Zwanenburgwal

Multatuli Statue This statue stands in honor of the Netherlands' most famous author, Eduard Dekker. Writing under the pen name Multatuli, he wrote *Max Havelaar*, a scathing indictment of the Dutch treatment of colonials in Batavia, now Indonesia. Singel at Oude Leliestraat

National Monument Standing in memory of the Dutch who died during World War II, this stone column—surrounded by urns containing earth from each of Holland's provinces as well as from Indonesia—is the focal point for remembrance each May 4. Dam Square

Ravensbrück Memorial Commemorating the women who were prisoners in the Ravensbrück concentration camp (1940-1945), this monument is a fitting one. Visitors stand inside of cold steel columns and are bombarded with disturbing lights and sounds. Museumplein

Major Highways

A1 runs east from the A10 toward Hilversum, Apeldoorn, and Enschede, and to Osnabrück and Münster in westernmost Germany.

A2 runs from Amsterdam toward Utrecht and continues on to Maastricht, the southernmost city in the Netherlands. A2 also links Amsterdam to A27, the highway to Antwerp and Brussels in Belgium, and A12, the highway to Düsseldorf in Germany.

A4 links Amsterdam to Schiphol, the city's international airport, as well as Leiden, The Hague, and Rotterdam via the A13.

A5 connects Amsterdam to Haarlem and the seaside resort towns of Bloemendaal and Zandvoort.

A9 runs parallel to the A10 on the south side of the city. Take it if you're driving to the famous Alkmaar cheese market.

A10 Ring is the key to leaving Amsterdam. In addition to circling the city, it's the nexus of all the major highways that serve Amsterdam.

Squares

The Dam Square is the geographical heart of Amsterdam, and the site of the Dom Paleis, "Dom Palace," the Queen's offices. It's always busy with locals and tourists alike. Street performers, concerts, and fairs add to the lively atmosphere.

Leidseplein The center of all that is tacky-touristy in Amsterdam is nonetheless a great place to flirt, people-watch, drink your worries away, and catch some street theater.

Museumplein Just south of the canal ring, the Rijksmuseum, Stedelijk, and Van Gogh Museum are situated here. The sprawling lawn is great for picnics, people-watching, and public festivals.

Rembrandtplein This former butter market is now a popular destination for drinking and dancing, but it isn't all neon signs and terraces; look for the Rembrandt statue in the garden at the center of the square.

Waterlooplein What used to be the Jewish market is now home to a huge daily flea market, as well as the Stopera—the building doing double duty as both the city hall and music theater.

HIT THE GROUND

Types of Cafes (and one that s not)

Bruin Cafés Traditional, dark, cozy, warm and often smoky, "brown cafes" are a great place for a beer with locals. Tiny table-top Persian rugs, used to soak up spilled suds, are a mark of authenticity.

Coffeeshops Not a cafe—don't show up looking for an espresso at the deceptively named "Coffeeshops." These are the famous places where soft drugs are sold and smoked. Ask for a menu—they don't advertise their stashes.

Eetcafés "Eat cafes" are places to grab a quick bite. The décor typically ranges from terrible to neutral and simple, but the food can be tasty and hearty and the price is always right.

Grand Cafés With vast, cavernous rooms, soaring ceilings and huge terraces, grand cafes have become big on style too. Amsterdam's 20- and 30- somethings con-gregate at grand cafes come lunch time.

Nachtcafés They're sometimes seedy and the food is never great, but when you're hungry after a night of clubbing and everything else has closed, the "Night Cafes" soldier on.

Main Canals

Herengracht (The Gentlemen's Canal) is widely accepted to be the grandest canal in the city-based on the residences that run along it. Highlight architecture on the Herengracht includes no. 527, where Peter the Great would crash when in town, and much more recently, no. 497, which played a cameo role in the hit movie *Ocean's Twelve*.

Keizersgracht (The Emperor's Canal), the centermost canal of the famous ring, offers visitors the chance to see stately residences, charming bridges, and some of the city's popular houseboats. The Metz & Co. department store, with its cupola designed by Gerrit Rietveld, is located on the Keizersgracht.

Prinsengracht (The Prince's Canal) is the outermost of the three canals that form the famous canal ring. On it you'll find the historic Westerkerk, offering stunning views from its tower; the Anne Frank House, where she hid during World War II; galleries; and cafes.

Teams

Ajax There's only one game in town: European voetbal, and the local club is Ajax, pronounced "eye-axe." Tickets are hard to get. Order a club card via the web, so you can purchase in advance. Amsterdam Arena, Arena Boulevard 1, ajax.nl. (Season runs mid-August through mid-April)

Amsterdam Admirals If you're homesick, check out the Amsterdam Admirals for a fix of Americana. They're the city's American football team and they claimed the World Bowl, Europe's top honors, in 2005. Amsterdam ArenA, ArenA Boulevard 1, admirals.nl. (Season runs first week of April through first week of June)

Singular Sensation

The Amstel River Running south to north into the city, the Amstel is arguably the city's lifeblood. The first settlements in the area were at the river mouth and the city's name was derived from "the dam on the Amstel" which once stood where the Dam Square does now.

Coffee (quick stops for a java jolt)

To the relief of many visitors, the Dutch are passionate coffee drinkers who prefer their drink strong and robust in flavor. It's rare to find a bad cup of coffee in Amsterdam—even the lowliest snack bar will conjure up a decent cup of joe—but these places rise above the crowd.

Caffe Esprit Notable lattes, trendy fashionable crowd, large streetside patio. (p.88) Spui 10 (Voetboogstr.), Nieuwe Zijde, 622-1967

Café de Jaren International newspapers and magazines, and a scenic waterside terrace. (p.87) Nieuwe Doelenstraat 20-22 (Binnengasthuisstr.), Oude Zijde, 625-5771

CaffePC Regular pit stop for Amsterdam's see-and-be-seen shopping set. (p.63) PC Hooftstraat 87 (v.d. Veldestr.), Museumplein, 673-4752

Coffee and Company Amsterdam's urban-hip coffee chain.
1e v.d. Helststraat 62b (Govert Flinckstr.), 673-1769
Beethovenstraat 43 (Brahmsstr.), 672-1258
Ferdinand Bolstraat 38 (Daniël Stalpertstr.), 573-0000
Haarlemmerdijk 62 (Korte Prisengracht), 626-3776
Kinkerstraat 330 (Jan Pieter Heijestr.), 489-8400
Leidsestraat 60 (Kerkstr.), 422-9423
Middenweg 32 (Wakkerstr.), 468-9682
Singel 457 (Raadhuisstr.), 422-9423
Nieuwe Doelenstraat 24 (Binnengasthuisstr.), 420-7364

HIT THE GROUND

Just for Business and Conventions

The RAI Convention Center is the focus of the business tourism scene and, thanks to the city's compact layout, most of Amsterdam's top tourist draws are only a quick taxi ride away. Some of the best museums in the world are close at hand, and the canal ring, the city center and De Pijp, a residential area known for great restaurants, are nearby too. Whatever you choose to do, don't settle for room service meals and pay-per-view movies. Amsterdam is so rich and lively that no matter which neighborhood you stay in, there are good restaurants, interesting cultural attractions, and friendly people just outside your hotel.

Addresses to Know

Convention Center

• RAI
Europaplein 22,
549-1212, rai.nl

City Information

• Amsterdam Tourism and Conventions Board
visitamsterdam.nl

• Amsterdam Chamber of Commerce
De Ruyterkade 5,
531-4000, kvk.nl

• Amsterdam Foreign Investment Office
Weesperstr. 89,
552-3536, ez.amsterdam.nl

• Customs Information
0800-0143

Business and Convention Hotels

These business hotels are in addition to those recommended in the Black Book.

Amsterdam Hilton Highrise hotel, close to eateries, between RAI and city center. €€€€ Apollolaan 138, 710-6000, hilton.com

Le Meridien Waterside, full-service international chain hotel with canal views. €€€€ Apollo Apollolaan 2, 673-5922, lemeridien.com

RAI (Convention Center) You can't stay any closer if you have business at the convention center. €€€€ Europaplein 22, 549-1212, rai.nl

Center City

Banks Mansion Canal views, centrally located. Breakfast, minibar, and internet included. €€€ Herengracht 519-525, 420-0055, carlton.nl

Marriott Amsterdam On a central tram line, near top museums and the canal ring. €€€ Stadhouderskade 12, 607-5555, marriott.com

Renaissance Amsterdam Close to train station, nightlife, attractions and restaurants. €€€€ Kattengat 1, 621-2223, marriott.com

Business Entertaining

Networking? Sealing a deal? Your business plan should include these places.

Altmann Restaurant and Bar (p.61) Global cuisine and cocktails in a chic brasserie setting. €€€€ Amsteldijk 25, 662-7777

De Compagnon (p.116) Quality French cuisine, wines, and service with water views. €€€€ Guldehandsteeg 17, 620-4225

De Kas (p.118) Modern Dutch dining in a buzzing greenhouse, attentive service. €€ Kamerlingh Onneslaan 3, 462-4562

Restaurant-Bar De Stijl Sleek hotel lobby bar catering to contemporary design fans. €€€ John M. Keynesplein 2, 718-9000

La Serre Bar Okura Hotel's lounge-bar, near the RAI; summer terrace. €€€ Ferdinand Bolstr. 333, 678-7111

La Terrasse (p.121) Waterside dining, traditional French dishes, summer terrace. €€€€ Nieuwe Doelenstr. 2, 531-1705

Also see: **Best Fine Dining** (p.27)
          Best Hot-Shot Chefs (p.31)

Ducking Out for a Half Day

Work hard. Play hard. Put down that laptop and recharge yourself.

Holland International Boat Tours Narrated one-hour boat tours of the canals. various locations, 622-7788

Negen Straatjes One-of-a-kind shopping, cafes and people-watching.

Also see: **Best Art Museums** (p.18)
          Best Dutch Design (p.24)

Gifts to Bring Home

Does anybody really want a pair of wooden shoes? Memorialize your trip to Amsterdam with a quality gift from one of these places.

Droog Design (p.100) Quirky, functional products from Holland's hottest design collection. Staalstr. 7b, 523-5050

The Frozen Fountain (p.75) Holland's best in contemporary porcelain and earthen-ware. Prinsengracht 645, 622-9375

Rijksmuseum Gift Shop (p.133) Iconic Dutch art on posters, souvenirs, and col-lectibles. Jan Luijkenstraat 1, 674-7000

Also see: **Best Dutch Design** (p.24)
          Cheat Sheet, Shopping Strolls (p.167)

HIT THE GROUND

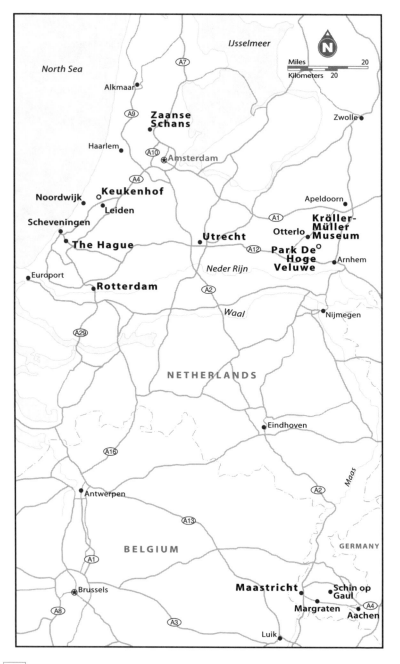

IJsselmeer

North Sea

N

Miles 20
Kilometers 20

Alkmaar

A7

A9

Zaanse Schans

Zwolle

Haarlem

A10

Amsterdam

A4

Keukenhof

Noordwijk

Leiden

Apeldoorn

Scheveningen

A1

Kröller-Müller Museum

Otterlo

The Hague

Utrecht

A12

Park De Hoge Veluwe

Arnhem

Europort

Neder Rijn

Rotterdam

A2

Nijmegen

Waal

A29

NETHERLANDS

Eindhoven

A16

Maas

Antwerpen

A2

A13

BELGIUM

GERMANY

A1

Brussels

Maastricht

Schin op Gaul

A8

Margraten

A4

A3

Aachen

Luik

LEAVING AMSTERDAM

If you want a break from Amsterdam's scene, a breathtaking variety of nearby excursions are yours for the choosing—from the cultural draw of The Hague to the exquisite canals of Utrecht. Many are only a few hours—or less—from the city, making them perfect for a quick day trip or an overnight excursion.

The Hague

Hot Tip: Crowds are largest in July and August, but the weather is great from mid-May through September, so visit then for the best of both worlds.

The Lowdown: When people think of The Hague, the International Court of Justice is usually the first thing that comes to mind and that's not exactly a sexy tourist draw. But don't be too quick to dismiss the city as being a wholly bureaucratic one. The Hague has aristocratic charm and it's a pleasant diversion from Amsterdam. No visit would be complete without wandering around Parliament's Binnenhof (Inner Court) and the adjacent Ridderzaal (Knight's Hall). Built in the 13th century, the ornate Binnenhof was once a hunting lodge belonging to the Counts of Holland, and the gothic Ridderzaal, intended as an elaborate banquet hall, now hosts the Queen's yearly "throne" speech. Outside of the Parliament, The Hague's top draws are undeniably its museums, the best of which are Mauritshuis and Gemeentemuseum (Municipal Museum) Den Haag. Mauritshuis, The Hague's nod to the old masters, is an elegant Dutch Classical building housing an outstanding collection of paintings, Vermeer's *Girl with a Pearl Earring* and Rembrandt's *The Anatomy Lesson of Dr. Nicolaes Tulp* the most famous among them. More modern in scope, Gemeentemuseum Den Haag shows off the world's most extensive Mondriaan collection and also focuses on exhibiting applied arts and fashion. Back on the streets, unleash your inner Churchill: Stop by De Graaff Tobacconist (Heulstraat 27), Sir Winston's smoke shop of choice, and wander the leafy Lange Voorhout to see stately embassies and residences. If you're feeling royal, shop in the footsteps of the House of Orange on Molenstraat, Denneweg, Hoogstraat and Den Plaats, the city's high-end shopping streets, or head to Scheveningen, the North Sea resort town. A short tram ride away, it offers seaside dining and lounging, although the water's a bit cold for all but the heartiest of visitors. Note: The Hague can be visited as a day trip, and nightlife in the city can be minimal.

Best Attractions

Binnenhof & Ridderzaal 13th-century former hunting lodge that houses Parliament, and a grand courtyard. € Binnenhof 8A, 070-364-6144, binnenhofbezoek.nl

Gemeentemuseum Den Haag Worthy collection of modern art. € Stadhouderslaan 41, 070-338-1111, gemeentemuseum.nl

Mauritshuis Museum Old Masters, including Vermeer's *Girl With a Pearl Earring*. € Korte Vijverberg 8, 070-302-3456, mauritshuis.nl

Peace Palace Library, museum and guided tour, including the International Court of Justice (book ahead for tour). € Carnegieplein 2, 070-302-4137, vredespaleis.nl

Best Restaurants

Bistro Mer Parisian-style bistro specializing in seafood; terrace in summer. €€€
Javastr. 9, 070-360-7389

Calla's Stark white interior, Michelin-star food, see-and-be-seen crowd. €€€
Laan van Roos en Doorn, 070-345-5866

Puck Smart bistro fare with an exotic twist. €€ Prinsestr. 33, 070-427-7649,
puckfoodandwines.nl

Watertanden Stylish South American food alongside stylish patrons; go for lunch.
€ Mallemolen 10a, 070-427-7888

Wox Top-notch creative Japanese fusion cuisine, views of Parliament. €€€
Buitenhof 36, 070-365-3754

Best Nightlife

Club OneFour Restaurant-bar-club with a Moulin Rouge-inspired interior, and DJs
at night that attract a 30-something crowd. Floow Plein 22, 070-302-0208

Floow Come one-come all dance club in the city center, busy Fridays and
Saturdays. Prinsengracht 14, 070-364-4177

Maliehuisje Small restaurant and club popular with a classic-minded set, with
DJs and live music. Maliestraat 8, 070-345-6482

Paard van Troje Concert hall hosting well-known bands, also award-winning club
on weekends. Prinsengracht 12, 070-360-1838

Best Hotels

Carlton Ambassador Conventions and embassies business hotel; ask for a room
with a balcony. €€ Sophialaan 2, 070-363-0363,carlton.nl/ambassador

Haagsche Suites Three-suite, all-inclusive, super-luxury B&B in the grand classic
style. €€€ Laan van Meerdervoort 155, 070-364-7879, haagschesuites.nl

Le Méridien Hotel Des Indes Luxury chain hotel located in a majestic manor
house. €€€ Lange Voorhout 54-56, 070-361-2345, starwoodhotels.com

Steigenberger Kurhaus Hotel Beachfront classic luxury hotel, some rooms with
kitchenette. €€€ Gevers Deynootplein 30, 070-416-2636, kurhaus.nl

Contacts

The Hague Tourism Board denhaag.com

LEAVING

Getting There
By Car: From the A10 Ring road, take the A4 Zuid (South) towards Den Haag
(The Hague). Takes about 45 minutes.
By Train: From Amsterdam Centraal Station, take the train to Den Haag Centraal.

Maastricht

Hot Tip: Summer has the best weather, and the height of the season is the wine and culinary festival of Preuvenemint during the last week of August—a must for gourmands.

The Lowdown: Founded by the Romans (circa. 50 BC), Maastricht is a walled city nestled in the gently rolling hills of Limburg province between Belgium and Germany. It has a thriving religious life, a relative intimacy with nature, and a rich culinary tradition that add up to an air of quiet sophistication.

If the Dutch talk about Maastricht, it's usually to praise the region's excellent food. Only the freshest ingredients appear in Limburg dishes and a visit to Maastricht should very well start, and end, at the table. Look for delicious vlai (fruit flans) year round. Visit mid-spring to do like the locals and indulge in heavenly white asparagus, the regional delicacy of legend, or come in the last week of August to catch Preuvenemint, the wine and culinary festival held on the historical city square. When it comes time to pry yourself away from the table and explore the city, you'll find much to enjoy, both inside the walls and outside Maastricht proper. Including two Romanesque cathedrals, six gothic churches, a Baroque church and a Walloon one, Maastricht's religious sites make this a history buff's paradise. Nevertheless, the city's premier attraction is the Aldo Rossi–designed Bonnefantenmuseum, where celebrated collections of modern art and art from the medieval age are complemented by first-rate temporary exhibitions. For a more solemn experience, head 10 km/6 miles east of Maastricht to Margraten, where you'll find the Netherlands' American Cemetery and Memorial. The 65-acre complex is a tribute to Americans who sacrificed their lives during World War II and it's the only one of its kind in Holland. Limburg's verdant hills are popular for hot air ballooning, and excursions combined with picnics are easily arranged. Back on earth, bike trips are possible, the Maas River provides excellent opportunities for scenic kayaking trips, and the nearby Valkenburg cave system affords adventurers the rare chance to take an 8km/5 mile subterranean mountain bike tour.

Best Attractions

ASP Adventure Mountain bike, ATV, and walking tours of Valkenburg cave system. €€–€€€ Oud Valkenburg 2, Schin op Geul, 043-604-0675, aspadventure.nl

Basilica of Our Lady Cathedral, ecclesiastical art and crafts. € Onze Lieve Vrouweplein

Bonnefanten Museum Contemporary art, medieval art and carvings, Flemish masters. € Avenue Céramique 250, 043-329-0190, bonnefanten.nl

Cycle-shop 'Aon de Stasie' Bicycle rentals with early morning/late night hours. € Parallelweg 40/a, 043-321-1100

Euregio Ballooning Hot air balloon excursions over the Province of Limburg. €€€€+ Weststraße 24, Aachen, Germany, +49 (0)241-8944-9555

Kajak Maasland Canoe/kayak trips on the Maas River, hotel pick-ups available. €€ 0032-89-717390, kajakmaasland.be

Netherlands American Cemetery and Memorial WW II military cemetery, visitors center, memorials. abmc.gov/ne.htm

St. Servatius Basilica Cathedral, collection of art, treasures and relics. € Keizer Karelplein, 043-325-1851

Best Restaurants

Beluga Two-Michelin-star design dining on the river Maas. €€€ Centre Céramique/Plein 1992 #12, 043-321-3364

Le Bon Bassin Waterside dining, the city's best seafood, simple but warm décor. € Bassinkade 11, 043-326-0927

Harbour Club The city's new hip and trendy hot spot, set 4-course menus. €€ Bassinkade 4, 043-450-6666

Rozemarijn Exclusive French food with service to match, terrace in summer. €€€ Havenstr. 19, 043-450-6505

Toine Hermsen Contemporized classical Dutch cuisine, Michelin star chef. €€€ Sint Bernardusstr. 2-4, 043-325-8400

Tout à Fait French rotisserie food with a Michelin star, warm interior. €€€ Sint Bernardusstr. 16, 043-350-0405

Zes Cocktails and tasting menus lure the city's trendiest crowds. €€ Onze Lieve Vrouweplein 6, 043-328-1300

Best Nightlife

De Kadans Traditional brasserie popular for drinks, with a lovely square terrace. € Desselskade 62, 043-362-8278

Night-Live Tradition meets the future in a renovated church that's now a dance-club. € Desselskade 43, 043-362-7238

Best Hotels

Derlon Hotel City center design hotel, champagne bar and trendy crowd. €€ Onze Lieve Vrouweplein 6, 043-321-6770, derlon.com

Design Hotel La Bergère Boutique design hotel, gym, media library. Lounge with DJs nightly. € Stationsstraat 40, 043-328-2525, la-bergere.com

Kruisherenhotel Once a 15th-century cloister, now a beautiful, luxury design hotel. €€€ Kruisherengang 19-23, 043-329-2020, chateauhotels.nl

Contacts

Maastricht Tourism vvvmaastricht.nl
Preuvenemint Food and Wine Festival preuvenemint.nl

Getting There
By Car: From the A10 Ring Road, take the A2 in the direction of Utrecht, continuing on to Maastricht. Takes about 2 hours.
By Train: From Amsterdam Centraal Station, take the train to Maastricht Centraal.

Rotterdam

Hot Tip: Arrive during Somer (Summer) Carnival to immerse yourself in the local culture, featuring Holland's largest Surinamese community.

The Lowdown: With world-famous contemporary architecture, innovative museums, thriving cultural venues, rockin' street festivals and an urban, cosmopolitan population, it's a wonder why Rotterdam is overlooked by so many visitors to the Netherlands. Granted, Rotterdam is not the prettiest of Dutch cities; bombed completely flat at the beginning of World War II, the rebuilt metropolis lacks Amsterdam's cozy charm. Nevertheless, Holland's second most populous city is an excellent choice for a day trip or overnight getaway. Visit Museum Boijmans Van Beuningen to view master paintings, applied arts and design, and a broad modern art collection showcasing Magritte and Dali. Jaded gallery-goers should head to the nearby Kunsthal—designed by local boy Rem Koolhaas, it has a unique mandate, and only shows exhibitions that have never been on display elsewhere. That theme of innovation continues on Rotterdam's streets where visitors encounter some of the icons of late 20th century architecture like the highly recognizable Erasmus Bridge, and the Cube Houses. Indoors, the Netherlands Architecture Institute (NAI) hosts rotating world-class exhibits on themes meant to expand the public understanding of modern architecture. On a more human note, Rotterdam has excellent nightclubs that mainly play electronic and hip-hop music. To sample global cuisine, pop into one of the countless Surinamese "Warung" that serve up delicious, albeit sometimes fiery, dishes. Festivals, like the Heineken Dance Parade (see p.144) and the Architecture Biennale (held in odd-numbered years only), draw huge crowds, and show off the city's best assets. Tulips and canals it ain't, but if you like your culture with a bit of an edge, Rotterdam is a must-do.

Best Attractions

Euromast Get a bird's eye view of the city from the top of Holland's tallest observation tower. € Parkhaven 20, 010-436-4811, euromast.nl

Kunsthal Rotterdam Thoughtfully planned, innovative art exhibitions in various media. € Westzeedijk 341, 010-440-0301, kunsthal.nl

Museum Boijmans Van Beuningen Classics, contemporary art and design under one roof. € Museumpark 18-20, 010-441-9400, boijmans.nl

Netherlands Architecture Institute Exhibitions on architecture and planned environments. € Museumpark 25, 010-440-1200, nai.nl

Netherlands Fotomuseum Up-to-the-minute, sometimes eyebrow-raising photo exhibitions. € Witte de Withstr. 63, 010-213-2011, nederlandsfotomuseum.nl

Rotterdam Roots Tailored guided trips of the city focusing on themes like architecture. €€€€+ Westzeedijk 80b, 010-411-3727, rotterdamroots.nl

Best Restaurants

Club Restaurant DeLoft Drink, dine, and lounge with hip 30-something locals; DJs on weekends. €€€ Van Vollehovenstr. 15, 010-241-7506, deloft.nl

De Engle Reserved style, substance, and noteworthy design make this a city favorite. €€€ Eendrachtsweg 19, 010-413-8256

Jackie Restaurant Club Stylish dining in one of the city's hottest all-in-one spaces. €€€ Maasboulevard 300, 010-280-0238

Parkheuvel Rotterdam's best is home to one of Holland's very few three-Michelin-star chefs. €€€€ Heuvellaan 21, 010-436-0766, parkheuvel.nl

Prachtig Design lunching on a riverside bistro terrace; sandwiches are tops. €€ Willemsplein 73-79, 010-411-5321

Warung Mini Surinamese cafe with awful décor and delicious food; go for lunch. € Witte de Withstr. 47, 010-404-7456

Best Nightlife

Las Palmas Big-name DJs and theme nights, a perennial favorite among hip locals. € Wilhelminakade 66, 010-215-1097

Now&Wow Groove till dawn, high-energy dance/hip-hop parties, hot DJs. €€ Maashaven Zuid Zijde 2, 010-477-1074, now-wow.com

Off Corso Dance, drink and experience new media in this "concept" space. €€ Kruiskade 22, 010-411-8541

Best Hotels

Hotel Bazar Super hip, internationally themed hotel for adventurous, trendy club-bers. € Witte de Withstr. 16, 010-206-5151

Hotel New York Trendy-chic harbor-side hotel with views of the city skyline. € Koningennenhoofd 1, 010-439-0500, hotelnewyork.nl

The Westin Rotterdam Contemporary five-star hotel, steps from shopping and entertainment. €€€ Weena 686, 010-430-2000, westin.com/rotterdam

Contacts

Tourism Rotterdam 010-413-3124, vvv.rotterdam.nl/uk

LEAVING

Getting There
By Car: From the A10 Ring Road, take the A4 Zuid (South) towards Den Haag (The Hague), then take the A13 to Rotterdam. Takes about 1 hour.
By Train: From Amsterdam Centraal Station take the train to Rotterdam Centraal.

Utrecht

Hot Tip: Utrecht's canals are considered some of the most beautiful in the country—rivaling even Amsterdam's.

The Lowdown: Just 30 km from Amsterdam, Utrecht offers visitors a glimpse of authentic Dutch city life. The Netherlands' fourth-largest city rewards visitors with canals that trump Amsterdam's for beauty, a bustling Saturday market, and a slew of one-of-a-kind shops. But if strolling more canals and stores doesn't inspire you, Utrecht does have some additional draws. Built in 1382, the 112-meter-high Dom Tower provides tourists with a bird's-eye view of the city as well as vistas that stretch all the way to Amsterdam. The Centraal Museum lures visitors with old master paintings, a wealth of new media, the work of famed illustrator Dick Bruna, and the most comprehensive collection of works by pioneering architect and designer Gerrit Rietveld—across town, his landmark Rietveld-Schröder house is also open to visitors. Built in 1924, and recently declared a UNESCO World Heritage Site, it still appears ahead of its time. History undeniably accounts for a large part of Utrecht's appeal, but the city continues to thrive: Creative dining on scenic canal-side terraces and a huge student population give the city a youthful flair. Still, when it comes to nightlife, even the locals head to Amsterdam. Note: Can be done as a day trip.

Best Attractions

Centraal Museum Outstanding Dick Bruna and Gerrit Rietveld collections, also master paintings and new media. € Nicolaaskerkhof 10, 030-236-2362, centraalmuseum.nl

Dom Tower and Dom Kerk Tour and climb the Gothic tower; free Saturday afternoon organ concerts. € Domplein 9-10, 030-233-3036

Museum Catharijneconvent Holland's tumultuous religious history is illustrated with master paintings, illuminated manuscripts, and assorted arts. € Lange Nieuwestr. 38, 030-231-7296, catharijneconvent.nl

Rietveld-Schröder House Tour an icon of modern architecture. Reservations required. €€ Prins Hendriklaan 50, 030-236-2310, centraalmuseum.nl

Best Restaurants

BIS Casual cafe-style dining, seasonal ingredients, canal views. € Lijnmarkt 26, 030-231-5831

Eggie Worldly French-fusion cuisine and excellent seafood attract locals. €€ Schoutenstr. 19, 030-240-0096

Goesting See-and-be-seen eatery, smart French-international menu with an edge. € Schoutenstr. 19, 030-240-0096 €€ Veeartsenijpad 150, 030-273-3346

Luce Trendy Italian dining, well known for set menus, service, and wines. € Visschersplein 75, 030-233-3008

Opium Asian fusion cuisine in a delicious purple and black design space. € Voorstraat 80, 030-231-5515

Best Nightlife

Café Belgie Forty beers on tap and 200 by the bottle make it a favorite hangout for suds-lovers. Oudegracht 196, 030-231-2666

Café Het Hart Hipster lounge scene, crowded until late, especially on Fridays. Voorstraat 10, 030-231-9718

Café Lust Design-ish lounge with a casual vibe, DJs on weekends, and good cocktails anytime. Nobelstraat 10, 030-239-2421

Monza Non Solo Utrecht's least student-oriented dance spot has a trendy vibe and is known for progressive music. Potterstraat 16-20, (no phone)

Best Hotels

Grand Hote Karel V Classic and grand, Utrecht's only five-star hotel. €€ Geertebolwerk 1, 030-233-7555, karelv. n l

NH Centre Modern facilities in a classic building, close to canals and shopping. € Utrecht Janskerkhof 10, 030-231-3169, nh-hotels.com

NH Utrecht Modern digs near the train station, shopping, market, and canals. € Jaarbeursplein 24, 030-297-7977, nh-hotels.com

Contacts

Utrecht Tourism 030-234-7388, utrechttourism.com

LEAVING

Getting There:
By Car: From the A10 Ring Road, take the A2 to Utrecht. Driving time is about 30 minutes.
By Train: From Amsterdam Centraal Station, take the train to Utrecht Centraal.

Keukenhof

Hot Tip: Seasonal weather conditions influence the specific dates, but the gardens typically open in the third week of March and stay open for eight weeks. The season is short and the gardens are famous; come mid-week to avoid the largest crowds.

The Lowdown: Can't think of Holland without dreaming of endless fields of flowers? Then the Keukenhof, the world's largest public garden, is a must. The gardens, which once belonged to the Duchess of Bavaria and were an inspiration to Claude Monet, feature traditional and modern landscaping, and are a sight to behold. Seven million bulbs blossom into countless varieties of flowers with pride of place reserved for the tulip. In addition to the flower beds, water features abound, as do various shrubs and larger trees that offer shade. The Keukenhof is also home to a Japanese garden, a maze, some outdoor sculpture, and a windmill. Should you still not have exhausted your passion for flowers, check out one of the many shows that are housed in covered pavilions. Since they focus on specific varieties of flowers and occur often, aficionados are advised to check the garden's website for the schedule of events. There is a comprehensive lunch cafe on-site, you can rent a bicycle to explore the neighboring commercial flower fields, and picnic baskets can be arranged in advance through the Keukenhof's website.

If walking the 32 hectare park still leaves you with energy to burn, consider combining your visit to the Keukenhof with a short bike tour. The Noordwijk Tourist Office offers a 25km/15.5 mile, round-trip bicycle tour (all of it on flat terrain) that starts in the scenic village of Noordwijk, meanders through commercial tulip fields, and includes coffee and pastries at a local cafe as well as admission to the gardens. Reservations are recommended.

Best Attractions

The Keukenhof The world's largest public garden. €€ Stationsweg 166a, Lisse, 025-246-5555, keukenhof.nl

VVV Holland Rijnland Tourist Office Noordwijk Bike through tulip fields; includes admission to the Keukenhof. €€ de Grent 8, 071-361-9321, vvv.noordwijk.nl

Getting There
By Car: Take the A4 in the direction of The Hague. Turn off at "Afrit (exit) 4" and follow the signs "N207-Lisse." Signposts will guide the way. Takes about 40 minutes.
By Train: From Amsterdam Centraal Station, take the train to Leiden. Then take bus 54 (Keukenhof Express) or a taxi.

Park De Hoge Veluwe and Kr ller-M ller Museum

Hot Tip: The 1,300 white bikes scattered around the Park De Hoge Veluwe are free for visitors to use—just grab one and hop on.

The Lowdown: Looking to get out of the tourist rut? Had enough of crowded cities? Feeling guilty for passing up another "all star" museum? Only 60 minutes from Amsterdam, the 5,000 hectare/12,000 acre Park De Hoge Veluwe, home to wild boar, deer, and Corsican sheep, and the Kröller-Müller Museum combine art, nature, and architecture in a way that's bound to leave you feeling recharged.

Grab a bike and enjoy the 43 km/27 miles of cycling trails that meander through the woodlands—some of them follow themes such as "Images in the Landscape" or "Creation," and some lead to the ornate St. Hubertus hunting lodge, but all of them eventually link up with the entrance of the Kröller-Müller Museum. The museum stages exhibitions that showcase the 20th-century's leading artists, but it's most famous for its excellent selection of Van Gogh's work, as well as paintings by Picasso and Mondriaan. Nonetheless, the indoor museum is only part of the Kröller-Müller attraction. Outside, Europe's largest sculpture garden holds a wealth of works by such luminaries as Rodin, Henry Moore, Richard Serra, Barbara Hepworth, and Alberto Giacometti. To see the highlights, take a "Ramble Route" map from the museum and follow the 6km/4-mile path to sculptural enlightenment. Admission to the museum can be combined with park admission. The museum is closed on Mondays. Guided tours of the museum and sculpture garden are available in English but remember to book ahead by calling 031-859-6155.

Best Attractions

Kröller-Müller Museum Van Gogh, Picasso, and Mondriaan works, 25-hectare/62-acre sculpture garden. € Houtkampweg 6, Otterlo, 031-859-1241, kmm.nl
Park De Hoge Veluwe Cycle and walk Holland's most natural setting; visit St. Hubertus, H.P. Berlage's lodge, lake, and rose garden. € hogeveluwe.nl

Getting There
By Car: From the A10 Ring Road, take the A1 East towards Hilversum, continuing until you see the signs for Park Hoge Veluwe/Kröller-Müller Museum. Takes about 40 minutes.
By Train: From Amsterdam Centraal Station, take the train to Apeldoorn. Catch bus 108 to Hoenderlo, and transfer to bus 106 which stops in front of the centre and the museum.

Zaanse Schans

Go mid-week—on weekends, it truly gets packed with tourists.

The Lowdown: If you're interested in seeing some of Holland's most readily identifiable symbols—cheese factories, working windmills, and wooden shoe-clad locals—head to the Zaanse Schans for a quick day trip, where you'll find a treasure trove of Dutch kitsch-classic set against flat-as-a-pancake, below-sea-level pasture land. It's equal parts open-air museum and working town. The quaint 17th-century wooden houses are still inhabited and the livestock isn't just for display, and the area offers fresh country air, some interesting history, a handful of tiny museums, and a glimpse into what could surely be described as "Ye Olde Holland" were in not for the fact that windmills and wooden shoes remain a part of life for the rural Dutch. In addition to the obvious draw of strolling through a pastoral, classic Dutch village, visitors come to experience exhibits on traditional life in the Netherlands and highlights of those include a small cheese factory, a wooden shoe museum complete with crowd-pleasing demonstrations on shoemaking, a working windmill where delicious creamy mustards are milled, and a boatyard where wooden boats are built and restored. When it comes time to rest your feet, choose from one of two restaurants serving typically Dutch dishes, including the omnipresent "pannekoek"—pancake—as well as a variety of delicious desserts, or earn your sea legs with a quick boat tour; 50 minutes in duration, the mini-cruises offer the best views of the storied windmills as well as the period neighborhood the Gortershoek on the bank of the River Zaan. Back on terra firma the requisite gift shops won't let you forget that you're visiting a tourist venue, but if you want your break from the city streets to offer a quick and charming glimpse of rural life, the popular-with-all-ages Zaanse Schans is a picture-perfect diversion.

Best Attractions

Zaan Boat Tours Fifty-minute scenic boat tours of the local windmills. €
Apr-Oct, Het Glop Jetty

Getting There
By Car: From the A10 Ring turn off at the A8 and then the A7 in the direction of Purmerend. Take the "Zaanse Schans" exit. Signposts will guide the way. Takes about 1 hour.
By Train: From Amsterdam Centraal Station take the train to Koog-Zaandijk. Then follow the signs to the Zaanse Schans.

AMSTERDAM BLACK BOOK

You're solo in the city—where's a singles-friendly place to eat? Is there a good lunch spot near the museum? Will the bar be too loud for easy conversation? Get the answers fast in the Black Book, a condensed version of every listing in our guide that puts all the essential information at your fingertips.

A quick glance down the page and you'll find the type of food, nightlife, or attractions you are looking for, the phone numbers, and the pages to turn to for more detailed information. How did you ever survive without this?

BLACK BOOK

Amsterdam Black Book

Hotels

NAME TYPE (ROOMS)	ADDRESS (CROSS STREET) WEBSITE	AREA PRICE	PHONE (020) 800 NUMBER	EXPERIENCE	PAGE
Amstel Hotel InterContinental Grand (79)	Professor Tulpplein 1 (Sarphatistr.) amsterdam.intercontinental.com	PL €€€€	622-6060 800-327-0200	Classic	111
Amsterdam American Hotel Timeless (174)	Leidsekade 97 (Leidsestr.) amsterdamamerican.com	CB €€€	556-3000 800-327-0200	Classic	111
Hotel Arena Trendy (127)	's-Gravesandestraat 51 (Mauritskade) hotelarena.nl	PL €	850-2400	Hip	85
Bilderberg Jan Luyken Modern (62)	Jan Luykenstraat 58 (PC Hooftstr.) janluyken.nl	MP €€	573-0730	Cool	57
Breaks and Butlers Trendy (1)	Groenburgwal 1 (Raamgracht) breaksandbutlers.nl	OZ €€€	638-9944	Cool	57
The College Hotel Trendy (40)	Roelof Hartstraat 1 (Balthasar Floriszstr.) thecollegehotel.com	MP €€	571-1511	Cool	57
EnSuite Apartment Trendy (1)	Keizersgracht 320 (Berenstr.) ensuite-logies.nl	JO €€	421-1887	Cool	58
Hotel V Trendy (24)	Victorieplein 42 (Vrijheidslaan) hotelv.nl	DP €	662-3233	Hip	85
The Grand Ams. Sofitel Demeure Timeless (182)	Oudezijds Voorburgwal 197 (Sint Agnietenstr.) thegrand.nl	OZ €€€€	555-3111 800-221-4542	Classic	112
Hotel Dylan Amsterdam Trendy (41)	Kreizersgracht 384 (Berenstr.) dylanamersterdam.com	JO €€€€	530-2010	Cool	58
Hotel de l'Europe Grand (100)	Nieuwe Doelenstraat 2-8 (Oude Turfmarkt) leurope.nl	OZ €€€	531-1777	Classic	112
Hotel Pulitzer Timeless (230)	Prinsengracht 315-331 (Westerchurch) starwood.com	JO €€€€	523-5235 800-326-3535	Classic	112
Hotel Seven One Seven Grand (8)	Prinsengracht 717 (Leidsestr.) 717hotel.nl	CB €€€€	427-0717	Classic	113
The Lloyd Hotel & Cultural Embassy Trendy (116)	Oostelijke Handelskade 34 (Lloydplein) lloydhotel.com	EH €€	561-3636	Hip	85
Lute Suites Trendy (7)	Amsteldijk Zuid 54-58 (Amsteldjk) lutesuites.com	VA €€€	472-2462	Cool	58
Miauw Suites Modern (3)	Hartenstraat 36 (Keizersgracht) miauw.com	JO €€	422-0561	Cool	59
NH Amsterdam Centre Modern (230)	Stadhouderskade 7 (Vondelstr.) nh-hotels.com	MP €€	685-1351	Cool	59

Neighborhood (Area) Key

CB = Canal Belt	**MP** = Museumplein	**VA** = Various Locations
DP = De Pijp	**NZ** = Nieuwe Zijde	**WE** = West
EA = East	**OZ** = Oude Zijde	**ZU** = Zuid
EH = Eastern Harbor	**PL** = Plantage	
JO = Jordaan	**RP** = Rembrandtplein	

Holland country code is 31. Within Amsterdam, local calls begin with 020, the city code, followed by the telephone number. See p.155 for more information.

NAME TYPE (ROOMS)	ADDRESS (CROSS STREET) WEBSITE	AREA PRICE	PHONE (020) 800 NUMBER	EXPERIENCE	PAGE
NH Barbizon Palace Timeless (275)	Prins Hendrikkade 72 (Zeedijk) nh-hotels.com	NZ €€	556-4564	Classic	113
NH Grand Krasnapolsky Timeless (468)	Dam 9 (Warmoesstr.) nh-hotels.com	NZ €€	554-9111	Classic	114
NL Hotel Trendy (10)	Nassaukade 368 (Derde Helmersstr.) nl-hotel.com	MP €	689-0030	Hip	86
The Okura Hotel Modern (315)	Ferdinand Bolstraat 333 (Jozef Israelskade) okura.nl	DP €€€€	678-7111	Cool	60
Wolvenstraat 23 Trendy (1)	Wolvenstraat 23 (Keizersgracht)	JO €	320-0843	Hip	86

Restaurants

NAME TYPE	ADDRESS (CROSS STREET) WEBSITE	AREA PRICE	PHONE (020) SINGLES/NOISE	EXPERIENCE 99 BEST	PAGE PAGE
Altmann Restaurant & Bar Fusion	Amsteldijk 25 (2e Jan v.d. Heijdenstr.) altmann.nl	DP €€	662-7777 - ☰	Cool	61
Arena:toDine* Continental	's-Gravesandestraat 51 (Mauritskade) hotelarena.nl	PL €	850-2460 - ☰	Hip	82, 87
De Badcuyp* Cafe	Eerste Sweelinckstraat 10 (Albert Cuypstr.)	DP €	675-9669 Ⓑ ☰	Hip	87
Balthazar's Keuken Mediterranean	Elandsgracht 108 (Looiersdwarsstr.) balthazarskeuken.nl	JO €	420-2114 - ☰	Hip	87
Bar Ça* Spanish	Marie Heinekenplein 30-31 (Ferdinand Bolstr.) bar-ca.com	DP €	470-4144 - ☰	Hip Restaurant-Lounges	87 42
Bazar North African	Albert Cuypstraat 182 (1e v.d. Helststr.)	DP €	675-0544 - ☰	Hip Tastes of the Exotic	80, 87 47
Beddington's Fusion	Utrechtsedwarsstraat 141 (Amstel) beddington.nl	CB €€	620-7393 - ☰	Cool	61
De Belhamel French	Brouwersgracht 60 (Herengracht) belhamel.nl	JO €€	622-1095 - ☰	Classic Tables with a View	115 46
Blauw aan de Wal French	Oudezijds Achterburgwal 99 (Barndesteeg)	OZ €€	330-2257 - ☰	Cool Only-in-Amsterdam	61 40
Blender Mediterranean	v.d. Palmkade 16 (Jacob Catskade) blender.to	ZU €€	486-9860 - ☰	Cool	61
Bond Mediterranean	Valeriusstraat 128b (Dufaystr.) restaurantbond.nl	ZU €€	676-4647 - ☰	Cool	61

Restaurant and Nightlife Symbols

Restaurants
Singles Friendly (eat and/or meet)
Ⓘ = Communal table
Ⓑ = Food served at bar

(G) = Gourmet Destination

Nightlife
Price Warning
Ⓒ = Cover or ticket charge

Restaurant + Nightlife
Prime time noise levels
⎵ = Quiet
☰ = A buzz, but still conversational
☰ = Loud

Note regarding page numbers: Italic = itinerary listing; Roman = description in theme chapter listing.

BLACK BOOK

Restaurants (cont.)

NAME TYPE	ADDRESS (CROSS STREET) WEBSITE	AREA PRICE	PHONE (020) SINGLES/NOISE	EXPERIENCE 99 BEST	PAGE PAGE
Bordewijk French-Mediterranean (G)	Noordermarkt 7 (Prinsengracht)	JO €€	624-3899 -	Classic	*108*, 115
Brasserie de Joffers Continental	Williamsparkweg 163 (Cornelis Schuytstr.)	ZU €	673-0360	Cool	*52*, 62
Brasserie Harkema* French	Nes 67 (Grimburgwal) brasserieharkema.nl	NZ €€	428-2222 -	Cool	62
Brasserie van Baerle French	Van Baerlestraat 158 (Ruysdaelstr.) brasserievanbaerle.nl	ZU €€	679-1532 -	Cool Brunches	*54*, 62 20
't Buffet van Odette en Yvette Dutch	Herengracht 309 (Oude Spiegelstr.) buffet-amsterdam.nl	JO €	423-6034 -	Cool	*53*, 62
Café de Jaren* Cafe	Nieuwe Doelenstraat 20-22 (Binnengasthuisstr.) cafe-de-jaren.nl	OZ €	625-5771 -	Hip	87
Café Luxembourg* Tavern	Spui 24 (Kalverstr.) cafeluxembourg.nl	NZ €	620-6264	Classic	115
Café Morlang Continental	Keizersgracht 451 (Leidsestr.) morlang.nl	CB €	625-2681 -	Hip	*81*, 88
Café Roux French	Oudezijds Voorburgwal 197 (Sint Agnietenstr.) thegrand.nl	OZ €€	555-3560 -	Classic	115
Café 't Schuim* Cafe	Spuistraat 189 (Wijdestr.)	NZ €	638-9357	Hip	88
Café Vertigo Cafe	Vondelpark 3 (R. Visscherstr.) vertigo.nl	MP €	612-3021	Classic	*106*, 115
Café Wildschut* Tavern	Roelof Hartplein 1-3 (Cornelis Anthoniszstr.)	MP €	676-8220	Classic	116
Caffe Esprit Cafe	Spui 10 (Voetboogstr.)	NZ € -	622-1967 -	Hip	*79*, 88
CaffePC Continental	PC Hooftstraat 87 (v.d. Veldestr.)	MP €	673-4752 -	Cool	*52*, 63
Chang-I Asian	Jan Willem Brouwersstraat 7 (Alexander Boersstr.) chang-i.nl	ZU €€	470-1700	Cool	63
Chez Georges French (G)	Herenstraat 3 (Herengracht)	JO €€	626-3332 -	Classic	*107*, 116
Christophe French-North African (G)	Leliegracht 46 (Keizersgracht) christophe.nl	JO €€€	625-0807 -	Classic	*106*, 116
Ciel Bleu* French (G)	Ferdinand Bolstraat 333 (Jozef Israelskade) okura.nl	DP €€€	678-7111 -	Classic Tables with a View	*108*, 116 46
Cinema Paradiso Italian	Westerstraat 184-186 (Tichelstr.) cinemaparadiso.info	JO €	623-7344 -	Cool Always-Trendy Tables	63 17
Coffee & Jazz Indonesian	Utrechtsestraat 113 (Herengracht)	CB €	624-5851 -	Hip	88
College* New Dutch	Roelof Hartstraat 1 (Balthasar Florisztr.) thecollegehotel.com	MP €€	571-1511 -	Cool Of-the-Moment Dining	*52*, 63 38
De Compagnon French	Guldehandsteeg 17 (Warmoesstr.) decompagnon.nl	NZ €€	620-4225 -	Classic	*107*, 116

| NAME | ADDRESS (CROSS STREET) | AREA | PHONE (020) | EXPERIENCE | PAGE |
TYPE	WEBSITE	PRICE	SINGLES/NOISE	99 BEST	PAGE
Côte Ouest French	Gravenstraat 20 (Blaeustr.) coteouest.nl	NZ €	320-8998 - ≡	Classic	117
De Duvel* Continental	1e v.d. Helststraat 59-61 (Daniël Stalpertstr.) deduvel.nl	DP €	675-7517 - ≡	Classic	117
The Dylan (formerly Blakes Amsterdam) Fusion (G)	Keizersgracht 384 (Berenstr.) dylanamsterdam.com	JO €€€	530-2010 - ⊟	Cool Always-Trendy Tables	63 17
Dynasty Asian	Reguliersdwarsstraat 30 (Sint Jorisstr.)	RP €€	626-8400 - ⊟	Classic	117
18 Twintig* Continental	Ferdinand Bolstraat 18-20 (Marie Heinekenplein) 18twintig.nl	DP €	470-0651 - ≡	Hip	88
11* Continental	Oosterdokskade 3-5 (De Ruyterkade) 	EH €	625-5999 - ≡	Hip Tables with a View	82, 88 46
L'Entrecôte et les Dames French	Van Baerlestraat 47-49 (Moreelsestr.) entrecote-et-les-dames.nl	MP €	679-8888 - ≡	Classic	117
Envy Italian	Prinsengracht 381 (Reestr.) envy.nl	JO €€€	344-6407 - ≡	Cool Of-the-Moment Dining	51, 64 38
Espressobar Puccini Deli	Staalstraat 21 (Zwanenburgwal) 	OZ €€	620-8458 - ⊟	Cool Lunch Spots	53, 64 37
Excelsior French (G)	Nieuwe Doelenstraat 2-8 (Oude Turfmarkt) leurope.nl	OZ €€€	531-1777 - ⊟	Classic	117
Fifteen Amsterdam* French	Jollemanhof 9 (Kattenburgerstr.) fifteen.nl	EH €€	0900-343-8336 - ≡	Cool Hot-Shot Chefs	54, 64 31
Le Garage French	Ruysdaelstraat 54-56 (Pieter de Hoochstr.) restaurantlegarage.nl	ZU €€	679-7176 - ≡	Cool Hot-Shot Chefs	51, 64 31
Gorgeous French	2e v.d. Helststraat 16 (Van Ostadestr.) gorgeousrestaurant.nl	DP €	379-1400 -	Cool	65
Hein Continental	Berenstraat 20 (Keizersgracht) 	JO €	623-1048 - ⊟	Hip	80, 89
Helden Continental	1e v.d. Helststraat 42 (Quellijnstr.) 	DP €	673-3332 - ≡	Hip	79, 89
Herengracht* Continental	Herengracht 435 (Leidsestr.) deherengracht.nl	CB €€	616-2482 - ≡	Hip	81, 89
Herrie French	Utrechtsestraat 30a (Keizersgracht) 	CB €€	622-0838 - ≡	Cool Of-the-Moment Dining	53, 65 38
Hostaria Italian	2e Egelantiersdwarsstraat 9 (Egelantiersstr.)	JO €	626-0028 - ≡	Classic Italian Eateries	117 33
Hudson's Terrace and Restaurant French	Prins Hendrikkade 72 (Zeedijk) 	NZ €€	556-4875 - ⊟	Classic	107, 118
In de Waag* French-Dutch	Nieuwmarkt 4 (Geldersekade) indewaag.nl	OZ €€	422-7772 - ≡	Classic	118
Incanto Italian	Amstel 2 (Muntplein) restaurant-incanto.nl	RP €€	423-3681 - ≡	Cool	65
Jean-Jean French	1e Anjeliersdwarsstraat 14 (Anjeliersstr.) jean-jean.nl	JO €€	627-7153 - ≡	Cool	65

Restaurants (cont.)

NAME TYPE	ADDRESS (CROSS STREET) WEBSITE	AREA PRICE	PHONE (020) SINGLES/NOISE	EXPERIENCE 99 BEST	PAGE PAGE
't Kalfje* Cafe	Prinsenstraat 5 (Keizersgracht)	JO €	626-3370 B ⊜	Classic Late-Night Scenes	108, 118 35
Kanis & Meiland Cafe	Levantkade 127 (Piraeusplein)	EH €	418-2439 - ⊜	Hip	81, 89
De Kas New Dutch (G)	Kamerlingh Onneslaan 3 (Middenweg) restaurantdekas.nl	EA €€	462-4562 - ⊜	Classic Dutch Dining	107, 118 25
Klein Paardenburg French (G)	Amstelzijde 59 (Oranjebaan)	VA €€€	496-1335 - ⊟	Classic	119
Het Land van Walem Continental	Keizersgracht 449 (Leidsestr.) cafewalem.nl	CB €	625-3544 - ⊜	Hip Lunch Spots	80, 89 37
Latei Cafe	Zeedijk 143 (Nieuwmarkt)	OZ € -	625-7485 - ⊜	Hip	80, 90
Letting Continental	Prinsenstraat 3 (Keizersgracht)	JO €	627-9393 - ⊜	Cool	65
Local Continental	Westerstraat 136 (Prinsengracht) local-amsterdam.nl	JO €	423-4039 ▯ ⊜	Hip	90
Lute Restaurant Fusion (G)	Oude Molen 5 (Amsteldijk) luterestaurant.nl	VA €€	472-2462 - ⊜	Cool Hot-Shot Chefs	53, 66 31
Mamouche Moroccan	Quellijnstraat 104 (1e v.d. Helststr.) restaurantmamouche.nl	DP €€	673-6361 - ⊜	Hip	80, 90
The Mansion* (formerly Vossius) Asian	Hobbemastraat 2 (Stadhouderskade) the-mansion.nl	MP €€€	616-6664 - ⊜	Cool	51, 66
Marius French-Mediterranean (G)	Barentszstraat 243 (van Linschotenstr.)	WE €€	422-7880 - ⊜	Classic	119
Nana Gentile Italian	Nieuwezijds Voorburgwal 289 (Paliesstr.) nanagentile.nl	NZ €€	420-0202 - ⊜	Cool	66
Nielsen Coffeehouse	Berenstraat 19 (Keizersgracht)	JO € -	330-6006 - ⊜	Hip	81, 90
NOA Asian	Leidsegracht 84 (Prinsengracht) tao-group.nl	JO €	626-0802 - ⊜	Hip	90
Nomads North African	Rozengracht 133 (Hazenstr.) restaurantnomads.nl	JO €€	344-6401 - ⊟	Hip Romantic Dining	91 43
Odeon* Continental	Singel 460 (Koningsplein) odeontheater.nl	CB €€	521-8555 - ⊜	Hip	91
De Ondeugd* Fusion	Ferdinand Bolstraat 13-15 (Daniël Stalpertstr.) ondeugd.nl	DP €	672-0651 - ⊜	Cool	66
Palladium Cafe	Kleine Gartmansplantsoen 7 (Leidsestr.)	CB €	620-5536 B ⊜	Hip	91
The Pancake Bakery Cafe	Prinsengracht 191 (Prinsenstr.) pancake.nl	JO €	625-1333 - ⊜	Classic	119
Le Pêcheur Seafood	Reguliersdwarsstraat 32 (SintJorisstr.) lepecheur.nl	RP €€	624-3121 - ⊟	Classic Romantic Dining	105, 119 43
Pont 13 French	Stavangerweg 891 (Tasmanstr.) pont13.nl	WE €	770-2722 B ⊜	Cool	66

NAME TYPE	ADDRESS (CROSS STREET) WEBSITE	AREA PRICE	PHONE (020) SINGLES/NOISE	EXPERIENCE 99 BEST	PAGE PAGE
Proeflokaal Janvier Fusion	Amstelveld 12 (Prinsengracht) proeflokaaljanvier.nl	CB €	626-1199 - ≡	Cool	51, 67
Pulitzer's French	Keizersgracht 234 (Reestr.) pulitzer.nl	JO €€€	523-5282 - ≡	Classic	119
Pygma-Lion South African	Nieuwe Spiegelstraat 5a (Herengracht) pygma-lion.com	CB €	420-7022 - ≡	Cool Tastes of the Exotic	54, 67 47
Quartier Sud French	Olympiaplein 176 (Parnassusweg)	ZU €€	675-3990 - ≡	Classic Lunch Spots	106, 120 37
Rain* Fusion	Rembrandtplein 44 (Utrechtsestr.) rain-amsterdam.com	RP €€	626-7078 - ≡	Cool Restaurant-Lounges	67 42
Restaurant Greetje Dutch	Peperstraat 23-25 (Rapenburg) restaurantgreetje.nl	OZ €	779-7450 Ⓑ ≡	Classic	120
Restaurante Bice Italian	Stadhouderskade 7 (Vondelstr.) bice.nl	MP €€	589-8870 - ≡	Cool Italian Eateries	67 33
Resto-Bar Knus* Fusion	Reguiiersdwarsstraat 23 (Sint Jorisstr.) restobarknus.nl	RP €	427-7828 Ⓑ ≡	Hip	91
La Rive French (G)	Professor Tulpplein 1 (Sarphatistr.) restaurantlarive.nl	CB €€€	520-3264 - ⊒	Classic Fine Dining	106, 120 27
Roberto's Continental	Apollolaan 138 (Breitnerstr.) amsterdam.hilton.com	ZU €€	710-6025 - ≡	Classic	107, 120
Rosario Italian	Peperstraat 10 (Rapenburg)	OZ €€	627-0280 - ≡	Classic	120
Royal Café de Kroon* Cafe	Rembrandtplein 17 (Halvemaansteeg)	RP €	625-2011 - ≡	Hip	79, 91
Sama Sebo Indonesian	PC Hooftstraat 27 (Stadhouderskade) samasebo.nl	MP €	662-8146 - ≡	Classic	121
Saskia's Huiskamer Dutch	Albert Cuypstraat 203 (1e v.d. Helststr)	DP €€	862-9839 Ⓘ ≡	Hip Dutch Dining	81, 91 25
Segugio Italian	Utrechtsestraat 96a (Prinsengracht) segugio.nl	RP €€	330-1503 - ⊒	Classic Italian Eateries	121 33
La Sirene Seafood	Apollolaan 2 (Bernhard Zweerskade) lasirene.nl	ZU €€€	570-5724 - ⊒	Classic Brunches	108, 121 20
Snel Dutch	Oostelijke Handelskade 34 (Lloydplein) lloydhotel.com	EH €	561-3636 - ≡	Hip	82, 92
Stout International	Haarlemmerstraat 73 (Herenmarkt) restaurantstout.nl	JO €	616-3664 Ⓑ ≡	Cool	67
SupperClub* Fusion	Jonge Roelensteeg 21 (Nieuwezijds Voorburgwal) supperclub.nl	NZ €€	344-6400 - ≡	Cool Always-Trendy Tables	53, 67 17
SupperClub Cruise* Fusion	Locations vary supperclubcruise.nl	VA €€	344-6404 - ≡	Cool On-the-Water	68 39
Tempo Doeloe Indonesian	Utrechtsestraat 75 (Herengracht) tempodoeloerestaurant.nl	CB €€	625-6718 - ⊒	Classic Tastes of the Exotic	108, 121 47
La Terrasse French (G)	Nieuwe Doelenstraat 2-8 (Oude Turfmarkt) leurope.nl	OZ €€	531-1705 - ≡	Classic Terraces	107, 121 48

Restaurants (cont.)

NAME TYPE	ADDRESS (CROSS STREET) WEBSITE	AREA PRICE	PHONE (020) SINGLES/NOISE	EXPERIENCE 99 BEST	PAGE PAGE
Tomo Sushi Sushi	Reguliersdwarsstraat 131 (Openhartsteeg)	RP €€€	528-5208 - ⊟	Cool	53, 68
Toscanini Ristorante Italian	Lindengracht 75 (Noorderkerkstr.) toscanini.nl	JO €	623-2813 - ⊟	Classic	122
Het Tuynhuys Continental	Reguliersdwarsstraat 28 (Sintjorisstr.) tuynhuys.nl	RP €€	627-6603 - ⊡	Classic	105, 122
Utrechtsedwarstafel French	Utrechtsedwarsstraat 107-109 (Utrechtsestr.) utrechtsedwarstafel.com €€	CB	625-4189 - ⊡	Classic	122
Vakzuid* Fusion	Olympisch Stadion 35 (Stadionplein) vakzuid.nl	ZU €€	570-8400 - ⊟	Cool Restaurant-Lounges	68 42
Van Vlaanderen French-Mediterranean (G)	Weteringschans 175 (Nieuwe Vijzelstr.)	CB €€€	622-8292 - ⊡	Classic Fine Dining	122 27
Vermeer French (G)	Prins Hendrikkade 72 (Zeedijk) restaurantvermeer.nl	NZ €€€	556-4885 - ⊡	Classic	106, 122
d'Vijff Vlieghen Dutch	Spuistraat 294-302 (Mosterdpotsteeg) thefiveflies.com	NZ €€	530-4060 - ⊡	Classic Dutch Dining	107, 123 25
Visaandeschelde Seafood (G)	Scheldeplein 4 (Scheldestr.) visaandeschelde.nl	ZU €€	675-1583 - ⊡	Classic	123
Voorbij Het Einde French (G)	Sumatrakade 613 (Javakade) voorbijheteinde.nl	EH €€	419-1143 - ⊡	Cool Romantic Dining	54, 68 43
Wolvenstraat* Fusion	Wolvenstraat 23 (Keizersgracht)	JO €	320-0843 - ⊟	Hip Brunches	82, 92 20
Yamazato Japanese (G)	Ferdinand Bolstraat 333 (Jozef Israelskade)	DP €€€	678-7111 - ⊡	Classic Fine Dining	123 27
Zaza's Fusion	Daniël Stalpertstraat 103 (1e v.d Helststr.)	DP €	673-6333 - ⊟	Hip	92
Zuid Zeeland Italian	Herengracht 413 (Beulingstr.) zuidzeeland.nl	JO €	624-3154 - ⊟	Classic	123

Nightlife

NAME TYPE	ADDRESS (CROSS STREET) WEBSITE	AREA COVER	PHONE (020) FOOD/NOISE	EXPERIENCE 99 BEST	PAGE PAGE
De Admiraal Bar	Herengracht 319 (Treeftsteeg)	JO -	625-4334 - ⊟	Classic Dutch Drinking	107, 124 26
Arc Lounge	Reguliersdwarsstraat 44 (Geel Vinksteeg) bararc.com	RP -	689-7070 - ⊟	Cool Gay Scenes	53, 69 28
Arena:toDrink* Hotel Lounge	's-Gravesandestraat 51 (Mauritskade) hotelarena.nl	PL -	850-2450 - ⊟	Hip	82, 93
Arena:toNight* Nightclub	's-Gravesandestraat 51 (Mauritskade) hotelarena.nl	PL Ⓒ	850-2541 - ⊟	Hip	82, 93
't Arendsnest Bar	Herengracht 90 (Korsjespoortsteeg) arendsnest.nl	JO -	421-2057 - ⊟	Classic Beer-Lovers' Spots	108, 124 19

NAME	ADDRESS (CROSS STREET)	AREA	PHONE (020)	EXPERIENCE	PAGE
TYPE	WEBSITE	COVER	FOOD/NOISE	99 BEST	PAGE
De Badcuyp*	Eerste Sweelinckstraat 10	DP	675-9669	Hip	*82*, 93
Jazz Club	(Albert Cuypstr.)	-	- ▤	Live Music	36
Bar Americain	Leidsekade 97 (Leidseplein)	CB	556-3000	Classic	124
Hotel Bar	amsterdamamerican.com	-	- ▤	Hotel Bars	32
Bar Bep	Nieuwezijds Voorburgwal 260	NZ	626-5649	Cool	*52*, 69
Bar/Restaurant	(Korte Lijnesteeg)	-	- ▤		
Bar Ça*	Marie Heinekenplein 30-31	DP	470-4144	Hip	*80*, 93
Theme Bar	(Ferdinand Bolstr.) bar-ca.com	-	- ▤	Restaurant-Lounges	42
Bierbrouwerij 't IJ	Funenkade 7 (Alexanderkade)	PL	622-8325	Classic	*108*, 124
Brewery	brouwerijhetij.nl	-	- ▤	Only-in-Amsterdam	40
Bimhuis	Piet Heinkade 3 (Vemenplein)	EH	788-2188	Cool	69
Performance	bimhuis.nl	Ⓒ	-	Jazz Scenes	34
Bitterzoet	Spuistraat 2 (Kattengat)	NZ	521-3001	Hip	*80*, 93
Nightclub		Ⓒ	- ▤	Live Music	36
Boom Chicago	Leidseplein 12 (Leidsestr.)	CB	423-0101	Classic	124
Comedy Club	boomchicago.nl	Ⓒ	▤		
Bourbon Street Blues Club	Leidsekruisstraat 6-8	CB	623-3440	Classic	*107*, 125
Live Music	(Prinsengracht) bourbonstreet.nl	Ⓒ	- ▤	Late-Night Scenes	35
Brasserie Harkema*	Nes 67 (Grimburgwal)	NZ	428-2222	Cool	69
Bar/Restaurant	brasserieharkema.nl	-	- ▤		
Brix*	Wolvenstraat 16 (Keizersgracht)	JO	639-0351	Hip	94
Jazz Club/Lounge	cafebrix.nl	-	- ▤		
Bubbles & Wines	Nes 37 (Pieter Jacobszstr.)	NZ	422-3318	Cool	*54*, 69
Wine Bar	bubblesandwines.com	-	- ▤		
Café Cuba	Nieuwmarkt 3 (Koningsstr.)	OZ	627-4919	Classic	*106*, 125
Theme Bar		-	- ▤		
Café Finch	Noordermarkt 5 (Prinsengracht)	WE	626-2461	Hip	94
Lounge		-	- ▤		
Café Gollem	Raamsteeg 4 (Spuistr.)	NZ	626-6645	Classic	*106*, 125
Bar	cafegollem.nl	-	- ▤	Beer-Lovers' Spots	19
Café Hoppe	Spui 18-20 (Kalverstr.)	NZ	420-4420	Hip	*81*, 94
Bar		-	▤	Dutch Drinking	26
Café de Jaren*	Nieuwe Doelenstraat 20-22	OZ	625-5771	Hip	94
Bar	(Binnengasthuisstr.) cafe-de-jaren.nl	-	- ▤	Terraces	48
Café Luxembourg*	Spui 24 (Kalverstr.)	NZ	620-6264	Classic	125
Pub/Tavern	cafeluxembourg.nl	-	- ▤	After-Work Drinks	16
Café Nol	Westerstraat 109 (Tichelstr.)	JO	624-5380	Classic	*106*, 125
Bar		-	- ▤	Only-in-Amsterdam	40
Café 't Schuim*	Spuistraat 189 (Wijdestr.)	NZ	638-9357	Hip	*81*, 94
Bar		-	- ▤	After-Work Drinks	16
Café 't Smalle	Egelantiersgracht 12	JO	623-9617	Classic	*108*, 126
Bar	(1e Egelantiersdwarsstr.)	-	- ▤		
Café Wildschut*	Roelof Hartplein 1-3	MP	676-8220	Classic	126
Pub/Tavern	(Cornelis Anthoniszstr.)	-	- ▤	After-Work Drinks	16

Nightlife (cont.)

NAME	ADDRESS (CROSS STREET)	AREA	PHONE (020)	EXPERIENCE	PAGE
TYPE	WEBSITE	COVER	FOOD/NOISE	99 BEST	PAGE
Chocolate Bar	1e v.d. Helststraat 62a	DP	675-7672	Hip	80, 95
Lounge	(Albert Cuypstr.)	-	- ☰		
Ciel Bleu Bar*	Ferdinand Bolstraat 333	DP	678-7111	Classic	126
Hotel Bar	(Jozef Israelskade) okura.nl	-	- ☰	Hotel Bars	32
Club Magazijn	Warmoesstraat 170 (Sint Jansstr.)	OZ	669-4469	Hip	81, 95
Nightclub		Ⓒ	- ☰	Dance Clubs	23
Club More	Rozengracht 133 (Ankoleienstr.)	JO	528-7459	Cool	70
Nightclub	expectmore.nl	Ⓒ	- ☰		
College Bar & Lounge*	Roelof Hartstraat 1 (Balthasar	MP	571-1511	Cool	51, 70
Hotel Bar	Floriszstr.) thecollegehotel.com	-	- ☰	Hotel Bars	32
Cristofori Salon	Prinsengracht 581-583 (Runstr.)	JO	624-4969	Classic	126
Live Music	cristofori.nl	Ⓒ	- ☰	Jazz Scenes	34
Diep	Nieuwezijds Voorburgwal 256	NZ	420-2020	Hip	82, 95
Lounge	(Wijdesteeg)	-	- ☰		
De Drie Fleschjes	Gravenstraat 18 (Blaeustr.)	NZ	624-8443	Classic	107, 126
Bar		-	- ☰		
De Duvel*	1e v.d. Helststraat 59 (Daniël	DP	675-7517	Classic	108, 126
Pub/Tavern	Stalpertstr.) deduvel.nl	-	- ☰		
18 Twintig*	Ferdinand Bolstraat 18-20	DP	470-0651	Hip	80, 95
Bar	(Marie Heinekenplein) 18twintig.nl	-	- ☰		
11*	Oosterdokskade 3-5 (De Ruyterkade)	EH	625-5999	Hip	82, 95
Nightclub		Ⓒ	- ☰		
En Pluche	Ruysdaelstraat 48 (Pieter	ZU	471-4695	Cool	51, 70
Lounge	de Hoochstr.) enpluche.nl	-	- ☰		
Escape	Rembrandtplein 11	RP	622-1111	Hip	80, 95
Nightclub	(Halvemaansteeg) escape.nl	Ⓒ	- ☰		
Escape deLux	Rembrandtplein 11	RP	622-1111	Cool	53, 70
Nightclub	(Halvemaansteeg)	Ⓒ	- ☰	Dance Clubs	23
Fifteen Amsterdam*	Jollemanhof 9 (Kattenburgerstr.)	EH	0900-343-8336	Cool	70
Restaurant/Lounge	fifteen.nl	-	- ☰		
GeSpot	Prinsengracht 422 (Raamstr.)	JO	320-3733	Hip	96
Bar	restaurant-gespot.nl	-	- ☰		
Herengracht*	Herengracht 435 (Leidsestr.)	CB	616-2482	Hip	96
Bar	deherengracht.nl	-	- ☰		
Het Proeflokaal Wynand	Pijlsteeg 31 (Oudezijds	NZ	639-2695	Classic	106, 127
Fockink Bar	Voorburgwal)	-	- ☰	Dutch Drinking	26
Holland Casino	Max Euweplein 62 (Weteringschans)	CB	521-1111	Classic	127
Casino		Ⓒ	- ☐		
De Huyschkaemer	Utrechtsestraat 137	CB	627-0575	Hip	96
Bar/Lounge	(Utrechtsedwarsstr.)	-	- ☰		
In 't Aepjen	Zeedijk 1 (Warmoesstr.)	OZ	626-8401	Classic	107, 127
Bar		-	- ☰		
In de Waag*	Nieuwmarkt 4 (Geldersekade)	OZ	422-7772	Classic	106, 127
Lounge	indewaag.nl	-	- ☰		

NAME	ADDRESS (CROSS STREET)	AREA	PHONE (020)	EXPERIENCE	PAGE
TYPE	WEBSITE	COVER	FOOD/NOISE	99 BEST	PAGE
Jazzcafé Alto	Korte Leidsedwarsstraat 115	CB	626-3249	Classic	106, 127
Jazz Club	(Leidsestr.) jazz-cafe-alto.nl	-	- ≡	Jazz Scenes	34
Jimmy Woo	Korte Leidsedwarsstraat 18	CB	626-3150	Cool	54, 70
Nightclub	(Leidsestr.) jimmywoo.com	Ⓒ	- ≡	See-and-Be-Seen	44
Joia	Korte Leidesedwarsstraat 45	CB	626-6769	Cool	54, 71
Lounge	(Leidsestr.) tao-group.nl	-	- ≡		
't Kalfje*	Prinsenstraat 5 (Keizersgracht)	JO	626-3370	Classic	127
Bar		-	- ≡		
Kamer 401	Marnixstraat 401 (Leidsegracht)	JO	620-0614	Hip	96
Bar		-	- ≡		
Lime	Zeedijk 104 (Molenstr.)	OZ	639-3020	Hip	81, 96
Lounge		-	- ≡		
Lux	Marnixstraat 403 (Rozengracht)	JO	422-1412	Hip	80, 96
Lounge		-	- ≡		
The Mansion* (formerly	Hobbemastraat 2	MP	616-6664	Cool	71
Vossius) Cocktail Bar	(Stadhouderskade) the-mansion.nl	Ⓒ	- ≡	See-and-Be-Seen	44
Melkweg	Lijnbaansgracht 234 (Lauriergracht)	CB	531-8181	Hip	81, 97
Nightclub/Performance	melkweg.nl	Ⓒ	- ≡		
NL Lounge	Nieuwzijds Voorburgwal 169	NZ	622-7510	Cool	52, 71
Lounge	(Nieuwezijds Armsteeg) clubnl.nl	-	- ≡		
Odeon*	Singel 460 (Koningsplein)	CB	521-8555	Hip	81, 97
Nightclub	odeontheater.nl	-	- ≡		
Odessa*	Veemkade 295 (Lloydplein)	EH	419-3010	Hip	82, 97
Lounge		-	- ≡		
Onassis	Westerdoksdijk 40 (Berentszstr.)	WE	330-0456	Cool	53, 71
Lounge	onassisamsterdam.nl	-	- ≡	See-and-Be-Seen	44
De Ondeugd*	Ferdinand Bolstraat 13-15 (Daniël	DP	672-0651	Cool	72
Bar/Restaurant	Stalpertstr.) ondeugd.nl	-	- ≡		
Panama	Oostelijke Handelskade 4 (Piet	EH	311-8686	Cool	54, 72
Nightclub	Heinkade) panama.nl	Ⓒ	- ≡	Dance Clubs	23
Pilsvogel	Gerard Douplein 14 (1e v.d. Helststr.)	DP	664-6483	Hip	79, 97
Bar		-	- ≡		
Proust*	Noordermarkt 4 (Prinsengracht)	JO	623-9145	Hip	97
Restaurant/Lounge		-	Ⓑ ≡		
Rain*	Rembrandtplein 44 (Utrechtsestr.)	RP	626-7078	Cool	53, 72
Restaurant/Lounge	rain-amsterdam.com	-	- ≡	Restaurant-Lounges	42
Reijnders	Leidseplein 6 (Leidsestr)	CB	623-4419	Classic	108, 128
Pub/Tavern	hoopman.nl	-	- ≡		
Royal Café de Kroon*	Rembrandtplein 17	RP	625-2011	Hip	97
Lounge	(Halvemaansteeg)	-	- ≡		
Soho	Reguliersdwarsstraat 36	RP	422-3312	Hip	98
Bar	(Openhartsteeg)	-	- ≡	Gay Scenes	28
De Still	Spuistraat 326 (Mosterdpotsteeg)	NZ	427-6809	Classic	108, 128
Bar		-	- ≡		

BLACK BOOK

Nightlife (cont.)

NAME	ADDRESS (CROSS STREET)	AREA	PHONE (020)	EXPERIENCE	PAGE
TYPE	WEBSITE	COVER	FOOD/NOISE	99 BEST	PAGE
Sugar Factory	Lijnbaansgracht 238 (Lauriergracht)	CB	627-0008	Hip	82, 98
Live Music	sugarfactory.nl	C	- ☰	Live Music	36
Suite Rest-O-Bar	Sint Nicolaasstraat 43 (Nieuwezijds	NZ	489-6531	Hip	98
Lounge	Voorburgwal)		- ☰		
SupperClub*	Jonge Roelensteeg 21 (Nieuwezijds	NZ	344-6400	Cool	72
Restaurant/Lounge	Voorburgwal) supperclub.nl	-	☰		
SupperClub Cruise*	various	VA	344-6404	Cool	53, 72
Restaurant/Lounge	supperclubcruise.nl	C	- ☰		
Suzy Wong	Korte Leidsedwarsstraat 45	CB	626-6769	Hip	80, 98
Lounge	(Leidsegracht) tao-group.nl	-	- ☰		
Theater Casa Rosso	Oudezijds Achterburgwal 106-108	OZ	627-8954	Classic	107, 128
Sex Show	(Stoofsteeg) janot.nl	C	- ☰	Sex-in-the-City	45
De Trut	Bilderdijkstraat 165 (Kinkerstr.)	WE		Hip	82, 98
Nightclub		C	- ☰	Gay Scenes	28
Twee Prinsen	Prinsenstraat 27 (Keizersgracht)	JO	624-9722	Classic	108, 128
Bar		-	- ☰		
De Twee Zwaantjes	Prinsengracht 114	JO	625-2729	Classic	107, 128
Bar	(Egelantiersgracht)	-	☰		
TWSTD	Weteringschans 157 (Vijzelgracht)	CB	320-7030	Hip	98
Nightclub	twstd.nl	-	- ☰		
Vakzuid*	Olympisch Stadion 35 (Stadionplein)	ZU	570-8400	Cool	53, 72
Lounge/Nightclub	vakzuid.nl	-	☰	Restaurant-Lounges	42
Vibing	Raamstraat 27 (Raamplein)	CB	624-4411	Cool	52, 72
Cocktail Bar	vibing.nl	-	- ☰		
Vuong	Korte Leidsedwarsstraat 51	CB	530-5577	Cool	54, 73
Lounge	(Leidsestr.) vuong.nl	-	- ☰		
Weber	Marnixstraat 397 (Leidsegracht)	JO	622-9910	Hip	80, 99
Lounge		-	- ☰		
Werck	Prinsengracht 277 (Westermarkt)	JO	627-4079	Cool	54, 73
Lounge	werck.nl	-	- ☰	Terraces	48
Westergasfabriek	Pazzanistraat 41 (Haarlemmerweg)	WE	586-0710	Hip	99
Nightclub	westergasfabriek.com	C	- ☰		
Wolvenstraat*	Wolvenstraat 23 (Keizersgracht)	JO	320-0843	Hip	99
Bar		-	- ☰		
Xtra-Cold Amsterdam	Amstel 194-196 (Amstelstr.)	RP	020-320-5700	Cool	73
Bar/Lounge	xtracold.nl	C	- ☰		
Youll Lady's Dancing	Amstel 178 (Engelse Pel Steeg)	RP	421-0900	Hip	81, 99
Nightclub	youii.nl	C	- ☰	Late-Night Scenes	35
Zebra Lounge	Korte Leidsedwarsstraat 14	CB	612-6153	Cool	54, 73
Lounge/Nightclub	(Leidsestr.)	C	- ☰		

Attractions

NAME	ADDRESS (CROSS STREET)	AREA	PHONE (020)	EXPERIENCE	PAGE
TYPE	WEBSITE	PRICE		99 BEST	PAGE
Albert Cuypmarkt	Albert Cuypstraat (btwn. Ferdinand	DP	-	Hip	79, 100
Market	Bolstr. and van Woustr.)	-		Outdoor Markets	41
Amstel Hotel Health Club	Professor Tulpplein 1 (Sarphatistr.)	PL	622-6060	Classic	108, 129
Spa	amsterdam.intercontinental.com	€			
Amsterdam Historical Msm.	Nieuwezijds Voorburgwal 357 (Wijde	NZ	523-1822	Classic	108, 129
History Museum	Kapelsteeg) ahm.nl	€		Historic Sites	30
Anne Frank House	Prinsengracht 267 (Westermarkt)	JO	556-7105	Classic	105, 129
Historic Site	annefrank.nl	€		Historic Sites	30
De Appel Centre for Cont. Art	Nieuwe Spiegelstraat 10 (Herengracht)	CB	625-5651	Hip	80, 100
Art Gallery	deappel.nl	€		Cont. Art Spaces	22
ARCAM (Ams. Centre for	Prins Hendrikkade 600 (Schippersstr.)	OZ	620-4878	Cool	54, 74
Architecture) Vis. Ctr.	arcam.nl	-			
Architectour	various	VA	625-9123	Cool	52, 74
Guided Tour	architectour@wish.net (email)	€€€€+		Guided Tours	29
ARTTRA Cultural Agency	Tweede Boomdwarsstraat 4 (Boomstr.)	JO	625-9303	Classic	106, 129
Guided Tour	arttra.nl	€€€€+		Guided Tours	29
De Balie	Kleine Gartmanplantsoen 10 (Leidseplein)	CB	553-5100	Hip	100
Art Gallery		€		Cont. Art Spaces	22
Begijnhof	Entry off Gedempte Begijnsloot (Spui)	NZ	622-1918	Classic	108, 130
Historic Site	begijnhofamsterdam.nl	-		Historic Sites	30
Christie's Auction House	Cornelis Schuytstraat 57	ZU	575-5255	Cool	52, 74
Auction House	(Willemsparkweg) christies.com	-			
City Picnic (Café Vertigo)	Vondelpark 3 (R. Visscherstr.)	MP	616-8727	Classic	130
Park	citypicknick.nl	€€€			
Cobra Museum of Modern	Sandbergplein 1 (Amstelveen)	VA	547-5050	Cool	53, 74
Art Art Museum	cobra-museum.nl	€ -			
Coffeeshop de Dampkring	Handboogstraat 29 (Heiligeweg)	NZ	638-0705	Classic	107, 130
Coffeeshop		-		Coffeeshops	21
Droog Design	Staalstraat 7b (Groenburgwal)	OZ	523-5059	Hip	81, 100
Art Gallery/Store	droogdesign.nl	-		Dutch Design	24
Dutch Flowers	Singel 387 (Heisteeg)	JO	624-7624	Classic	107, 130
Coffeeshop		-		Coffeeshops	21
Dutch Resistance Museum	Plantage Kerklaan 61 (Plantage	PL	620-2535	Classic	130
History Museum	Muidergracht) verzetsmuseum.org	€			
Erotic Museum	Oudezijds Achterburgwal 54 (Oude	OZ	624-7303	Hip	81, 101
Cultural Museum	Kennisteeg)	€		Sex-in-the-City	45
Female and Partners	Spuistraat 100 (Nieuwe Spaarpotsteeg)	NZ	620-9152	Hip	101
Store	femaleandpartners.nl	-			
Flower Market	The Singel (Koningsplein)	RP	-	Classic	107, 131
Market		-		Outdoor Markets	41
FOAM Photography Museum	Keizersgracht 609 (Vijzelstr.)	CB	551-6500	Cool	53, 75
Art Museum	foam.nl	€			
The Frozen Fountain	Prinsengracht 645 (Leidsestr.)	CB	622-9375	Cool	75
Store	frozenfountain.nl	-		Dutch Design	24

Attractions (cont.)

NAME TYPE	ADDRESS (CROSS STREET) WEBSITE	AREA PRICE	PHONE (020)	EXPERIENCE 99 BEST	PAGE PAGE
Game Over? Retrogames Amsterdam Store	Hasselaerssteeg 12 (Nieuwendijk) gameover.nl	NZ -	624-7841	Hip	101
Gassan Diamonds Guided Tour/Store	Nieuwe Uilenburgerstraat 173-175 (Houtkopersburgwal) gassandiamonds.com -	OZ	622-5333	Cool	52, 75
The Hash Marihuana & Hemp Msm. Cultural	Oudezijds Achterburgwal 148 (Stoofsteeg) hashmuseum.com	OZ €	623-5961	Hip	81, 101
Heineken Experience Brewery	Stadhouderskade 78 (PC Hooftstr.) heinekenexperience.com	DP €	523-9666	Hip Beer-Lovers' Spots	79, 101 19
Hermitage Amsterdam Art Museum	Nieuwe Herengracht 14 (Amstel) hermitage.nl	PL €	530-8755	Classic	131
Holland Intl. Boat Tours Guided Tours	various hir.nl	VA €€	622-7788	Classic On-the-Water	105, 131 39
Hortus Botanicus Botanical Gardens	Plantage Middenlaan 2 (Plantage Parklaan) dehortus.nl	PL €	625-9021	Classic	131
Huis Marseille: Foundation for Photography Art Museum	Keizersgracht 401 (Hartenstr.) huismarseille.nl	JO €	531-8989	Hip	81, 102
Jacobus Toet . Store	Hobbemastraat 4 (PC Hooftstr.) jacobus-toet.nl	MP -	679-9162	Cool	75
Jewish Historical Museum History Museum	Nieuwe Amstelstraat 1 (Turfsteeg) jhm.nl	OZ €	531-0310	Classic	131
Kadinsky Coffeeshop	Rosmarijnsteeg 9 (Nieuwe Spaarpotsteeg) 	NZ -	-	Hip Coffeeshops	81, 102 21
Koan Float and Massage Centre Spa	Herengracht 321(Raamsteeg) koan-float.com	JO €€€€	555-0333	Cool	54, 75
Lambiek Comics Shop Store	Kerkstraat 132 (Leidsegracht) lambiek.net	CB -	626-7543	Hip	80, 102
Loods 6 Art Gallery	KNSMlaan 143 (Levantkade) loods6.nl	EH -	418-2020	Cool Cont. Art Spaces	52, 76 22
Looier Art & Antique Centre Market	Elandsgracht 109 (1e Looiersdwarsstr.) looier.nl	JO -	624-9038	Classic	132
MacBike Bicycle Rentals Bicycle Rentals	Stationsplein 12 (Centraal Station) Weteringsschans 2 (Nieuwe Vijzelstr.) Mr. Visserplein 2 (Jodenbreestr.) macbike.nl	OZ CB OZ €	620-0985	Hip	81, 102
Marlies Dekkers Store	Cornelis Schuytstraat (Van Breestr.) marliesdekkers.nl	ZU -	471-4146	Cool Sex-in-the-City	76 45
Museum Van Loon Historic Site	Keizersgracht 672 (Leidsegracht) museumvanloon.nl	JO €	624-5255	Classic	132
Museum Willet-Holthuysen Historic Site	Herengracht 605 (Utrechtsestr.) willetholthuysen.nl	CB €	523-1822	Classic	132
Nieuwe Kerk Art Museum	Dam Square (Mozes en Aaronstr.) nieuwekerk.nl	NZ €	638-6909	Classic	132
Oude Kerk Historic Site	Oudekerksplein 23 (Oudezijds Voorburgwal) oudekerk.nl	OZ €	625-8284	Classic	132
Paradis Private Boat Tours Guided Tours	various privateboattours.nl	VA €€€€+	684-9338	Cool On-the-Water	51, 76 39

NAME	ADDRESS (CROSS STREET)	AREA	PHONE (020)	EXPERIENCE	PAGE
TYPE	WEBSITE	PRICE		99 BEST	PAGE
Platform 21 Ams. Design Center Art Gallery	Prinses Irenestraat 19 (Beethovenstr.) platform21.com	ZU -	344-9449	Cool Dutch Design	54, 76 24
Puccini Bomboni Store	Staalstraat 17 (Kloveniersburgwal) puccinibomboni.com	OZ -	626-5474	Cool	76
Rembrandt House Art Museum	Jodenbreestraat 4-6 (Houtkopersdwarsstr.) rembrandthuis.nl	OZ €	520-0400	Classic	106, 132
Rijksmuseum Art Museum	Jan Luijkenstraat 1 (Hobbemastr.) rijksmuseum.nl	MP €€	674-7000	Classic Art Museums	106, 133 18
Royal Palace Historic Site	Dam Square (Paleisstr.) koninklijkhuis.nl	NZ €	620-4060	Classic	108, 133
Scheepvaart Museum (Netherlands Maritime)	Kattenburgerplein 1 (Prins Hendrikkade) Museum scheepvaartmuseum.nl	OZ €	523-2222	Classic	133
Sexmuseum Amsterdam Cultural Museum	Damrak 18 (Karnemelksteeg) sexmuseumamsterdam.com	NZ €	622-8376	Hip	102
Soap Treatment Store Spa	Spuistraat 281 (Palelsstraat) soapcompany.com	NZ €€€€	428-9660	Cool	77
Splash Healthclub Health Club	Looiersgracht 26-30 (Hazenstr.); Lijnbaansgracht 241 (Leidsegracht) healthclubsplash.nl	JO CB €€	624-8404 422-0280	Hip	82, 103
Stedelijk Museum CS Art Museum	Oosterdokskade 5 (Piet Heinkade) stedelijk.nl	EH €	573-2911	Hip Art Museums	82, 103 18
Tropenmuseum Cultural Museum	Linnaeusstraat 2 (Mauritskade) kit.nl	PL €	568-8215	Classic	133
Van Gogh Museum Art Museum	Paulus Potterstraat 7 (Van de Veldestr.) vangoghmuseum.nl	MP €€	570-5200	Classic Art Museums	107, 134 18
Van Ravenstein Store	Keizersgracht 359 (Huidenstr.)	JO -	639-0067	Cool	54, 77
Waterlooplein Market Market	Waterlooplein (Mr. Visserplein)	OZ -		Hip Outdoor Markets	103 41
Westerkerk Church	Prinsengracht 281 (Westerstr.) westerkerk.nl	JO -	624-7766	Classic	134
Wonderwood Store	Rusland 3 (Oudezijdsachterburgwal) wonderwood.nl	OZ -	625-3738	Cool	77
World of Ajax - Ajax Museum Sports Museum	Arena Boulevard 3 (Haakbergweg) ajax.nl	EA €	311-1336	Hip	103
Yellow Bike Tours Guided Tour	Nieuwezijds Kolk 29 (Nieuwezijds Voorburgwal) yellowbike.nl	NZ €€	620-6940	Classic Guided Tours	106, 134 29

BLACK BOOK

Amsterdam Unique Shopping Index

NAME	PHONE (020)	AREA	PRODUCTS	PAGE
Oger	676-8695	PC	High end/casual men's wear	56
Perrysport	624-7131	KA	Sporting goods store	110
Pol's Potten	419-3541	EH	Contemporary furnishings	56
Pompadour Chocolaterie	624-7919	NS	An Amsterdam institution	110
Puccini Bomboni	626-5474	OZ	Chocolaterie	76
Rituals Boutique	344-9222	KA	Skin care products	110
Shoebaloo	671-2210	PC	Great shoes in a chic shop	56
Sissyboy Homeland	419-1559	EH	Trendy clothing, accessories	56
Skins Cosmetics	528-6922	NS	Luxe lines for both sexes	56
Van Ravenstein	639-0067	NS	Belgian designer clothing	56, 77
De Vlieger	625-7030	NS	Contemporary art	56
Wonderwood	625-3738	OZ	Galllery fillled with wooden accessories	77

Amsterdam Black Book By Neighborhood

Canal Belt (CB)

De Pijp (DP)

Code: H-Hotels; R-Restaurants; N-Nightlife; A-Attractions. Blue page numbers denote listings in 99 Best. Black page numbers denote listings in theme chapters. The Amsterdam Neighborhoods Map is on p.208.

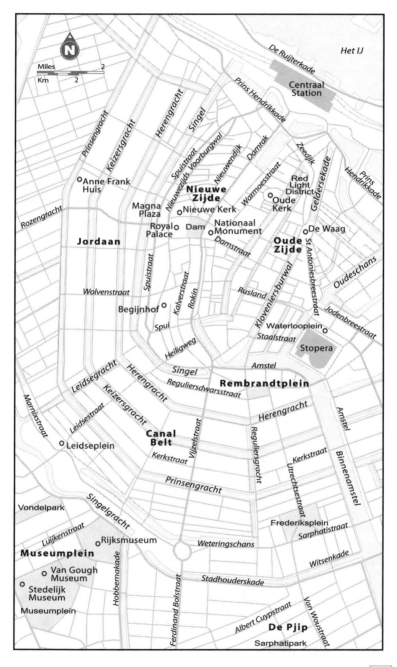

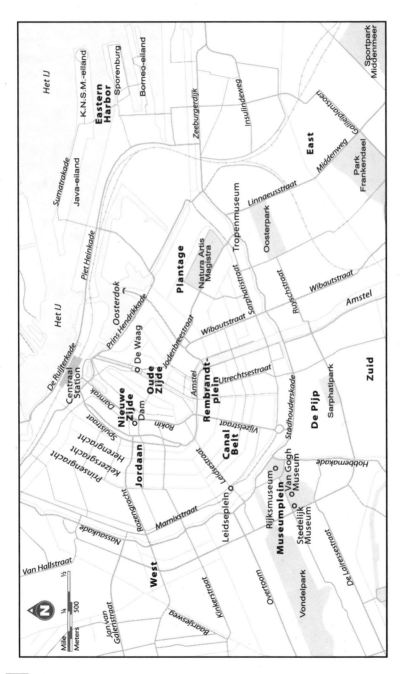